Making
Political Choices

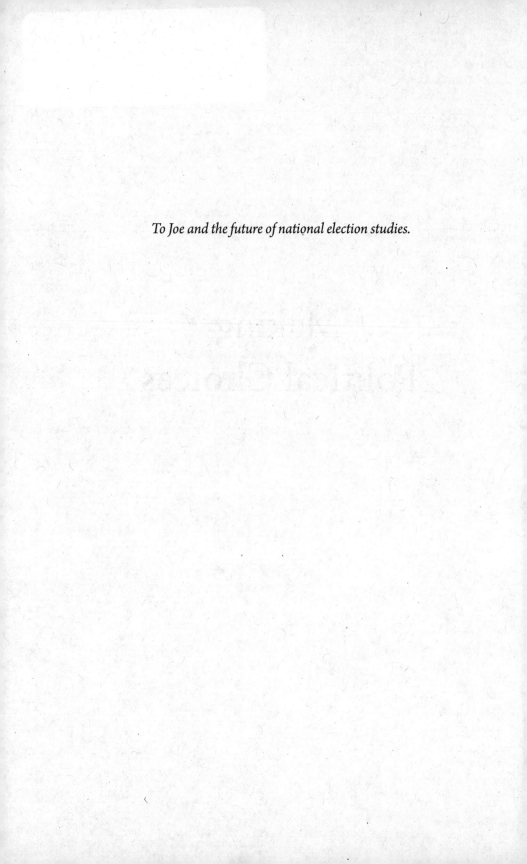

To Joe and the future of national election studies.

Making
Political Choices

CANADA AND
THE UNITED STATES

Harold D. Clarke, Allan Kornberg, and Thomas J. Scotto

UNIVERSITY OF TORONTO PRESS

LIBRARY AND ARCHIVES CANADA CATALOGUING IN PUBLICATION

Clarke, Harold D., 1943-
      Making political choices : Canada and the United States / Harold D. Clarke, Allan Kornberg, and Thomas J. Scotto.

Includes bibliographical references and index.
ISBN 978-0-8020-9674-6 (pbk.). — ISBN 978-1-4426-0136-9 (bound)

      1. Elections — Canada — History — 21st century. 2. Elections — United States — History — 21st century. 3. Voting research — Canada. 4. Voting research — United States. 5. Canada — Politics and government — 1993-2006. 6. United States — Politics and government — 2001-. 7. United States — Politics and government — 1993-2001. I. Kornberg, Allan, 1931- II. Scotto, Thomas J. III. Title.

JL193.C53 2008   324.971   C2008-906592-1

We welcome comments and suggestions regarding any aspect of our publications—please feel free to contact us at news@utphighereducation.com or visit our internet site at www.utphighereducation.com.

North America	*UK, Ireland, and continental Europe*
5201 Dufferin Street	NBN International
Toronto, Ontario, Canada, M3H 5T8	Estover Road, Plymouth, PL6 7PY, UK
	TEL: 44 (0) 1752 202301
2250 Military Road	FAX ORDER LINE: 44 (0) 1752 202333
Tonawanda, New York, USA, 14150	enquiries@nbninternational.com

ORDERS PHONE: 1-800-565-9523
ORDERS FAX: 1-800-221-9985
ORDERS EMAIL: utpbooks@utpress.utoronto.ca

This book is printed on paper containing 100% post-consumer fibre.

The University of Toronto Press acknowledges the financial support for its publishing activities of the Government of Canada through the Book Publishing Industry Development Program (BPIDP).

Cover design by Michel Vrána, Black Eye Design.
Interior design by Michel Vrána, Black Eye Design.

Printed in Canada

CONTENTS

LIST OF FIGURES

LIST OF TABLES

PREFACE

This is a book about the political choices Canadian and American voters make. The story we tell focuses on voting in several recent elections—the 2004 and 2006 Canadian federal elections, and the 2000, 2004, and 2006 American national elections. To help us understand the decisions voters made in these consequential contests, we employ data gathered in national surveys of the opinions, attitudes, and behavior of several thousand voters in the two countries. We test the generality of our findings about factors that affect voting by studying the choices voters made in three important earlier elections—the 1988 and 1993 Canadian federal elections, and the 1980 American presidential election. And since voters must choose not only which party or candidate they prefer but also whether to cast a ballot, we investigate factors that promote or inhibit electoral participation.

Viewed generally, our analyses of voting in these eight elections provide strong support for what has become known as the valence politics model of electoral choice. The valence politics model has its origins in a path-breaking analysis of election issues by Donald Stokes in the early 1960s. A closely related "Absent Mandate" model was then developed in studies of voting behavior in Canada in the 1970s and 1980s by one of the authors of the present volume (Harold Clarke) and his colleagues (Jane Jenson, Larry LeDuc, and Jon Pammett). Research in the 1990s on voting in American state- and local-level referendums by Arthur Lupia and Matthew McCubbins, and several studies by Paul Sniderman and his colleagues provided valuable insights about how voters decide. The results of these studies of voter psychology fit very well with the conjectures and empirical findings that were shaping the development of the valence politics model. Recently, the model has been elaborated in studies of party choice in Britain by Clarke and his colleagues David Sanders, Marianne Stewart, and Paul Whiteley.

The valence politics model emphasizes the importance of the images of party leaders and presidential candidates as "heuristic devices" or cues that guide voters' choices in political contexts of high stakes and abundant insecurity. Stated simply, voters use leader images as guides to political decision-making because they are "smart enough to know that they are not smart enough" to behave in accordance with the canons of classic rational choice theory. Voters are endowed with agency, but not with omniscience.

Issues are also important in the valence politics model. What typically matter are issues where political debate focuses on "who" and "how" rather than "what." Good examples of valence issues include economic well-being, accessible health care, protection from terrorism, and honesty in government. In every case, there is strong public consensus on the goal, and competing parties try to convince voters that they are best able to do the job. Voters' psychological attachments to political parties matter too but, *pace* the many researchers who have claimed that such attachments are durable lifelong bonds, we find that substantial numbers of Canadians and Americans have flexible party ties that are products of ongoing evaluations of the performance of parties and their leaders. A party that does not perform well will find that its partisan base erodes and its public support fades. As analyses in this book demonstrate, these dynamics can be rapid, sizable, and consequential.

A variety of individuals and organizations have assisted our efforts. We are very pleased to have the opportunity to acknowledge their assistance. First and foremost, we thank the National Science Foundation (NSF) (US), and its Political Science Program Director Frank Scioli. Starting in the early 1980s, two of the authors, Harold Clarke and Allan Kornberg, began a series of NSF-sponsored studies of political support in Canada. Over the years, Frank Scioli and his colleagues in the political science program—Rick Wilson and Jim Granato—have expressed interest in our "Political Support in Canada" research and have provided us with much helpful advice. We are also extremely grateful for generous financial assistance from the University of Texas at Dallas. Provost Hobson Wildenthal's interest in and support for Clarke's election study research program is greatly appreciated. In addition, we are very appreciative of the financial support Daniel Abele, academic relations officer, Canadian Embassy,

Washington, DC, and the academic relations staff, Canadian High Commission, London, provided Tom Scotto so he could conduct ancillary projects linked to our election studies. We are also pleased to acknowledge the support of the Canadian Studies Program and John Aldrich's Program for Advanced Research in the Social Sciences at Duke University.

As this is written, the research methodology of national election studies is experiencing its greatest change in a half century. The advent of Internet surveys promises to change—is changing—the science of election studies in very beneficial ways. Our analyses of two of the elections studied in the present volume, the 2006 Canadian federal election and the 2006 American congressional election, were made possible by national pre- and post-election panel surveys fielded via the Internet. These surveys were conducted on our behalf by YouGov, with Joe Twyman serving as project director. We are extremely grateful to Joe and his colleagues at YouGov for making these opportunities available to us. Simply fantastic! Thanks so much, Joe—we owe you a deep debt of gratitude.

Prior to the recent Internet surveys, Clarke, together with Jane Jenson, Larry LeDuc, and Jon Pammett, conducted national surveys for the 1974, 1979, and 1980 Canadian National Election Studies, and Clarke and Kornberg conducted several national surveys between 1983 and 2004 for the Political Support in Canada project. Initially, these surveys were carried out using in-person interviews, and later they were done using an RDD-CATI system. In every case, the field work was conducted by TNS-Canadian Facts. For many years, Mary Auvinen was our project director there. Her extremely careful, extremely hard work and her always helpful advice are greatly appreciated. More recently, we have benefited in similar ways from the efforts of Peter Wearing and John MacLeod. We are very pleased to thank Peter and John for their help.

Over the years, we have benefited greatly from a cornucopia of insightful ideas offered by our colleagues. In some cases, their thoughts were voiced in the course of prosecuting collaborative ventures whereas, in others, they were expressed in stimulating, sometimes contentious, conference meetings or in laid-back casual conversations (more than occasionally in suitable settings for scientific discourse, such as the Wivenhoe House Bar at the University of Essex). We especially wish to thank (in alphabetical order): John Aldrich, André Blais, Ray Duch, Charles Franklin, Mark Franklin, Jim Gibson, Simon Jackman, Richard Johnston, Larry LeDuc, Mike Lewis-Beck, Allan McCutcheon, Bill Mishler, Tony Mughan, Skip Lupia, Mike Munger, Neil Nevitte, Helmut Norpoth, Jon Pammett, Jason Reifler, David Sanders, Peter Schmidt, Joel Smith, Paul Sniderman, Marianne Stewart, Norm Thomas, John Thompson, Cees van der Eijk, Paul Whiteley, and Guy Whitten. Tom Scotto also wishes to thank Antoine Bilodeau, Nicki Doyle, and Mebs Kanji for their assistance and hospitality during his visits to Concordia University, and Bob Duval,

Kevin Leyden, and Donley Studlar for facilitating his work while he was at West Virginia University.

Last, but certainly not least, we thank Michael Harrison and Judith Earnshaw at University of Toronto Press, Higher Education Division. We would also like to thank Greg Yantz and Kirsten Craven. Michael's interest in the idea for the book encouraged us to proceed, and Kirsten did a great job copy-editing. Greg's cheerful enthusiasm for the project and his patience (a lot of patience) were extremely helpful. Thanks very much.

CHAPTER ONE

Political Choices
and Valence Politics

This is a book about voting in national elections, one of the most important and by far the most frequent political act in which citizens in mature democracies engage. Our focus is on eight national elections in Canada and the United States, two of the world's oldest democracies. In Canada the four elections we have selected for analysis are the 1988, 1993, 2004, and 2006 federal elections. In the United States our concern is with the 1980, 2000, and 2004 presidential elections, and the 2006 congressional election. We have selected these elections largely because we view them as offering strong tests of the principal models of electoral choice that have been employed to address two central questions about political life in democracies. These are whether people will vote, and for whom they will vote. The first of these questions has a corollary—why some people do not vote. The latter topic has generated particular concern recently among political scientists since levels of electoral participation in many mature democracies, including Canada, have fallen noticeably in the past two decades. This is not true in the United States, but voting turnout in American elections was already quite low when the downward trend began elsewhere. Why people do not vote is also one of the concerns of this book.

The outcome of some national elections may seem to many voters and observers to be "cut and dried." However, uncertainty, anticipation, and anxiety are the hallmarks of most national election campaigns. Consider, for example, the 2004 American and Canadian elections. In the United States, an incumbent president, despite facing a plethora of seemingly insurmountable foreign and domestic policy problems, nonetheless appeared well-positioned for re-election until his Democratic Party opponent, Senator John Kerry, seemed to rise like Lazarus from the political dead following their first presidential debate. Energized in the run-up to election day, Democratic activists celebrated when early exit polls suggested Senator Kerry might be the next president. In Canada the run-up to the 2004 election was somewhat different. The recently installed head of the governing Liberal Party, Prime Minister Paul Martin, Jr., appeared to be in big trouble. Faced with a new Conservative Party and a widely publicized and very embarrassing scandal that refused to go away, he seemed destined to lose his office before he was even familiar with the furniture.

In both countries the election results gainsaid predictions, and the incumbent president and prime minister were returned to office. However, there were notable differences. In President Bush's case, unlike the 2000 election that first brought him to power, he won a majority of the popular vote, as well as gaining a majority in the electoral college. Adding to the glow of victory, Republican majorities retained control of both houses of Congress. Martin, in contrast, remained prime minister as head of a minority government—a far cry from the powerful majorities his predecessor, Jean Chrétien, had enjoyed for more than a decade. Also, because both elections were considered to be highly competitive ones involving substantial, highly publicized policy differences between the contestants, voter turnout was expected to rise substantially. In the United States it did, although still remaining well below the average for other mature democracies. In Canada turnout actually declined to the lowest level in the country's history.

In Chapters Three and Four we will explain why these elections turned out as they did, and in Chapter Eight we address the issue of nonvoting. In these and other chapters we will take advantage of the availability of a half-century of high-quality cross-sectional and panel surveys of the political attitudes, opinions, and voting behavior of the citizens of each country. For the American analyses, we rely primarily on the American National Election Studies (ANES) survey data, but also make use of the data gathered in the recent National Annenberg Election Studies (NAES), and the 2006 Political Support in America Study (PSA). For Canada, we employ data from the Canadian Election Studies (CES) and the Political Support in Canada Studies (PSC).

Why, the reader may ask, focus on Canada and the United States? We do so because Canada and the United States are "naturals" for comparative political inquiry. The many similarities and differences in the social, economic, and political systems of the two countries facilitate systematic comparative research. Similarities include, *inter alia*, populations characterized by ethno-linguistic, racial, regional, and religious diversity; quasi-free-market economies and very high average standards of living; federal systems of government; written constitutions with bills of rights; single-member plurality electoral systems; and competitive party systems at the national and sub-national levels of government.

There are a number of differences in the origins and development of Canada and the United States (e.g., Lipset, 1990) that also encourage and facilitate comparative analysis. For example, unlike the United States, Canada has long had genuine (if oftentimes limited) multiparty competition at both the national and sub-national levels of government (Epstein, 1964). As a result, the political choices offered Canadians in successive elections are more varied than those available to Americans. Also, some important political differences between the two countries are not static. For example, in the early 1990s, Canada witnessed a major change in its national party system. Voting turnout is another relevant example. Over the past 100 years, levels of participation in Canadian national elections have typically surpassed those in American elections by wide margins. However, over the past two decades, patterns of turnout have been quite different in the two countries. Levels of nonvoting have fluctuated without trend in the United States, whereas turnout in Canadian national elections has fallen sharply to levels that are approaching those typical of recent American presidential elections.

Another major difference is the status of Quebec within the Canadian federal system. The Canadian provinces, in part because there are only 10 of them, generally have been much more important political actors than have the states within the American system. In addition, for generations Québécois nationalists have argued that Quebec is a province *"pas comme les autres."* Given their 400 years of history, their common language, religion, and culture, francophones claim that they are now, and have long been, a nation that is domiciled within the province of Quebec. As a consequence, in less than a generation, separatist provincial governments twice held referendums designed to initiate Quebec's departure from Canada. The last one, in 1995, came within the proverbial eyelash of succeeding. Although following that event the fires of Quebec separatism were banked for several years, the strong showing of the Bloc Québécois in the 2004 federal election indicated that the idea of an independent Quebec, especially among younger voters, retained considerable appeal. Nationalist sentiments could be a powerful political force.

Similarities and differences such as those mentioned above make comparisons of voting behavior in Canada and the United States an interesting enterprise with potentially large payoffs. We begin with an overview of the ways political scientists have tried to comprehend the act of voting. As noted above, we will compare and evaluate four alternative models that have been employed to explain how voters decide. These are the sociological or "Columbia School" model; the social-psychological or "Michigan" model; the issue-proximity or "Downsian" model; and the "valence" model. Analyses of voting in several American and Canadian elections provide opportunities to compare the performance of these competing models. This assessment exercise may be viewed as a "tournament of models" (Clarke et al., 2004). We also will determine whether a composite model that includes all of these models generates explanatory power over and above that provided by the individual models. The generality of the findings is enhanced by analyzing voting for varying political offices, at different times, and in different political settings.

COMPETING MODELS OF ELECTORAL CHOICE

As the 2006 Canadian federal election and the 2006 US congressional election demonstrated rather vividly, elections in democracies are by their very nature "a risky business." The question of what an election outcome will be continues to agitate and confound not only the candidates for public office but also those who, in democracies such as Canada and the United States, literally constitute small armies of "election experts" comprised of political scientists, pollsters, media mavens, public relations experts, and strategic advisors versed in the black arts of running successful campaigns for high office. Some of the earliest scholarly attempts to explain voting behavior and election outcomes through systematic research were undertaken in the United States in the 1940s. Studies of voting in Erie County, Ohio, in 1940 and Elmira, New York, in 1948 by Bernard Berelson, Paul Lazarsfeld, and their associates at Columbia University are especially noteworthy. Samuel Popkin (1991: 12–13) has rightly noted that their research and the insights flowing from it laid the groundwork for modern electoral studies.

Although the Columbia team originally focused on the dynamic processes by which people made up their minds in reaction to campaign stimuli, their findings led them to conclude that voting "is essentially a group experience" (Lazarsfeld, Berelson, and Gaudet, 1948: 137). Lazarsfeld et al.'s core argument is that voting behavior reflects social group memberships shaped by socioeconomic and demographic forces. Major societal cleavages such as ethnicity, religion, gender, social class, and region matter a great deal when explaining how voters cast their ballots. In this regard, they reported that an "index of political predispositions" based on such characteristics was a good predictor of voting behavior. The basic conclusion was that, when all was said and done, social location was political destiny. Not surprisingly, the Columbia team's approach has been termed the sociological perspective on electoral choice.

In the years following these pioneering studies by Lazarsfeld and his colleagues, various sociological models continued to attract the attention of students of electoral choice. However, the popularity of such models has waned over time. The reason is simple—sociological variables typically have only very limited ability to explain variations in voting behavior. Also, since many sociological variables seldom, if ever, exhibit significant individual-level variation, the sociological perspective is inadequate for understanding inter-election changes in people's voting behavior. Sociological models do even less well in explaining short-term change. Monthly changes in party support in public opinion surveys and, *a fortiori*, daily movements in parties' poll ratings, such as those that occurred in the 2006 Canadian federal election, are completely outside the purview of sociological models. Reacting to these shortcomings, political scientists have tended to treat sociological variables as distal antecedents in the skein of causal forces that drive voting behavior and election outcomes. They are not irrelevant, but they are far back in the "funnel of causality" (Campbell et al., 1960) that leads to the vote. What was needed was a model that could explain both stability and change over short and medium time horizons. Enter socio-psychological models of voting.

Given the inadequacy of sociological perspectives for explaining individual- and aggregate-level variation in electoral choice, analysts soon were attracted to the social-psychological model pioneered by Angus Campbell and his associates at the University of Michigan (e.g., Campbell et al., 1954, 1960, 1966). The Michigan model, as it came to be known, emphasizes the primacy of party identification, conceptualized as voter loyalties to a party grounded in feelings of "oneness" with it. Identifications with parties are similar to self-identifications people develop with ethnic, religious, and other social groups. Party identifications typically develop early in life, as a result of socialization processes occurring during childhood and adolescence (Jennings and Niemi, 1974). Once formed, partisan attachments are directionally stable and tend to strengthen over time, as people reinforce their partisanship by voting repeatedly for the same party (Converse, 1969).

Party identifications affect voting behavior directly and also function as a "perceptual screen" through which candidates and issues are viewed and evaluated. However, this screening process is imperfect. In any given election, positive and negative messages about competing candidates and issues can get through and create short-term forces that produce changes in voting behavior and election outcomes. That said, since candidates come and go, and many voters generally seem to lack any great awareness or interest in policy issues (e.g., Converse, 1964), party identification is typically designated as a key explanatory variable by analysts who adopt the Michigan model of voting behavior.

For many years after its introduction, the Michigan model enjoyed wide acceptance among students of voting and elections. This is not to say there were no dissenters. There were, and the model was challenged by scholars in the United States, Canada, and elsewhere, especially with respect to the pride of place assigned to party identification. In the United States the two most extended criticisms were by Norman Nie, Sidney Verba, and John Petrocik (1976), and by Morris Fiorina (1981). Nie et al. contended that time, new information, changes in the composition of the electorate, and other contextual factors influenced the relative salience and explanatory power of party identification, issue concerns, and candidate images. Their argument was that by the mid-1960s, voters' positions on highly charged issues such as the Vietnam War, civil rights, feminism, homosexuality, and the recreational use of drugs deeply divided the American electorate in ways that cut across party lines. As a consequence, by the 1970s, candidates and issues were becoming more important and partisan identifications less important as determinants of electoral choice.

Fiorina's critique was informed by utility maximization principles in rational choice theory, and it involved a fundamental reconceptualization of party identification. Rather than viewing party identification as akin to an unchanging identification of oneself in terms of sociological categories, Fiorina claimed that partisan attachments were psychological storehouses of information about the performance of parties and their leaders. The contents of these storehouses were mutable—over time, voters acquire new information about the activities of governing and opposition parties that they use to update the strength and direction of their partisan attachments. When doing so, they give more weight to recent as opposed to earlier information. The updating process is continuous, and it can either reinforce or erode an existing partisan attachment. In a widely quoted phrase, Fiorina wrote that party identification is a "running tally" of party performance evaluations. Other scholars soon offered similar reconceptualizations, i.e., partisan attachments have dynamic properties and are grounded in ongoing judgments voters make about the performance of parties and their leaders (e.g., Achen, 1992, 2002; Franklin, 1992; Franklin and Jackson, 1983; Stewart and Clarke, 1998).

A related stream of criticism came from congressional scholars. Initially, it was argued that with the weakening of the two major American political parties as organizations able to elect their congressional candidates, by the late 1960s the latter increasingly turned to an emerging group of experts in the use of surveys and focus groups, of advertising and marketing techniques, and the use of media, in particular television, to craft the kind of public images that would get them elected. Those who were successful in such candidate-centered campaigns were harder to organize into coherent party coalitions (e.g., Broder, 1972; Pomper, 1977). Relatedly, the lack of cohesion in the congressional parties helped to erode both the incidence and intensity of partisanship in Congress, as well as in the parties' core support groups in the electorate.

However, by the middle and late 1980s, first the Republican and then the Democratic congressional parties became more unified and ideologically polarized (Jacobson, 2001). So much so, that by 1994 the entire Republican congressional campaign was organized around the so-called Contract with America. That document may not have had much impact on average Americans, but it had an enormous impact on the Republican Party (e.g., Riley, 1995). Republican leaders believed the contract, a laundry list of promises to, *inter alia*, cut taxes, fight crime, restore "family values," end the rapacious practices of so-called trial lawyers, and curtail the powers of Congress and its members, had enabled them to win majorities in both houses of Congress after a very long period in the electoral wilderness. Campaigning hard on ideologically charged "hot button" issues paid handsome political dividends.

A related argument is that there has been a polarization of support for the president since the election of George W. Bush in 2000. Members of Congress are now less likely to cross party lines and form coalitions either to support or to oppose legislation initiated by the president. And, as the two parties became more coherent and ideologically distinct, the same happened to their core supporters in the electorate. Partisanship in the American electorate reflects deepening elite-level ideological divisions.

In Canada, the Michigan model was initially well received by students of voting and elections. In addition to three Canadians (John Meisel, Peter Regenstreif, Mildred Schwartz), one of the principal investigators of the first Canadian national election study (CES) was Philip Converse, a co-author of *The American Voter* (1960) and other seminal studies that expounded the Ann Arbor wisdom (e.g., Campbell et al., 1960, 1966; Converse, 1964, 1969). In addition to the theoretical direction the Michigan model provided to the 1965 CES, the study was methodologically informed by the design of the American election studies. Key design features included a national probability post-election sample of the electorate and in-person interviews to gather information on Canadians' political attitudes and behavior.

The 1965 CES data were intriguing. Answers to a question asking respondents whether they had ever identified with a party other than the one with which they currently identified suggested that partisanship in Canada had dynamic qualities. It was not the "unmoved mover" of Michigan lore. Reacting to this evidence, John Meisel, a member of the 1965 CES team (and the sole investigator of the subsequent 1968 CES), concluded that other variables, particularly party images, were the key to understanding voting in Canada (e.g., Meisel, 1975). Meisel's critique was soon echoed by other scholars (e.g., Jenson, 1976; Clarke et al., 1979). It was again argued that partisanship in Canada was not necessarily a "durable" psychological attachment. Indeed, many Canadians not only had party ties that were weak and unstable, but partisan attachments also could be directionally inconsistent across levels of the federal system. An identifier with the federal Liberal Party could be a provincial Conservative or NDP identifier. Although it was acknowledged that current partisanship was a powerful predictor of voting behavior at any time, the "flexibility" of partisanship suggested that a revised model of electoral choice was required for Canada.

Canadian party scholars had long argued that the Liberals and Conservatives were "brokerage" organizations whose long-running dominance was due largely to their ability to win elections by exploiting the country's deep-seated ethno-linguistic and regional cleavages for their political advantage (e.g., Engelmann and Schwartz, 1967; Schwartz, 1974; Meisel, 1975; see also Carty, 2002). They did this by brokering policy deals that favored national and sub-national socioeconomic and political elites, with the two "heavyweight" provinces/regions, Ontario and Quebec, dominating the process to their advantage at the expense of the Atlantic provinces and Western Canada, as well as working-class people in all parts of the country (Porter, 1965; Wilson, 1968).

Besides providing a normative critique of the brokerage model, party scholars noted that it focused on election outcomes rather than on whether and for whom people voted. Empirically, the brokerage model failed to account for the fact that periodically position issues have achieved a very high salience in an election. Among the examples cited were the heated parliamentary and public debates over the use of conscripts in military service during World War I and World War II, the 1974 debate over the utility and fairness of implementing wage and price controls to curb inflation, and the 1988 "mother of all debates" over the Free Trade Agreement. In addition, some observers argued that the post-1993 party system appeared to be rooted in ideological differences that divided both the parties and the electorate. As in the United States, such differences encouraged the use of spatial (issue-proximity) models that emphasize varying combinations of pro-con issues and more closely mirror the traditional cleavage lines of Canadian society (Gidengil et al., 1999; Nevitte et al., 2000; Blais et al., 2002; Scotto et al., 2004).

The issue-proximity model had earlier been labelled the "Rochester" model after the work of a pioneering group of political scientists at the University of Rochester. The spatial modelling approach is based on rational choice theories of human behavior. It received its impetus from Anthony Downs's pioneering study of inter-party competition. Downs (1957) proposed that voters try to maximize their utilities by comparing the positions of competing parties in uni- or multidimensional ideological or policy space with their own positions in that space. Voters choose parties that are closest to them. For their part, parties try to position themselves in the space so as to maximize their support. The spatial modelling approach has generated a large formal theoretical literature and numerous empirical analyses (see Merrill and Grofman, 1999; Adams, Merrill, and Grofman, 2005).

Variations of Downs's initial formulation have proved attractive to investigators despite the powerful critique of it offered by Donald Stokes. Stokes (1963) did not dismiss the importance of issues in voter decisions, but instead argued for the importance of special types of issues that he termed *valence issues*. In developing his argument, Stokes carefully distinguished these issues from "pro-con" positional issues, such as those that currently divide people on matters such as gay and lesbian marriage, women's reproductive rights, and the desirability of strict restrictions on immigration. Valence issues, in contrast, concern conditions on which virtually all voters are in agreement or are opposed. Examples of the former include economic conditions; almost everyone favors low rates of inflation and unemployment, and rising economic prosperity. Examples of the latter include terrorism and crime in the streets, which virtually everyone abhors.

Clarke et al. (1979) believed that Stokes's contentions could be combined with aspects of brokerage politics, such as leaders' ability to deliver policy goods, into a powerful theory of electoral choice. Empirically, 1974, 1979, and 1980 CES data indicated that not only did many people have flexible partisan attachments but also party identifications changed in response to short-term leader and issue forces, and not just in response to cataclysmic events such as wars and economic depressions. Additionally, when given an opportunity to cite important election issues, people repeatedly emphasized what Stokes (1963, 1992) had termed valence issues. Party leader images were also important determinants of voting behavior—and not just when charismatic figures such as Ronald Reagan or Pierre Trudeau were at the center of the political stage. Instead, the effects of leader images on electoral choice were very general. Voters used leader images as cues for making decisions in contexts in which reliable information was in short supply or existing information was in conflict (see Lupia and McCubbins, 1998; Sniderman et al., 1991). Voters were wise enough to know what they did not know or were uncertain about. They reacted by looking for "a safe pair of hands" when making decisions about who should govern.

Investigations in the 1980s and 1990s by Clarke, Kornberg, and their associates as part of the Political Support in Canada project (PSC) replicated earlier CES studies. In *Citizens and Community* (1992), Kornberg and Clarke broadened the argument and contended that assessments about leaders and parties were a part of one of the principal pillars of support for a democratic political regime and community such as Canada's. The continuing significance of valence issues and public perceptions of leaders and their performance (Clarke, Kornberg, and Wearing, 2000; Clarke et al., 2004) has led to this model being labelled the valence model of electoral choice.

To recapitulate, why people vote as they do and whether people vote at all have been fundamental questions that have motivated electoral inquiry for more than a half-century. Systematic attempts to answer these questions have generally relied on models that privilege the strength and direction of partisan identification, models that focus on the relative congruence of voters and parties on salient positional issues, and models that emphasize the importance of valence issues and party leader images. Still other explanations have been grounded in variations in demographic and regional variables and voting as a form of social behavior. We will investigate which is the single most powerful explanatory model of voter choice, and demonstrate that it is repeatedly the valence model. However, we will also consider whether other models, such as the issue-proximity model, when combined into a more general composite model, add significantly to our understanding of the political choices people make.

(NOT) AT THE POLLS

Traditionally, high turnout in Canadian national (federal) elections has been very much the rule, not the exception. For the first 15 federal elections that began after World War II (1945) and ended in 1988, on average over three-quarters of the eligible electorate cast a ballot. Given that so many people voted, with the exception of recent works by André Blais (2000), and Jon Pammett and Lawrence LeDuc (2003), turnout in Canadian elections inspired relatively little scholarly inquiry. The image of Canadian voters streaming to the polls could easily be accepted as an enduring fact. However, in the five most recent elections, turnout has fallen sharply. Clearly, the decision to not vote has become an important feature of political choice in contemporary Canada, as well as in the United States.

In the United States turnout rates have long been lower than those in virtually all other mature democracies. This, and the widespread perception that turnout was falling further, prompted widespread concern among political scientists and other observers. However, there have been surprisingly few systematic studies of the phenomenon. Generally, attention has focused on a series of ad hoc explanations featuring the various problems related to voter registration (Wolfinger and Rosenstone, 1980; Mitchell and Wlezien, 1995); the frequency and types of elections (Boyd, 1989; Jackson, 1997); the long ballot (Bowler, Donovan, and Happ, 1992); the age at which people become eligible to vote (Franklin, 2004); the weakening of parties as organizations (Dalton and Wattenberg, 2002); simple voter fatigue (Rallings, Thrasher, and Borisyuk, 2003); and racism (Filer, Kenny, and Morton, 1991).

The decline of electoral participation in Canada to the low levels prevalent in the United States parallels similar downward trends in other mature democracies (Blais and Dobrzynska, 1998; Dalton and Wattenberg, 2002; Franklin, 2004; Pammett and LeDuc, 2003). This clear negative trend in the central form of citizen political activity in democratic polities (Held, 1996) prompts us to consider factors governing decisions to (not) vote.

Election studies in both countries have included a number of variables pertinent to research on turnout (e.g., political efficacy, interest, knowledge, and perceived inter-party competition). However, there has been little attention devoted to assessing the explanatory capacity of alternative models of electoral participation. Here, we will investigate five such models. These are civic volunteerism (e.g., Verba, Schlozman, and Brady, 1995); cognitive mobilization (Dalton and

Wattenberg, 2002); social capital (Jackman and Miller, 1998; Putnam, 2000); modified rational actor (Aldrich, 1993; Clarke et al., 2004); and general incentives (Whiteley and Seyd, 1994, 2002).

OVERVIEW OF CHAPTERS

In this section we briefly describe the contents of the several chapters that follow. In Chapter Two we consider voting in the 2006 Canadian election. The new Conservative Party of Canada (CPC), under the leadership of Stephen Harper, ran an almost prefect campaign. For one, ideologically extreme members of the new party were effectively muzzled so that the Liberals could not again claim, as they did in the 2004 election, that Harper and the CPC were right-wing extremists out of touch with the Canadian mainstream. To demonstrate how wrong that claim was, Harper promised to cut the GST (Goods and Services Tax) and increase family allowance benefits, two matters dear to the hearts of many Canadians.

Adding to the CPC's advantage was the continuing stream of revelations pertinent to the sponsorship scandal that had plagued the Liberals since the 2004 election. Liberal leader Paul Martin, try as he might, could not distance himself from that event. The media and many Canadians derided Martin's claim of ignorance. Critics charged that if, as both long-term finance minister in the Chrétien government and the senior Liberal MP from Quebec, he was ignorant of the affair, he was either incompetent, a liar, or both. In 2006 francophone support for the Liberals in Quebec significantly eroded, while Conservatives made gains after promising to right what many Quebeckers saw to be a serious imbalance in the division of revenues between Ottawa and the provinces.

The Conservatives also had an edge over the Liberals and other parties on issues deemed most important by the voters. Why then, it may be asked, did they only manage to win a plurality rather than a majority of parliamentary seats? In our view, it was in great part a function of two major valence politics variables. One was the relative paucity of Conservative partisans—as voters prepared to go to the polls, less than one voter in five was a CPC identifier. The other was that Stephen Harper, the Conservative leader, did not project a strong enough image as a leader. Although Harper outscored Martin, he was not especially warmly received by the electorate, and even his staunchest supporters could not argue that he was a dominant figure in the mold of a Diefenbaker or a Trudeau.

The focus of Chapter Three is the Canadian election of 2004. This election is of interest because it presents an interesting test of valence and spatial models of voting. As noted above, people's images of party leaders have served as cost-effective heuristic devices for making political choices in contexts of uncertainty. For example, the Progressive Conservatives of Joe Clark and Brian Mulroney came to power not so much by emphasizing their policy differences with Pierre Trudeau or John Turner, respectively, as they did their leadership attributes. But when the Clark-led PCs were defeated in the 1980 federal election, Clark was widely derided for his seeming lack of leadership qualities. As for Mulroney, his 1984 platform promised no major policy departures from those of the Liberal government. In fact, during the campaign he frequently emphasized his commitment to Canada's cherished social programs, claiming he regarded them as a "sacred trust" (Bercuson, Granatstein, and Young, 1986). Mulroney also hammered away at Trudeau's patronage appointments and what he claimed was John Turner's appalling lack of leadership in meekly accepting them.

In 2004 voters trying to measure the leadership qualities of the new Conservative leader, Stephen Harper, must have experienced considerable difficulty. For one thing, despite the name, the new Conservative Party of Canada (CPC) lacked the familiar "brand appeal" of the old Progressive Conservative Party. Also, Harper had so recently been installed as party leader that many voters probably had a hard time using his image as an information shortcut in any decision to either support or oppose his party. Yet another difficulty was that voters who might have tried to locate the new party in issue space may have assumed it was either too much or not enough like the Reform and Alliance parties that were the principal predecessors of the CPC. Enhancing this possibility was that Harper was so new to the leadership; and, as observed, his failure to muzzle ideological extremists in the party enabled the Liberals to paint Harper and the CPC as a group of right-wing nutcases. Thus, despite the avalanche of criticism and derision directed at Martin and the Liberals because of the sponsorship scandal, the best Harper could do was to limit the Liberals to a minority government.

In Chapter Four we consider the 2004 American presidential election. This contest was won handily by incumbent President George W. Bush and his fellow Republicans in Congress because they convinced enough Americans that they were best able to deal with terrorism—perhaps the contemporary exemplar of a valence issue. They were able to do this despite the erosion of the president's support for his handling of the ongoing war in Iraq. Nor was that Bush's only problem. He had taken over in 2000 in an environment of huge budget surpluses and had turned the surpluses into record deficits. Mounting monthly trade deficits running into the billions compounded the problem. So, the reader may ask, how did the president not only win the electoral college but also manage to win 500,000 more popular votes than his Democratic opponent, Senator John Kerry.

We argue that President Bush won in great part because, on the highly salient valence issue of terrorism, 85 per cent of the public judged that he was doing a good or very good job. This huge number made it possible for the president to have an overall three to two favorable margin on evaluations of what was the most important issue in the election. These kudos cut across party lines. Not only did President Bush get a universally positive rating from Republican identifiers, he was also lauded by over one-third of Democrats and, importantly, by over half of Independents.

Bush also came out ahead on another major component of valence politics: his positive image. Most important in the image contest with Kerry was that Bush was regarded as a stronger leader. The president was also fortunate in having an opponent who conducted a considerably less than exemplary campaign. On the campaign trail Kerry was verbose, rambling, and at times seemingly disinterested. He was also unable to address people's concerns about the economy, another valence issue on which Bush and the Republicans were vulnerable. Perhaps most disastrous for Kerry's image, and most perplexing to both reporters who covered the campaign and to Democrats more generally, was why Kerry did not respond to his "Swift Boat attackers" about his military service in Vietnam.

Here was a situation that was ripe with irony. Kerry, who *volunteered* for service in Vietnam (rather than being drafted), and then *volunteered* again for a hazardous combat assignment as a commander on a Swift Boat, who was twice wounded and decorated, nonetheless was being attacked by groups associated with and funded by supporters of Bush-Cheney. In contrast to Kerry, neither Bush nor Dick Cheney had served in Vietnam, in combat nor otherwise. Bush spent his Vietnam years in the United States, in less than scintillating service in the Texas Air National Guard, and Cheney asked for and received multiple draft deferments because he was a graduate student. Ironic or not, Kerry's failure to defend himself against such scurrilous charges did little to boost public confidence that he could be trusted to defend the United States in an age of international terrorism.

Our focus in Chapter Five is the 2000 presidential election in which George W. Bush's opponent was former congressmen, senator, and two-term vice president Albert Gore, Jr. Gore had a very different problem than Kerry's—how to square the political circle, a problem on which his election as president might well hinge. Most political elites, members of the media, and average citizens undoubtedly believed that the 2000 presidential election was a contest that Gore and his running mate, Senator Joseph Lieberman, could not lose. The economy was robust, high inflation and unemployment rates were but fading memories, and the stock market, fuelled by the dot-com revolution, had soared to unprecedented heights. The huge budget deficits that had accrued during the Reagan and Bush, Sr. presidencies were also things of the past. The booming economy had turned the deficits of the 1970s and 1980s into equally large surpluses in the late 1990s. Even the widely feared implosion of the world's computing system as the millennium drew to a close—the so-called Y2K meltdown—did not occur.

There were, of course, domestic and foreign policy problems. However, the Democratic faithful who gathered at the convention in Los Angeles had high hopes that the presidency would remain Democratic and, with luck, the party might even regain control of Congress. Both Gore and Lieberman were seasoned intelligent professionals who in their personal lives embodied the "family values" that were presumed to be of such electoral importance to millions of American voters. But in the latter lay a problem for the Gore-Lieberman team. How could they claim credit for eight years of plenty without at the same time embracing William Jefferson Clinton, the presumed chief architect of those eight good years, but also a president who had been recently impeached on charges stemming from his illicit sexual affair with White House intern Monica Lewinsky. The choice that Gore made—to distance himself as far as possible from Clinton—proved to be very costly.

To be sure, there were also serious questions that could be raised about their Republican opponents. Dick Cheney, Bush's choice as a running mate, was regarded by most political observers as an able and effective political professional, a former congressman and secretary of defense who had left politics and had become a very successful businessman. The problem was that he had suffered several serious cardiac episodes. The question was whether the long electoral campaign and, if the Republicans won, the stress of returning to public life as the holder of the second-highest office in the land might prove to be too much for him. As for Bush, which "W" would the country be getting? Would it be the confessed former heavy drinker, the less-than-successful businessman and take-no-prisoners political partisan who was the hatchetman and loyalty enforcer for his father's two presidential campaigns? Or would it be the two-term governor of Texas with a reputation as a "unifier rather than a partisan divider," a Republican who told other Republicans that it was wrong to try to balance the budget on the backs of the poor, a Republican who was a different kind of conservative, a "compassionate one"?

Given these several considerations, why did the Gore-Lieberman team lose the election? In a narrow sense, they lost in the end because of a 5–4 decision by the Supreme Court of the United States that had the effect of giving Bush the electoral votes of Florida and, with them, a slight majority in the electoral college. They thus lost the presidency, despite receiving 500,000 more popular votes than Bush. But there are other reasons. The vice president could not even carry his own state, Tennessee, or former President Clinton's home state, Arkansas. A win in either would have given Gore and his running mate the victory they sought. They failed to win these and other states, it will inevitably be argued, because of their decision to distance themselves from a very popular outgoing president. We will show that Gore also lost because of his relative weakness on one of the major variables in the valence politics model, namely, his image as a political leader. Gore's image was significantly diminished by his performance in three presidential debates he not only was expected to win but to dominate. It was not to be.

Over the past decade, it has become a virtual cliché among students of American congressional elections to endorse former Speaker of the House of Representatives Tip O'Neill's widely quoted aphorism that "all politics are local." Not everyone agrees. Some observers, disputing the universality of the wisdom of the former speaker, contend that periodically congressional elections become "nationalized." This is because one or more major issues affecting the country, because of their divisiveness and complexity, fail to be resolved for a substantial period of time. Public discontent with the situation boils over in particular elections, such as the 1932 contest that led to a long period of Democratic majorities in the House and Senate, and to Roosevelt's "New Deal," which forever changed the scope and power of the federal government.

In Chapter Six we argue that the 2006 congressional election was just such a nationalized contest. The major issue focus of that election was the war in Iraq and President Bush's (mis)handling of it and other problems. Like the 2004 and 2006 Canadian federal elections, the 2006 congressional election was also about scandals. Some of these scandals were sexual, others were financial. But, the "big beast" was Iraq. The war was in its third year, and it appeared to many observers that precious little progress was being made. Military and civilian casualties were rising steadily, and Bush's monthly presidential approval ratings were in free fall. On the eve of the election, the president's popularity stood at a dismal 37 per cent.

We were especially interested in this election because it provides a test of the generality of the valence model of electoral choice. If the model could do as good a job of explaining a congressional election as it does for presidential ones, we would have demonstrated that, regardless of the level of the office involved, individual voters make their choices in great part because of valence considerations.

The distinction between explaining individual voting behavior and explaining election outcomes is important here. The distinction can be easily blurred when it comes to studying congressional elections. Many scholars studying these contests focus on wining and losing seats, and not on what motivates the choices that individual voters make. Thus, political scientists have argued that congressional elections, particularly "off-year" ones that are devoid of an accompanying presidential contest, are decided almost entirely by incumbency, the balance of Democratic and Republican identifiers in the congressional districts, and the human and financial resources available to congressional candidates (e.g., Box-Steffensmeier et al., 2003; Cover, 1977; Fenno, 1978; Kimball, Meinke, and Tate, 2003; Romero, 2006, but see Campbell, 1997). Incumbent congressmen use these resources to build large campaign war chests to deter potential challengers, and to engage in a variety of other activities that help ensure their re-election (e.g., Mayhew, 1974). Without gainsaying the validity of these arguments, we contend that the 2006 congressional election demonstrates how nationally generated valence politics forces can drive the behavior of millions of voters participating in elections for members of the House of Representatives.

The elections analyzed in Chapters Two through Six are very recent. Accordingly, in Chapter Seven we investigate the generality of various models of electoral choice by considering three important twentieth-century elections. These are the 1980 American presidential election and the 1988 and 1993 Canadian federal elections. In the 1980 presidential election, Republican candidate Ronald Reagan emphasized that he was an ideological conservative who aimed not only to stop but to actually roll back the tide of "big government" that had begun with FDR's New Deal, which had then been reinvigorated by Harry Truman's "Fair Deal," and dramatically extended by Lyndon Johnson's "Great Society" programs. Reagan also promised to pursue, in contrast to the incumbent Democratic President Jimmy Carter, an aggressive foreign policy vis-à-vis the former Soviet Union, which he would openly label an "Evil Empire." Consistent with his conservatism, Reagan also promised massive tax cuts because, as he frequently observed, ordinary Americans know better than the government how they want to spend their money.

The 1988 Canadian federal election has become known as the "free trade" election. Liberal leader John Turner and his media experts succeeded in making free trade virtually the only issue in an election that, according to Turner, would decide Canada's future as an independent nation-state. If the Conservatives under Prime Minister Brian Mulroney were successful in passing free trade legislation, he argued, they would "sell out" their country. Rather than being the "True North, Strong and Free," Canada would become an economic, political, and cultural vassal of the American empire. The problem for the Liberals, as we will demonstrate, was that sometimes you *do* have to be careful what you wish for. The Liberals succeeded in making free trade *the issue* of the 1988 election, but a substantial proportion of the Canadian electorate did not share Turner's views of Mulroney or how the free trade deal would affect the future of Canada.

By 1992 Prime Minister Mulroney and his government faced a virtual tsunami of problems, a number of which angry and disappointed Conservative stalwarts attributed to Mulroney himself. Western Conservatives complained that Mulroney had made a number of symbolic and substantive decisions to woo Quebec that proved to be both wrong and in vain. Mulroney's efforts to broker a constitutional deal that would quell the fires of separatism and turn Quebec into a Conservative electoral stronghold had "crashed and burned." According to his critics, both the failed Meech Lake Accord and the lost referendum on the Charlottetown Accord were Mulroney-initiated disasters—end of story.

In hindsight, these judgments of the man may seem excessively harsh since the Conservatives had other major problems as well. For example, the economy had gone into a serious recession in the early 1990s, and it was easy to blame the "Mulroney free trade deal" for the job losses and continuing economic distress. Also, many Canadians were exercised by the Conservative government's decision to ignore public opinion and pass the massively unpopular Goods and Services Tax (GST). Voters were reminded of the GST with the 7 per cent charge added to virtually every purchase they made.

The political consequences for the Conservatives were dire. In the 1993 federal election, they elected only two members of Parliament, fully 167 fewer than they had in the previous (1988) election. The New Democrats, although they did not suffer as harsh an electoral fate as the Conservatives, were also decimated. Out of these ruins arose two new parties, the Western-based Reform Party, and the separatist Quebec-only Bloc Québécois. Our analyses of the 1993 PSC survey data indicate that the limping economy, a quintessential valence issue, and the widespread unpopularity of the new Conservative leader, Kim Campbell, were key factors in the Conservatives' demise.

As observed above, most of the research on voting behavior in Canada and the United States has focused on party and candidate choice. Less attention has been devoted to turnout. In Canada, until relatively recently, nonvoting had never been regarded as a serious problem. In the United States much of the focus, for good reason, was on the paucity of African Americans voting in the South because of the chilling effect of voter registration requirements designed to keep nonwhites from exercising their franchise. In Chapter Eight we employ data from the 2004 Political Support in Canada and the 2004 American National Election surveys to investigate the efficacy of several different models of electoral participation. These analyses show that a variety of factors affect the turnout decision. Some of these factors, particularly, sense of civic duty, are very strongly related to age. Although the American survey does not include the requisite question, the Canadian survey does and it shows a huge civic duty gap between younger and older people. Many younger people simply do not view voting as an obligation of citizenship. Other important factors affecting turnout include, *inter alia*, variables such as strength of party identification, perceptions of inter-party competition, and efforts by the parties to mobilize supporters. No one model can explain the decision to (not) vote.

In Chapter Nine we conclude by addressing three questions. First, why do valence issues resonate so strongly with both Canadian and American voters? Second, why does electoral participation vary strongly with age, and what are the possible future consequences of this relationship? Third, we briefly consider what our findings tell us about the quality of citizen participation in Canada and the United States—two of the world's oldest continuing functioning democracies—and attendant implications for understanding the problems and prospects for democratic governance in the twenty-first century.

Note: We encourage readers who are unfamiliar with key differences between the American presidential-congressional and Canadian parliamentary systems to refer to this chapter's appendix, where we briefly compare the two systems.

Two Democratic Polities

A Comparative Primer

The American president and the Canadian prime minister are the heads of their parties and their governments, but the president, unlike the prime minister, is also the head of state and embodies in his office the sovereignty of the United States. He is elected for a four-year term and remains president regardless of whether his party is in the majority in either or both the House of Representatives and the Senate. In Canada if a prime minister's party loses an election, he is no longer prime minister. Moreover, in Canada, the de facto head of state is the Governor General. The Governor General's role is purely symbolic and devoid of any real political power. In contrast, an American president derives very substantial substantive and symbolic power and authority from being head of state.

His constitutional authority as head of state contained in Article 2, Section 2 of the American Constitution makes the president commander-in-chief of the American armed forces, gives him the power to grant pardons, and the power to make treaties for the United States, by and with the consent of the Senate. However, he can also employ executive agreements that do not require senatorial consent to conduct foreign policy. The ability to project American military force anywhere in the world and to make treaties and executive agreements, as well as to grant pardons, are formidable powers indeed. Although a president through his power as commander-in-chief can involve the United States in prolonged armed conflicts, or through an executive agreement significantly change not only foreign but also the domestic status quo with the stroke of a pen (as President Truman did when he desegregated the American armed forces), these powers are not the kind a president exercises on a day-to-day basis. More important to his popularity and image, and to his potential to be re-elected if he is eligible, as well as to get others to do what he wants, are the symbolic powers he derives from being head of state.

There is first the pomp and circumstance that have become attached to the office of president. When he enters a room at a dinner or other formal occasion, customarily everyone rises, and a band strikes up "Hail to the Chief." When he travels to the presidential retreat at Camp David, it is in one of his fleet of helicopters, and when he is travelling a substantial distance within the country or abroad, he flies on his specially appointed jet, Airforce One.

The president is frequently in the public eye. He will often visit places that have been struck by a flood, a hurricane, a forest fire, or some other disaster, where he can be shown to look sympathetic on the nightly news, inspecting the area, chatting with citizens and local officials, and almost always promising federal aid to address the calamity. There are also the periodic "photo ops" provided by visits with championship college and professional sports teams. During these events, a smiling president will appear on national television surrounded by team members who present him with souvenirs, such as team jerseys, jackets, and game balls. The president can also be seen on television presiding at various events that range in significance and solemnity from laying a wreath to honor America's fallen in battle on Memorial Day, to declaring open National Girl Scout Cookie Week. The president lights the nation's Christmas tree, he and his wife often lead the hunt for Easter eggs on the White House lawn in the company of dozens of smiling children, and every Thanksgiving, by presidential decree, he saves one of two turkeys destined for the White House table—an act of clemency duly recorded for television both within and outside the United States.

In Canada, some prime ministers, such as the charismatic Pierre Trudeau or the colorful orator John Diefenbaker, become household names throughout the country. Other prime ministers, although not quite as well known, also have considerable salience. Similar to US presidents, Canadian prime ministers attempt to enhance their public standing by availing themselves of opportunities to generate favorable publicity whenever possible. The range of such opportunities may be smaller than those available to American presidents, but media scrutiny of prime ministers is nevertheless intense. Like their American counterparts, prime ministers are preeminent figures on the national political stage.

Although they are selected in different ways, both presidents and prime ministers are leaders of their parties. Most incumbent presidents who are eligible for a second and final term are virtually certain of the nomination of their party. When a two-term president such as William Jefferson Clinton left office, his vice president for eight years, Albert Gore, received his party's nomination as did Bush, Sr. after eight years as Ronald Reagan's vice president. Since the current vice president, Richard Cheney, has evidenced no desire to seek his party's nomination, a half-dozen or so contestants, including governors, senators, and congressmen, and even a former mayor, became aspirants for the Republican nomination. Similarly, when the party that lost the presidency last time around begins the process of choosing its new presidential candidate, a large number of contenders typically throw their hats in the ring.

In the United States, since the 1960s, the candidates of both parties have been chosen as a result of winning a requisite number of state primary and caucus contests. The New Hampshire primary and the Iowa caucuses come first. A candidate must win a majority of the delegates of the several states to the party's national convention, which meets every four years. The road to a nomination since the 1960s has been a long and hard one, and serious contenders tend to follow the lead of Jimmy Carter, who began his quest more than two years before the actual election. The winning candidates select their presidential running mates at their respective conventions, and the period between the national conventions and the first Tuesday in November (Election Day) is devoted to intensive campaigning.

When Americans go to the polls to vote for a president, they are voting for an individual, but they do so by voting for a slate of state electors who are pledged to their party's candidate. The number of electors in each state is equivalent to the combined number of the state's senators and congressmen and women, which gives a minimum of three electors to even the smallest states. Together, these slates of electors comprise the 538 members of the electoral college (equal to the 535 members of Congress from the 50 states plus 3 members from the District of Columbia). Almost always the winning candidate in the electoral college is also the person who won the popular vote. Occasionally, however, the winner of the popular vote does not always become president. The most recent example was in 2000, when George W. Bush received a majority in the electoral college (with the assistance of a 5–4 vote in the Supreme Court) despite the fact that his Democratic opponent, Vice President Al Gore, had received some half-million more popular votes.

In Canada the leader of a party which has won a majority or plurality of the contests in 308 parliamentary ridings is asked by the Governor General to become prime minister. Both president and prime minister select their cabinets, the men and women who will become the heads of the several departments of government. They are termed "secretaries" in the United States and "ministers" in Canada. These choices are influenced by a variety of constraints. For example, in Canada there is a convention that each of the provinces will be represented by a minister chosen from among the Members of Parliament (MPs) of the prime minister's party elected from the province. A problem arises when a province has not elected a Member of Parliament from the winning party. There is also the necessity of recognizing representatives of key demographic groups, as well as from the parties' "base" of core electoral supporters. A president must also make sure that socioeconomic, demographic, and sectional interests are taken into consideration in making his cabinet selections. A major difference between the two systems is that because of the formal separation of powers doctrine enshrined in the US Constitution, a sitting Member of Congress or the holder of a judicial position cannot be a member of the cabinet. In Canada no one can serve in the cabinet who is not a Member of Parliament.

Most American presidents rarely rely on cabinet secretaries for advice on major policy issues. For this purpose, presidents look more often to their chief of staff, to the White House Council, and to other key members of the White House staff and the executive office of the presidency. A Canadian prime minister, although much more than a "first-among-equals," relies more often on the collective opinion of his cabinet in setting and carrying out the agenda for a parliamentary session. Although like a president he can fire any cabinet minister he appoints, normally too many dismissals or resignations call into question the leadership ability of the prime minister. Consequently, a prime minister is more likely to treat his cabinet as a key advisory group whom he must consult regularly. An American president, apart from a ritualistic first meeting with the cabinet he has appointed after an election, rarely meets with that entire body. Presidents also rarely, if ever, attend caucuses of their congressional party. Prime ministers do so regularly, in great part because a prime minister has no independent statutory base for his status as does a president. By convention, a prime minister remains in office only as long as he has the support of a majority of Parliament which, given the convention of disciplined and cohesive parliamentary parties, means that he has to have the support of a majority of the members of his own caucus. If and when he should lose that support, a new leader will be chosen.

Though elections have usually taken place in four-year intervals, historically parliaments are elected for a maximum of five years. If the prime minister judges the timing to be advantageous, he or she has the ability to dissolve parliament and ask the governor general to call an election. A new fixed election law may make four years the rule, but how the law will be interpreted remains to be seen. In the United States, a president is elected for a fixed four-year term, the 435 members of the House of Representatives are elected for fixed two-year terms, and the 100 senators are elected for fixed six-year terms. Staggered elections to the Senate result in one-third of its members facing re-election every two years together with all members of the House of Representatives.

A final notable difference is that individual members of both the House and Senate in the United States are important political actors in their own right. Any congressperson or senator can introduce legislation and every senator or House member serves on two or more committees or sub-committees. These committees or sub-committees are miniature legislatures in which the real business of evaluating legislative proposals that may become law takes place. Service on committees of interest to House and Senate members is highly prized. The committees are hierarchically organized in the sense that occupancy of a committee chairmanship position or becoming a ranking minority member is largely determined by a seniority system. A House member or senator who becomes committee chair or ranking minority member usually has the longest period of uninterrupted service on the committee.

In contrast, parliamentary committees in Canada, although more important than in the past, still are of relatively little importance for the outcome of legislation. As is well known, only cabinet members and opposition "front benchers" are important actors in the legislative process. The importance of the latter, although they have no effect on the content of legislation, lies in their constant criticism of the government's policy proposals and in the alternative policies they offer to a supposedly attentive country.

The great strength of the American presidential-congressional system is held to be that Congress is both a representative and a law-making body. All of the 435 members of the House and the 100 members of the Senate are important public policy actors, but they are also first and foremost the representatives of the interests of their districts and states. The great weakness of the system is in its inability to deal with major public problems by generating coherent legislative enactments that are substantial departures from the status quo. Because of the separation of powers, and the fragmented character of Congress (because of the committee and sub-committee systems), as well as the power of major interest groups, it is extremely difficult to enact major legislation to address pressing public problems. For the same reasons, it is difficult for the American public to assign responsibility to someone or some group when nothing or little is done about a major problem, or when legislation that is enacted produces unintended and unwanted outcomes.

The great strength of Canada's Westminster-model parliamentary government is the ability of a government with a majority to address any major public problem with whatever legislative and financial remedies it desires, and then to be held accountable to the electorate for what it has done. Since a majority government can pass any legislation or budget it desires within reason, by doing so that government also accepts responsibility for unfavorable as well as favorable outcomes. Lines of accountability are clear.

A major weakness of parliamentary government is held to be that the great majority of backbench MPs have no real role in the policy process. As a result, many talented people elected to Parliament resign after one or two terms because they feel underutilized and underappreciated. Unlike the United States Congress, the Canadian Parliament does not offer the great majority of MPs opportunities to enjoy a career. As a consequence, Canadian Parliaments, unlike the US Congress, have very substantial membership turnover following an election, with each election bringing up to 40 per cent of new members who, it can be argued, have difficulty providing their ridings with the kind of effective representation that the average member of the House of Representatives or Senate does. These, then, are some of the key similarities and differences for the reader to keep in mind in the chapters that follow.

CHAPTER TWO

Flawless Campaign, Fragile Victory

The 2006 Canadian Federal Election

C anada's 23rd federal election was held on January 23, 2006. Only 20 months earlier, on June 28, 2004, the governing Liberals—in power continuously since 1993—had been reduced to a minority in Parliament, winning 135 of 308 seats and 37 per cent of the popular vote. Minority governments in Canada typically have quite short half-lives, and the Liberal government formed in 2004 was no exception. After narrowly avoiding defeat on its budget bill in May 2005, the government lost a vote of confidence in the House of Commons on November 28, and Canadians faced the prospect of a winter trek to the polls. And, since the holiday season was fast approaching, election day was deferred until late January, making the campaign an atypically long one by Canadian standards. It also proved to be a very exciting one.

A DYNAMIC AND CONSEQUENTIAL CAMPAIGN

The issues in play in the 2006 campaign strongly resembled those in 2004. Most salient was the "Adscam" or sponsorship scandal. In the run-up to the 2004 election, the Auditor General's annual report revealed that former Prime Minister Jean Chrétien's government had allocated millions of dollars to pro-Liberal advertising agencies in Quebec, ostensibly to inform Quebeckers of the many good things Ottawa was doing on their behalf. In fact, much of the work was not done, and proper records were not maintained. The scandal prompted a judicial inquiry (the Gomery Commission), which reported on November 1, 2005, that although Liberal leader Prime Minister Paul Martin was not personally culpable, Chrétien and several other prominent Liberals bore responsibility for fostering a "culture of entitlement." In addition, the report described a massive kickback scheme whereby large sums of money had been funnelled into party coffers. The scandal had tarnished Martin's image and damaged Liberal fortunes in 2004 and, reinvigorated by the Gomery findings, it threatened to do so again in 2006.

At first this did not seem to be the case. Early November public opinion surveys showed a sharp drop in Liberal support immediately after the Gomery revelations, but the party's poll numbers quickly rebounded. When the campaign began in late November, several surveys reported that the Liberals were running well ahead of their principal rivals, the Conservative Party of Canada (CPC), with vote intention shares very similar to the parties' respective vote tallies in the 2004 election. The Liberals maintained their sizable lead in the polls for nearly three weeks into the campaign, prompting observers to conclude that the campaign was nothing more than "déjà vu all over again." A Liberal victory was inevitable.

The conclusion was decidedly premature. Canadians traditionally have prided themselves that their country—in sharp contrast to their giant neighbor to the south—is a land of "peace, order, and good government." Events in late December 2006 caused them to reconsider. Violent crime has been on the increase in Canada in recent years, prompting widespread media attention and mounting public concern. The problem was dramatized on December 26, when a teenage girl became an innocent victim of gang violence after being shot in midtown Toronto. Sensational accounts of the horrific slaying prompted public outrage, and the Martin government was criticized for allowing "peace" and "order" to be jeopardized.

More bad news for the prime minister and his colleagues quickly followed when two new financial scandals made national headlines, putting "good government" into question again. One of the stories concerned yet more misdeeds in the sponsorship scandal, whereas the second—the "income trust affair"—involved charges of insider trading using information obtained from the office of Minister of Finance Ralph Goodale. A senior Liberal cabinet minister, Goodale rejected calls for his resignation, claiming that he had done nothing wrong, and that the public release of information about an RCMP investigation into the charges constituted a highly irregular attempt to influence the election.

Figure 2.1 suggests the finance minister had good reason to be concerned.[1] As 2005 drew to a close, Liberal poll numbers were sliding downward, and CPC support—already increasing—was surging. The events of late December seemingly acted like a booster rocket for the Conservatives, propelling their upward trend. In early January they pulled ahead of the Liberals in the polls and never relinquished the lead afterwards. Trends in party support in Ontario and Quebec were particularly important. In Ontario, the Conservatives and New Democratic Party (NDP) both benefited at the Liberals' expense, and in Quebec, increasing numbers of so-called soft nationalists began to desert the Bloc Québécois (BQ), which had been leading in the polls, in favor of the Conservatives.

Although scandals and violent crime dominated the news at a crucial juncture in the campaign, other issues were being discussed as well. As is typical in Canadian elections, the competing parties tried to convince voters that they would deliver a bountiful supply of health care and other cherished public services. Hospital care waiting times and child care were focal points of concern. Attempting to demonstrate that he was very much in the mainstream, and not the "right-wing nut" the Liberals portrayed him as being in 2004, Conservative leader Stephen Harper promised

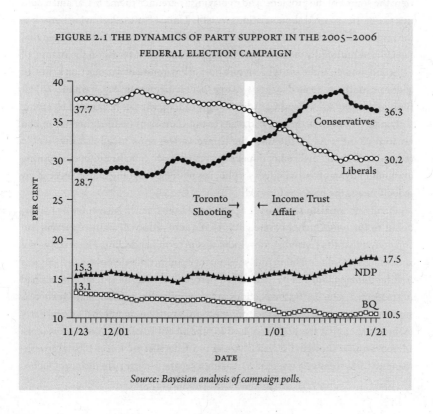

FIGURE 2.1 THE DYNAMICS OF PARTY SUPPORT IN THE 2005–2006 FEDERAL ELECTION CAMPAIGN

Source: Bayesian analysis of campaign polls.

that a CPC government would boost health care funding, implement a guaranteed hospital waiting time scheme, and give families an annual $1,200 per child allowance, "no strings attached." Possible merits aside, Harper's child-care proposal had an immediate political payoff when Prime Minister Martin's communications director, Scott Reid, ill-advisedly quipped to the media that parents would simply blow it on "beer and popcorn." The Conservatives responded that Reid's comment exemplified the Liberals' deep disrespect for average Canadians, and their arrogance fuelled by years—too many years—in power.

Another 2004 issue enjoying an encore was same-sex marriage. Gay and lesbian marriages were endorsed as a "Charter right" by both the Liberals and the NDP, and also supported by the BQ. However, the Conservatives promised that same-sex marriage would be subject to a free vote in Parliament should they win the election. Gun control, US-Canada relations, and the Goods and Services Tax (GST) also made return engagements. In the wake of heavy criticism of their gun registry program and the aforementioned wave of highly publicized shootings in major cities, the Liberals proposed eliminating all handguns. The Conservatives responded that the Liberals (and NDP) were mistaking pistols for perpetrators, and that the latter, not the former, were the source of the problem. And, replaying a perennial theme in Canadian politics, the parties sparred about relations with the United States. Portraying himself as the resolute defender of Canadian sovereignty, Prime Minister Martin charged that the US had repeatedly violated NAFTA regulations about tariffs on the import of softwood lumber, and was negligent on a host of environmental protection issues. In addition, Martin reiterated his 2004 charge that Harper was in league with President Bush and had plans to send Canadian troops to Iraq. Harper responded by saying that, in fact, it was Martin who had plans to put Canadians on the firing line in that wartorn country. As for the GST, the Conservatives announced that they would reduce the heartily disliked national sales tax by 2 per cent. The Liberals, touting low unemployment and a budget surplus, countered by arguing that an income tax reduction was the best way forward.

Finally, national unity was once again on the front burner. After the very narrow defeat of the 1995 Quebec sovereignty referendum proposal, many observers had concluded that the separatist movement was in terminal decline. However, as the 2004 election result and numerous subsequent opinion polls demonstrated, this was wishful thinking. Fuelled by widespread perceptions that the federal Liberals had "disrespected" Quebec by their actions in the sponsorship scandal, Bloc Québécois support skyrocketed. Early in the 2006 election campaign, an internal Liberal Party memo warned that the BQ was poised to take all but 10 of the province's 75 seats. Moreover, polls showed that Jean Charest's pro-federalist provincial Liberal government was also massively unpopular, making a separatist victory in the next Quebec provincial election a distinct possibility. If the Parti Québécois regained power in Quebec City, this would set the stage for another sovereignty referendum.

The apparent strength of pro-sovereignty forces in Quebec early in the campaign was both a problem and an opportunity for the federal Liberals. It was an obvious problem for them because the growth of separatist sentiment had occurred on their watch. Yet, it was an opportunity as well. Historically, the Liberals have reaped political profits by portraying themselves to voters outside of Quebec as the only party that can keep Quebec in Confederation. Equally, the Liberals have been able to convince many Quebeckers that they are the only party that can keep the separatists in check, while advancing Quebec's interests in the national political arena. In the 2006 election campaign, Martin and his party played this familiar double-edged gambit one more time. The Conservatives countered by arguing that Quebeckers' support for federalism could be best secured by redressing the "fiscal imbalance" whereby Ottawa starved Quebec and other provinces of much-needed tax revenue. The idea proved popular.

An air of desperation and disorganization hung over the Liberal campaign in the waning days of the campaign. Sensing their peril, the Liberals "went negative." Replaying their 2004 strategy, they unleashed a barrage of somber TV advertisements that portrayed CPC leader Harper as an ideological zealot. Viewers were warned that Harper had a "hidden agenda." He would dismantle the health care system and other highly valued public services, implement secret schemes for military occupation of major Canadian cities, and do the United States' bidding by placing Canadian soldiers in harm's way in Iraq and other danger zones. Also similar to 2004, the Liberals tried to convince supporters of the left-of-center NDP that they should behave tactically, voting Liberal to stop the right-wing bogeyman. However, as it became increasingly evident that the Liberals' scare tactics were not working and they were poised for defeat, NDP leader Jack Layton tried to turn the logic of tactical voting on its head. He appealed to Liberal supporters to "lend us your vote" to ensure a strong progressive voice in Ottawa to oppose a Harper-led CPC government. For his part, Harper stuck to his carefully scripted game plan of emphasizing relatively popular policies such as cutting the GST and providing an unmonitored child-care allowance, while restraining enthusiastic colleagues tempted to engage in ideological diatribes.

The Conservative plan worked and the party's lead in the polls held. On election day turnout was up slightly (64.7 per cent versus 60.9 per cent in 2004), with the Conservatives attracting 36 per cent of the vote, almost a 7 per cent increase over 2004. This was less than party strategists had hoped for, but it was enough to give the CPC a small plurality (124) of seats in Parliament, and the opportunity to form a minority government. In contrast, the Liberals' seat total dropped from 135 to 103 and their vote share fell from 36.7 per cent to 30.2 per cent. The Liberals' 13-year hold on national power had ended. Upon learning the disappointing news, Liberal leader Paul Martin immediately resigned.

The fortunes of the smaller parties also varied. The NDP was relatively successful, capturing 17.5 per cent of the vote and 29 seats, 10 more than in 2004. However, the Bloc Québécois faltered. Although the BQ captured 51 of Quebec's 75 seats (only three less than in 2004), its vote total declined from 48.9 per cent to 42.1 per cent. A new era in Canadian politics had begun.

MAKING ELECTORAL CHOICES

As discussed in Chapter One, Canadian political scientists have often emphasized that a triumvirate of factors—valence issues, leader images, and partisanship—are crucial elements in voters' decision-making processes (e.g., Clarke et al., 1996; Clarke, Kornberg, and Wearing, 2000; see also Blais, 2000). Unlike the "pro-con" position issues, such as the desirability of free trade with the United States that divided the Canadian electorate in 1988 or the 2004 debate on same-sex marriage, valence issues are ones upon which there is widespread consensus (Stokes, 1963, 1992). A healthy economy, accessible health care, and public security are good examples. For valence issues, political debate centers on which party or leader can do the best job in achieving goals that virtually everyone shares.

Data gathered in the 2006 Political Support in Canada (PSC) survey enable us to investigate the mix of issues that informed the choices Canadians made in the 2006 election.[2] We begin with the sponsorship scandal, an issue that had bedevilled Prime Minister Martin and his Liberal government in the 2004 election. As noted above, the scandal was reinvigorated by the Gomery Commission's findings. It continued to receive widespread media coverage in 2006 with new revelations, including those about the income trust affair, helping to keep possible Liberal misdeeds in office on the front burner throughout much of the campaign. In one sense, we may take it as given that the sponsorship scandal was a valence issue; the vast majority of people view corruption as a "bad thing." However, the implications of the scandal for evaluating the Liberals' ability to govern are another matter.

As Figure 2.2A shows, the PSC respondents were divided regarding the lessons to be drawn from the sponsorship scandal. A small majority (51 per cent) thought the scandal proved the Liberals could not govern effectively, and a somewhat larger number (58 per cent) thought the scandal demonstrated that corruption was widespread in the Liberal Party. However, another small majority (52 per cent) concluded that it was unfair to blame the whole party for the scandal. These divisions were strongly correlated with voting. For example, the percentage of PSC respondents voting Conservative declined from 56 per cent among those strongly agreeing that there was widespread corruption in the Liberal Party to only 4 per cent among those

FIGURE 2.2 THE SPONSORSHIP SCANDAL AND ELECTORAL CHOICE, 2006

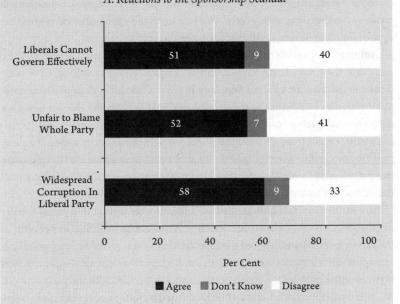

A. Reactions to the Sponsorship Scandal

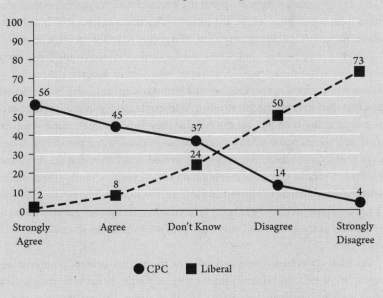

B. Liberal and Conservative Voting by Judgments that
Scandal Proves that There Is Widespread Corruption in the Liberal Party

strongly disagreeing (see Figure 2.2B). Liberal support demonstrates precisely the opposite pattern rising from 2 per cent among those who strongly agreed with the corruption charge to 73 per cent among those who strongly disagreed. Below, we will consider whether these strong correlations are sustained when statistical controls are applied for other possible causes of voting behavior.

Although evaluations of the implications of the sponsorship scandal divided the electorate, there were clearly large numbers of voters who were willing to believe it demonstrated that the Liberals were unfit to govern. The Liberals hoped to counter this impression by pointing to the strength of Canada's economy. The economy is a quintessential valence issue—everyone wants economic good times—and governing parties expect to profit from them. Accordingly, the Liberals wanted to claim credit for successful stewardship of the country's economic affairs, and to emphasize that party leader, Prime Minister Paul Martin, had engineered the healthy economy during his lengthy term as finance minister during the Chrétien years.

The PSC survey data indicate that the Liberals were correct to try to get voters to focus on the economy as an election issue. A substantial majority (62 per cent) of the survey respondents believed the Liberals had done a "good" or "very good" job managing the economy (see Figure 2.3A) and, again, there was a strong correlation between attitudes about the government's economic performance and party support. As Figure 2.3B illustrates, Liberal voting increased by fully 74 per cent as judgments about the party's stewardship of the economy move from negative to positive. And, as also expected, Conservative voting moved in exactly the opposite direction, declining by 47 per cent as judgments about the government's economic performance shifted from negative to positive. The economy clearly was an issue with potential to help the Liberals. Getting voters to focus on it proved to be the problem.

As in the 2004 election, politicians and the media devoted considerable attention to selected position issues—issues upon which voters disagree—in 2006. Two of these issues were same-sex marriage and relations with the United States. In both cases, the electorate was deeply divided. As illustrated in Figure 2.4, 43 per cent of the people in the 2006 PSC survey said that they favored same-sex marriage and 39 per cent were opposed. On relations between Canada and the United States, 32 per cent favored looser ties, 27 per cent wanted closer ones, and the remainder preferred the status quo. Public opinion on a third position issue—the trade-off between tax reductions and increased public services—was different. On this issue a substantial majority (60 per cent) favored tax reduction, 37 per cent opted to keep things as they were, and only 3 per cent were willing to shoulder a heavier tax burden.

The relatively even divisions of opinion on the first two of these position issues suggest that there were relatively small *aggregate gains* to be made by the parties if voters were making their choices based on these issues. What a party would gain

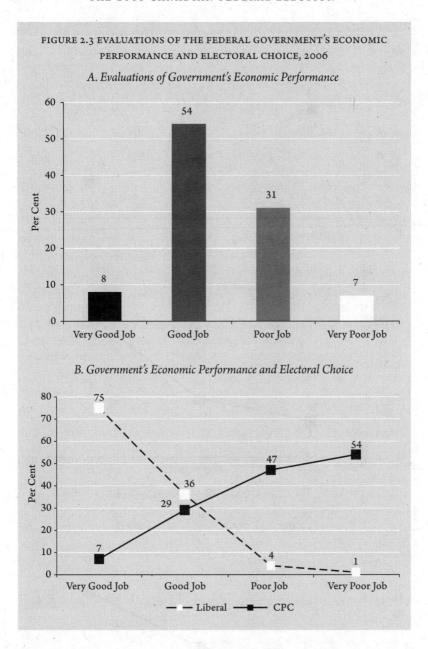

FIGURE 2.3 EVALUATIONS OF THE FEDERAL GOVERNMENT'S ECONOMIC PERFORMANCE AND ELECTORAL CHOICE, 2006

A. Evaluations of Government's Economic Performance

B. Government's Economic Performance and Electoral Choice

from one group of voters, it would lose from another. However, as Figures 2.4A and 2.4B show, these issues did have considerable potential to influence *individual* voting behavior. For example, the percentage voting Conservative increased from 18 per cent to 53 per cent as opinions on same-sex marriage moved from positive to negative. The

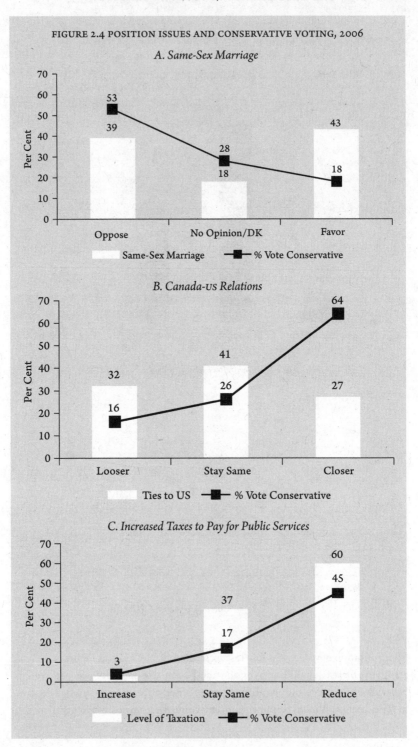

FIGURE 2.4 POSITION ISSUES AND CONSERVATIVE VOTING, 2006

A. Same-Sex Marriage

B. Canada-us Relations

C. Increased Taxes to Pay for Public Services

correlation between voting and relations with the United States was similar, with the percentage casting a CPC vote moving upward from 16 per cent among those who favored looser ties with the US to 64 per cent among those who favored closer ties. The relationship between CPC voting and taxation was also strong, with the percentage opting for the CPC increasing from 3 per cent to 45 per cent as opinions on the desirability of tax reduction moved from negative to positive. These simple bivariate correlations between position issues and voting are impressive. Below, we will see if they are sustained in more sophisticated analyses that control for a variety of possible causal factors.

When trying to determine what causes people to vote the way they do, it is important to recognize that voters do not attach equal weight to all issues. As is typical in Canadian federal elections, valence issues topped the "most important issue" list in 2006. Figure 2.5 shows that concerns about health care and other public services were mentioned by nearly one-third of those participating in the PSC survey, with government dishonesty (including the sponsorship scandal) being cited by nearly one-quarter more of the respondents. All other issues were mentioned much less frequently. Especially noteworthy in this regard were same-sex marriage and relations with the United States. Although these position issues received considerable media attention, less than 3 per cent mentioned one of them as "most important." Two other "hot button" position issues, abortion and immigration, were cited by less than 1 per cent.

Economic issues also had relatively little resonance. Taxation was mentioned by slightly over 10 per cent—typically by people endorsing the Conservative plan to reduce the GST. All other economic issues, including clearly valenced ones such as unemployment, accounted for an additional 11 per cent. As noted above, the Liberals had hoped that voters would credit them for the country's healthy economy and, indeed, a plurality of people mentioning an economic issue other than the GST selected the Liberals as the party closest to them. However, the problem for the Liberals was that relatively few voters accorded priority to the economy in 2006. Consistent with the conjecture advanced by many political economists, it appears that Canadian voters are much less likely to make an issue of good economic news and credit a government for delivering prosperity than they are to emphasize economic bad news and blame a government for its inability to manage the economy effectively (e.g., Bloom and Price, 1975; see also Clarke et al., 1996).

In 2006 the prosperity the Liberals hoped to profit from was seemingly taken for granted. This hurt because they did not do well on most of the issues voters *were* emphasizing. Overall, only 22 per cent preferred the Liberals on an issue deemed most important. The Conservatives did somewhat better (28 per cent), with 17 per cent, 8 per cent, and 4 per cent favoring the NDP, the BQ, or one of the minor

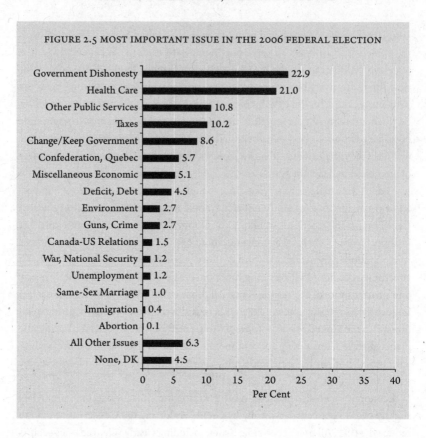

FIGURE 2.5 MOST IMPORTANT ISSUE IN THE 2006 FEDERAL ELECTION

parties, respectively. An additional 22 per cent said no party was closest or that there were no important issues.

Leader Images

As stated in the preface, party leader images typically have large effects on voting behavior in Canada and other mature democracies such as the United States and Great Britain. Voters' assessments of the leaders' character and competence provides them with cost-effective cues to guide their electoral choices in a political world of high stakes and considerable uncertainty (e.g., Clarke, Kornberg, and Wearing, 2000; Clarke et al., 2004). The importance of leader effects on electoral choice suggests why a serious protracted scandal such as the sponsorship affair could do major damage to Liberal prospects. Indeed, many voters had a decidedly negative view of Prime Minister Martin in the run-up to the 2006 election. In the PSC pre-election survey, Martin's average score on a 0–10 "feeling thermometer" scale was only 4.4 in English-speaking Canada and a dismal 3.0 in Quebec (see Figure 2.6). Feelings about the prime minister were powerfully correlated (-.74) with overall reactions to the scandal. People making very harsh judgments about the scandal had a very low opinion of the prime minister, giving him an average score of less than one on the 0–10 point feeling thermometer scale. In sharp contrast, those who considered the scandal unimportant gave him an average score of over eight on this scale.

Martin was not the only leader to experience a chilly public reception. Most important, his principal rival Stephen Harper scored only 4.1 in the rest of Canada (ROC) and 4.8 in Quebec. Again, feelings about Harper were strongly correlated with opinions about the sponsorship scandal, with his average thermometer score ratings on the 0–10 point scale climbing from less than one among those minimizing the importance of the scandal to well over six among those reacting very negatively to it. Other party leaders fared somewhat better, although few voters expressed strong enthusiasm for them. NDP leader Jack Layton scored 5.2 in Quebec and 5.4 in the ROC, while BQ chieftain Gilles Duceppe achieved a 5.7 rating in Quebec, the only locale that mattered for him. Although feelings about Layton were largely unrelated to reactions to the sponsorship scandal, like Martin and Harper, Duceppe's thermometer scores were much higher among Quebeckers who made very negative judgments about the scandal than among those who believed it inconsequential.

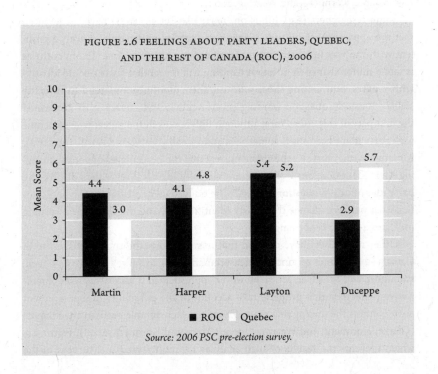

FIGURE 2.6 FEELINGS ABOUT PARTY LEADERS, QUEBEC, AND THE REST OF CANADA (ROC), 2006

Source: 2006 PSC pre-election survey.

Partisanship

Party identification is a third variable that typically has strong effects on voting behavior in Canada and many other countries. As observed in Chapter One, party identification is one of the most important theoretical concepts in voting behavior research. In the original "University of Michigan" studies of the American electorate (e.g., Campbell et al., 1960), the idea was that a large majority of people acquired identifications with political parties analogous to their self-identifications as members of important social groups defined in terms of characteristics such as nationality, ethnicity, or religion. Usually formed during childhood or adolescence, these partisan attachments tended to be very stable over time, and to increase in strength as people aged (Converse, 1969). However, the early Canadian election studies (e.g., Meisel, 1975; Jenson, 1976) suggested that this "Michigan" model of stable party identifications was unsuitable for Canada. Canadians' psychological attachments to political parties are not "fixed in stone," but rather vary over time as voters respond to a changing mix of political events and conditions. Subsequent analyses have confirmed this finding by indicating that large numbers of Canadians have flexible partisan attachments, and are prepared to move from one party to another in response to judgments about the performance of parties and party leaders (e.g., Clarke et al., 1996; Clarke, Kornberg, and Wearing, 2000).

Some researchers (e.g., Johnston, 1992; Blais et al., 2001) have conjectured that the apparent instability in Canadians' party identifications reflects a problem with the way in which those identifications are measured. The hypothesis is that a minor change in question wording will reveal that fewer people identify with a party, but, among those who do, their identifications tend to be quite stable.[3] Recently, question-wording experiments in PSC surveys have confirmed the first part of this conjecture, although differences in the percentage of people with party identifications is sometimes quite small (Clarke and Kornberg, 2008). Moreover, panel survey experiments reveal that the percentages of people changing their identifications over time are virtually identical regardless of how the party identification question is asked. The traditional question wording indicates that 40.4 per cent change their party identification, and the alternative wording indicates 40.6 per cent change.

Other researchers have claimed that measured instability in partisanship in Canada is a product of random measurement error in survey data (e.g., Green, Palmquist, and Schickler, 2002). However, sophisticated statistical analyses of multiwave panel data that properly take account of the possibility of measurement error confirm the finding that many Canadians lack durable partisan attachments (Clarke, Kornberg, and Wearing, 2000; Clarke and Kornberg, 2008). Figure 2.7, which presents the results of such analyses for multiwave panel surveys of the

Canadian electorate conducted since the late 1970s, consistently indicate that many people are partisan "movers" rather than partisan "stayers," i.e., they are willing to change their party identifications over time. For example, between 1979 and 1984, fully 45 per cent were in the "mover" group. The comparable figure for the 2004–06 period is only slightly smaller, 41 per cent. This latter figure is particularly noteworthy because the data used for the analysis were generated by the Canadian national election survey (CES), which uses the revised party identification question wording discussed in the preceding paragraph. The widespread absence of strong stable partisan attachments makes large-scale shifts in party support an ongoing possibility.

This flexibility in partisan attachments has important implications for voting behavior and election outcomes. Although some political scientists have concluded that election campaigns are inconsequential (e.g., Curtice and Steed, 1982; Gelman and King, 1993; see Clarke et al., 2004), this is definitely not the case in Canada. Large changes in voter intentions, such as those that occurred in 2006, are distinct possibilities. Over the past two decades, dramatic movements in party support have occurred in several federal election campaigns (Clarke et al., 2005; Johnston et al., 1992). The fact that many Canadian voters' attitudes towards political parties are not firmly rooted in durable partisan attachments means that they are susceptible to information presented to them as a campaign progresses. Sometimes, as in 2006, events happen during campaigns that cause voters to reconsider their choices.

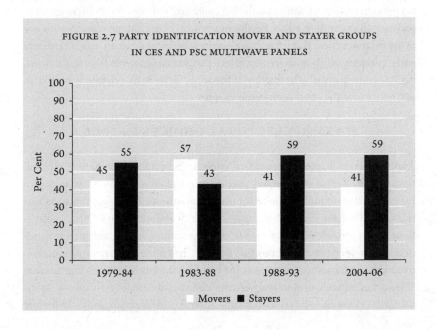

FIGURE 2.7 PARTY IDENTIFICATION MOVER AND STAYER GROUPS IN CES AND PSC MULTIWAVE PANELS

Competing parties can use campaigns to persuade voters to change their minds, and a party that begins a campaign with a sizable lead is not a guaranteed winner.

The dynamics of federal party identification as measured in several PSC surveys conducted since 1988 are presented in Figure 2.8. This figure shows that the number of Liberal identifiers has declined substantially after reaching a high-water mark in 1997. During the 2006 campaign, only 29 per cent of the respondents claimed to be Liberal identifiers (see Figure 2.8A). This is the smallest cohort of Liberal partisans recorded in any national election survey conducted since 1965. However, it is considerably larger than the percentage of identifiers with any of the other parties, including the victorious Conservatives. The latter's number of party identifiers was remarkably low for a winning party. In the run-up to the 2006 election, 19 per cent were CPC identifiers—only 1 per cent more than the number who identified with the CPC's predecessor, the Progressive Conservative (PC) Party at the time of the disastrous 1993 election that effectively ended that party's status as a major player in federal politics (Figure 2.8B).

NDP and BQ partisan shares are also noteworthy. Although the New Democrats were encouraged by the 2006 election outcome, their achievement did not reflect an increase in the cohort of NDP identifiers. On the contrary, the percentage (12 per cent) of NDP partisans in the 2006 post-election survey was actually 1 per cent less than that recorded in 1965 when the first Canadian election study was conducted.[4] The Bloc Québécois percentage in Figure 2.8A (10 per cent) is a national figure, and in Quebec, 41 per cent said they were BQ partisans. Although the latter is 5 per cent smaller than in 2004, the BQ continued to have a much larger group of partisans than any of its rivals. Finally, nearly 30 per cent did not identify with any of the federal parties. This latter figure emphasizes the point that Canada's national party system is lightly anchored by voters' partisan attachments. This is not novel, but it is consequential. The fragility of the 2006 Conservative victory is a topic we will return to in the conclusion of this chapter.

MAKING ELECTORAL CHOICES IN 2006

As observed in Chapter One, political scientists have offered a variety of explanations for why people vote the way they do. Some of these explanations are sociological accounts of political behavior that emphasize sociodemographic cleavages related to characteristics such as region, ethnicity, and social class. Other explanations focus narrowly on voters' evaluations of government economic performance or their stands on prominent position issues such as same-sex marriage, reproductive rights, or Canada-US relations. The latter are the kinds of issues that animate "Downsian" models of electoral behavior and spatial competition among political parties (Downs, 1957; see also Adams, Merrill, and Grofman, 2005). Still other

FIGURE 2.8 FEDERAL PARTY IDENTIFICATION, 1988–2006

A. Aggregating "All Conservative" Identifiers

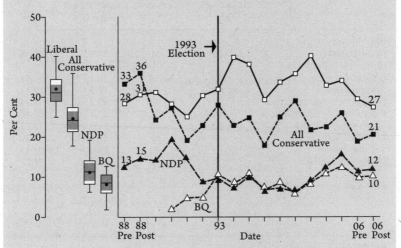

Note: All Conservative = PC + Reform+ Alliance + CPC

B. Decline of Progressive Conservative Identification and Emergence of CPC Identification

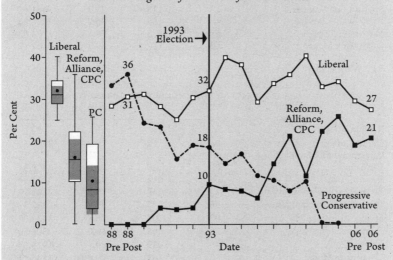

Source: Political Support in Canada (PSC) Surveys, 1988–2006.

TABLE 2.1 SUMMARY OF PERFORMANCE OF RIVAL MODELS OF VOTING IN
THE 2006 FEDERAL ELECTION (ALL CANADA)

A. *Liberal Voting*

	MCFADDEN R^2	MCKELVEY R^2	PER CENT CORRECTLY CLASSIFIED	AIC†
Rival Models				
Demographics	.05	.10	73.9	3731.38
Government Economic Performance	.19	.39	76.2	3180.61
Position Issues	.02	.04	72.5	3819.64
Federal Party Identification	.27	.45	80.2	2855.94
Party Best Important Issues	.40	.55	81.2	2368.40
Sponsorship Scandal	.36	.55	81.3	2510.22
Party Leader Images	.43	.65	85.0	2233.22
Valence Politics	.53	.71	89.3	1871.13
Composite Model	.56	.74	89.4	1771.25

B. *Conservative Voting*

	MCFADDEN R^2	MCKELVEY R^2	PER CENT CORRECTLY CLASSIFIED	AIC†
Rival Models				
Demographics	.03	.05	66.5	4118.36
Government Economic Performance	.04	.07	70.8	4045.12
Position Issues	.22	.36	74.9	3321.18
Federal Party Identification	.30	.42	81.8	2975.28
Party Best Important Issues	.47	.56	88.6	2235.82
Sponsorship Scandal	.13	.23	78.7	3661.65
Party Leader Images	.48	.68	86.7	2226.90
Valence Politics	.59	.73	90.1	1774.83
Composite Model	.62	.77	89.7	1661.42

C. *NDP Voting*

	MCFADDEN R^2	MCKELVEY R^2	PER CENT CORRECTLY CLASSIFIED	AIC†
Rival Models				
Demographics	.06	.12	78.8	3256.57
Government Economic Performance	.00	.00	78.8	3438.34
Position Issues	.06	.12	78.7	3221.46
Federal Party Identification	.27	.39	75.3	2523.91
Party Best Important Issues	.35	.45	87.4	2232.71
Sponsorship Scandal	.00	.00	78.8	3434.37
Party Leader Images	.28	.45	83.0	2500.50
Valence Politics	.45	.59	89.1	1925.04
Composite Model	.50	.63	90.0	1846.11

†—Akaike Information Criterion (AIC)—smaller values indicate better model
performance.

explanations stress the importance of party identifications, judgments of government performance on a range of valence issues that include, but are not limited to, the economy, and party leader images. Here, we consider the ability of these rival models of electoral choice to account for voting behavior in the 2006 federal election. ·

We use various "goodness-of-fit" statistics to assess the explanatory power of the rival models (Long, 1997). Technical details aside, the key idea is to assess how well competing explanatory models perform in terms of reproducing the choices the voters actually made. One such statistic is a measure of the models' ability to classify these choices. For example, if we know people's ages, their level of education, or their province of residence, can we accurately predict their voting behavior? Other statistics such as the McFadden and McKelvey R^2 (Long, 1997) measure the strength of competing models along a 0 to 1 scale, with larger numbers indicating better model performance. Still others, such as the Akaike Information Criterion (AIC), discount the explanatory power of models by the number of predictor variables needed to achieve that power (e.g., Burnham and Anderson, 2002).

Table 2.1 summarizes the results of applying these various statistical yardsticks to assess the performance of rival models of voting in the 2006 election.[5] The results speak clearly, with some models performing much better than others according to all measurement criteria. Regardless of whether one is trying to explain Liberal, Conservative, or NDP voting, the sociodemographic and economic performance models perform very poorly. And, despite the attention that they receive in the press's coverage of recent election campaigns, this is also true for the position issue model that includes same-sex marriage, US-Canada relations, and the taxation-public services trade-off as predictor variables. The sponsorship scandal model also has relatively weak effects on Conservative and NDP voting, but does considerably better for Liberal voting. In contrast, models that include party identification and the party selected as best on most important issue consistently perform relatively well. Of the several specific models, party leader images do the best in the cases of Liberal and Conservative voting, and second-best in the case of NDP voting. Indicative of their explanatory power, leader images by themselves are able to correctly classify 85 per cent of Liberal voters, nearly 87 per cent of Conservative voters, and 83 per cent of NDP voters.

Table 2.1 has two additional important messages for students of Canadian voting behavior. The first of these messages, what we call the *valence politics* model, performs very well. As discussed in Chapter One, this model includes party identification, assessments of which party is best on important issues (typically valence issues), and party leader images. Indicative of its explanatory power, the valence politics model correctly classifies more voters, has higher R^2 statistics, and lower (i.e., superior) AIC values than any of the more specific models of Liberal, Conservative, or NDP voting.

The second message is that, although an impressive performer, the valence politics model does not have the playing field entirely to itself. Rather, a more general composite model that includes all of the predictor variables from the several specific models outperforms the valence politics model. The composite model has the largest R^2s and classifies more voters correctly than does any of its competitors. Also, despite its much richer parameterization (i.e., it has many more predictor variables than any of its competitors), the composite model has the lowest AIC values. Thus, these statistics testify that although the valence politics model is the dominant model, rivals based on other theoretical traditions can contribute to explaining why Canadians vote as they do.

The behavior of the several specific predictor variables in composite models of voting is documented in detail in Tables 2.2 and 2.3 that present the results of analyzing electoral choice in Quebec and the other provinces (the ROC) separately. Each table presents two analyses; one contrasts Liberal voting against voting for any of the opposition parties, and the second considers voting for various opposition parties, with Liberal voting as the reference category. The analyses show that a variety of predictor variables have significant and "properly signed" effects on voting. Component variables in the valence politics model behave as expected. For example, in the model of Liberal voting in the ROC (Table 2.2, Panel A), all of the party leader image variables have statistically significant effects, with positive attitudes towards Prime Minister Martin having a positive impact on Liberal voting, and positive attitudes towards Stephen Harper and Jack Layton having negative impacts. As also expected, judgments about party performance on important issues come into play, with selection of the Liberals as best on such issues bolstering Liberal voting, and selection of any of the opposition parties inhibiting Liberal voting. Party identification works well, too; controlling for all other factors, Liberal identifications are associated positively, and identifications with other parties are associated negatively, with Liberal voting.

In most respects, the valence politics variables also do well in predicting Conservative and NDP voting. For example, feelings about Stephen Harper and Jack Layton positively affect Conservative and NDP voting, respectively. Selecting the CPC as best on the most important issues has a similar effect, positively affecting the likelihood of casting a Conservative ballot. Similarly, selecting the NDP as best on important issues positively influences the probability of voting NDP. The only anomaly concerns party identification. Although a New Democratic identification has the predictable positive effect of enhancing the probability of voting for the NDP, a Conservative identification does not have a positive effect on CPC voting. This finding, in turn, suggests the weakness of CPC partisanship in the skein of causal forces affecting electoral choice in 2006. We will return to this point in the conclusion of this chapter.

TABLE 2.2 COMPOSITE MODELS OF LIBERAL, CONSERVATIVE, AND NDP VOTING IN THE 2006 FEDERAL ELECTION, REST OF CANADA (ROC)

	PANEL A	PANEL B	
	LIBERAL	CPC	NDP
Predictor Variables			
Age	-.00	.01	-.00
Gender	.13	-.71***	.12
Income	.08*	-.02	-.11**
Region:			
Atlantic	.03	.59*	.00
Prairies	-.69***	1.19***	.61**
British Columbia	-.45*	.60*	.47*
Government			
Performance on Economy	.30***	-.29*	-.33**
Position Issues:			
Canada-US Relations	-.26**	.52***	.08
Same-Sex Marriage	.05	-.21*	.08
Taxation	.10	.38*	-.26*
Party Identification:			
Liberal	.45**	-.12	-.58***
Conservative	.15	.21	-.83*
NDP	-.78***	-.61	.71**
Other Party	-2.66***	1.89*	2.13**
Party Best			
Important Issue:			
Liberal	.71***	-.40	-.50*
Conservative	-1.62***	1.81***	.14
NDP	-.93***	-.05	1.33***
Other Party	-1.33***	.19	.65
Sponsorship Scandal	-.19***	.22***	.18***
Leader Images:			
Martin	.25***	-.26***	-.25***
Harper	-.17***	.46***	.04
Layton	-.20***	.01	.32***
Tactical Voting	.90***	.63***	-1.40***
Constant	.13	-2.49***	-.93
McFadden R^2	.56	.59	
McKelvey R^2	.74	X	
Per Cent Correctly Classified	88.8	81.5	
AIC†	1445.39	2746.82	

Note: Two analyses are shown. Panel A is a binomial logit analysis of Liberal versus voting for all other parties. Panel B is a multinomial logit analysis of CPC and NDP voting with Liberal voting as the reference group. (Other party voting is included in the analysis but not shown.)

†—Akaike Information Criterion (AIC)—smaller values indicate better model performance.

x—McKelvey R^2 is not defined for multinomial logit analysis.

*** $p < .001$; ** $p < .01$; * $p < .05$; one-tailed test.

Among the other significant predictors, it is noteworthy that evaluations of the government's economic performance have predictable effects, with positive evaluations boosting the likelihood of a Liberal vote, and lowering the likelihood of CPC or NDP voting. Attitudes towards the sponsorship scandal also work as expected, with people who are exercised about the scandal being less likely to vote Liberal and more likely to vote CPC or NDP than are those who minimize the seriousness of the affair. Effects of position issues are mixed; although attitudes towards same-sex marriage, Canada-US relations, and taxation all influence CPC voting in predictable ways, only Canada-US relations affects Liberal voting, and only taxation affects NDP voting. These results are consistent with the finding reported above that the position issue model, by itself, has stronger effects in analyses of CPC voting than in analyses of Liberal or NDP voting (see Table 2.1).

Finally, we note that tactical voting considerations were in play in 2006. Tactical voting occurs when voters, believing that the party they prefer cannot win, move to another party to prevent a least-preferred alternative from winning. In 2004 (see Chapter Three) some voters, fearing a CPC victory, abandoned the NDP in favor of the Liberals. As noted earlier, in the closing days of the 2006 campaign, NDP leader Jack Layton attempted to counter this type of behavior by arguing that the Liberals were sure losers, and that progressively minded voters should move to the NDP to provide a "real" opposition in Parliament to a Harper-led Conservative government. However, the significant negative coefficient on the tactical voting variable in the NDP vote analysis in Table 2.2 suggests that Layton's appeal was not successful. Further, the significant positive coefficients on the tactical voting variable in the Liberal and CPC analyses suggest that both major parties, not just the Liberals, benefited from tactical voting in 2006.

In many respects, the analyses of voting behavior in Quebec echo those for the ROC. Party leader images and party preferences on the issues people deemed most important have significant, properly signed effects on Liberal and opposition party voting (see Table 2.3). The same is true for government economic evaluations and attitudes towards the sponsorship scandal. People who thought the Martin government had done a good job on the economy were more likely to vote Liberal than for any of the opposition parties, whereas those who thought the scandal reflected badly on the Liberals were less likely to vote for them and more likely to opt for one of the opposition parties. And, similar to the ROC, the effects of party identification were not completely consistent. Although being a Conservative identifier had a positive effect on CPC voting, the effect of being a BQ identifier did not have a significant impact on BQ voting.

As for the impact of position issues in Quebec, the findings are mixed. Canada-US relations, same-sex marriage, and the taxation-public services trade-off all failed to influence Liberal, NDP, or BQ voting. However, the latter two issues did affect

TABLE 2.3 COMPOSITE MODELS OF LIBERAL, CONSERVATIVE, NDP, AND
BLOC QUÉBÉCOIS VOTING IN THE 2006 FEDERAL ELECTION, QUEBEC

| | PANEL A | PANEL B | | |
	LIBERAL	CPC	NDP	BQ
Predictor Variables				
Age	.02**	-.03**	-.03**	.00
Gender	.50*	.61*	.36	.23
Income	-.14*	.13*	.10	.10
Francophone	-1.21***	1.15**	1.27**	1.48***
Government				
Performance on Economy	.46**	-.55***	-.43*	-.50**
Position Issues:				
Canada-US Relations	-.34	.36	.35	.25
Same-Sex Marriage	.24	-.32*	.27	-.12
Taxation	-.36	.57*	-.16	.29
Party Identification:				
Liberal	.69*	-.26	-.85*	-.81*
Conservative	-2.41*	2.63**	2.13*	2.14*
NDP	-1.01	-.39	1.34*	1.40
Bloc Québécois	.33	-.83	-1.68**	-.08
Other Party	-1.99	.09	1.18	.50
Party Best Important Issue:				
Liberal	.37	.26	-1.90**	-.22
Conservative	-1.78***	2.29***	.96*	.45
NDP	-2.25***	1.33*	2.26***	1.38*
Bloc Québécois	-2.27***	1.79**	.94	2.16***
Other Party	-1.37*	.98	.06	1.74**
Sponsorship Scandal	-.17***			
Leader Images:				
Martin	.18***	-.21***	-.17*	-.13*
Harper	.05	.12*	-.17**	-.14**
Layton	.00	-.03	.37***	-.11*
Duceppe	.04	-.15***	-.11*	.24***
Quebec Sovereignty	-1.59***	1.27***	1.18***	1.71***
Tactical Voting	-.30	.65*	-.81*	.13
Constant	-.94	-.33	-.45	-2.41*
McFadden R²	.62	.58		
McKelvey R²	.78	X		
Per Cent Correctly Classified	93.5	80.1		
AIC†	570.32	2111.45		

Note: Two analyses are shown. Panel A is a binomial logit analysis of Liberal versus
voting for all other parties. Panel B is a multinomial logit analysis of CPC, NDP, and BQ
voting with Liberal voting as the reference group.
†—Akaike Information Criterion (AIC)—smaller values indicate better
model performance.
x—McKelvey R² is not defined for multinomial logit analysis.
*** p < .001; ** p < .01; * p < .05; one-tailed test.

Conservative voting, with opposition to same-sex marriage and the desire for lower taxes positively affecting the likelihood of choosing the CPC. The consistently influential position issue in Quebec was attitudes towards sovereignty. As anticipated, Quebeckers favoring sovereignty were likely to vote BQ and those opposed to sovereignty were likely to choose one of the opposition parties. The Bloc was not the only beneficiary of pro-sovereignity sentiments; the Conservatives and the NDP also benefited.

Regarding other predictors, tactical voting helped the CPC and hurt the NDP in Quebec, perhaps because voters seeking a non-Liberal federalist alternative saw the former party as their best bet in 2006. Also, net of all other factors, being a francophone was negatively associated with Liberal voting and positively associated with BQ voting. Being a member of the francophone community was also positively associated with support for the CPC and NDP. There were various other demographic effects as well; men, with younger people and those with higher incomes tended to support the Conservatives, and older people, women, and those with lower incomes tended to favor the Liberals.

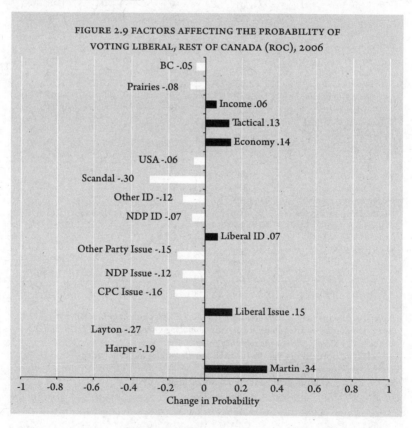

FIGURE 2.9 FACTORS AFFECTING THE PROBABILITY OF
VOTING LIBERAL, REST OF CANADA (ROC), 2006

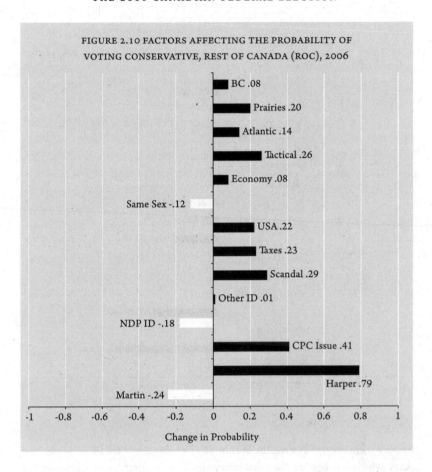

FIGURE 2.10 FACTORS AFFECTING THE PROBABILITY OF
VOTING CONSERVATIVE, REST OF CANADA (ROC), 2006

The analyses in Tables 2.2 and 2.3 tell us which variables have significant effects on electoral choice. However, they are not informative about the *size* of various effects. To appreciate which predictor variables were particularly important for electoral choice in 2006, we construct scenarios in which all of the predictors in an analysis are held at their mean values (in the case of continuous variables) or at zero (in the case of categorical variables). We then manipulate the values of each significant predictor, noting how the probability of voting for a party changes. Results for Liberal, CPC, and NDP voting in the ROC are shown in Figures 2.9, 2.10, and 2.11.[6]

These analyses testify to the importance of party leader images. In the Liberal analysis, as feelings about Martin moved from very negative to very positive, the probability of a Liberal vote increased by 34 points (see Figure 2.9). Increasingly positive feelings about Harper and Layton were also influential, lowering the probability of a Liberal vote by 19 and 27 points, respectively. The sponsorship scandal was another major predictor in the Liberal analysis; as attitudes towards the scandal

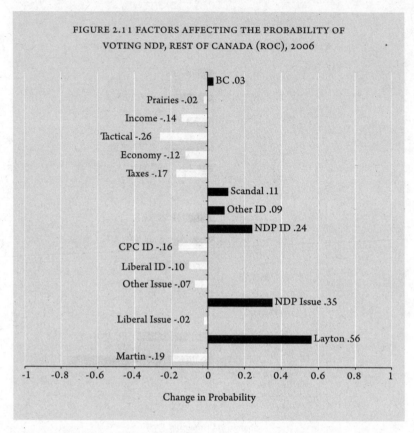

FIGURE 2.11 FACTORS AFFECTING THE PROBABILITY OF
VOTING NDP, REST OF CANADA (ROC), 2006

became increasingly negative, the likelihood of a Liberal vote fell by 30 points. The party selected as best on the most important issue mattered, too. Choosing the Liberals rather than the CPC as best increased the probability of a Liberal vote by 31 points (-.16 to .15).

The Conservatives and the NDP pictures are similar. As Figure 2.10 shows, other things being equal, the effect of feelings about Stephen Harper on Conservative support were huge. As feelings about him moved from very negative to very positive, the likelihood of voting Conservative increased by fully 79 points. Selecting the Conservatives as best on the most important issue also had a very large effect, increasing the probability of choosing the CPC by 41 points. The sponsorship scandal was also influential; changing attitudes towards the scandal shifted the probability of a Conservative ballot by 29 points. In the NDP analysis, varying feelings about Jack Layton moved the likelihood of a New Democratic vote by 56 points, and selecting the NDP as best on the most important issue had a 35-point effect (see Figure 2.11). Two other big predictors of NDP support were being an NDP identifier and tactical voting. The former increased the likelihood of a New Democratic ballot by 24 points, and thinking tactically lowered it by 26 points.

For Quebec, we focus on BQ voting. The numbers presented in Figure 2.12 once again confirm the importance of party leader images. As feelings about the BQ leader, Gilles Duceppe, moved from very negative to very positive, the probability of choosing the Bloc increased by fully 74 points. Feelings about other party leaders mattered too, with the Harper and Layton effects being 36 and 34 points, respectively. Feelings about Martin were less influential (11 points). Another big predictor of BQ voting was the sponsorship scandal. People who did not believe the scandal reflected badly on the Liberals and Martin were 36 points less likely to support the Bloc than were those who believed the scandal constituted a damning indictment of the party and its leader. Finally, controlling for all other factors, attitudes towards sovereignty were another powerful predictor of Bloc voting, having the capacity to shift the probability of casting a BQ ballot by 24 points.

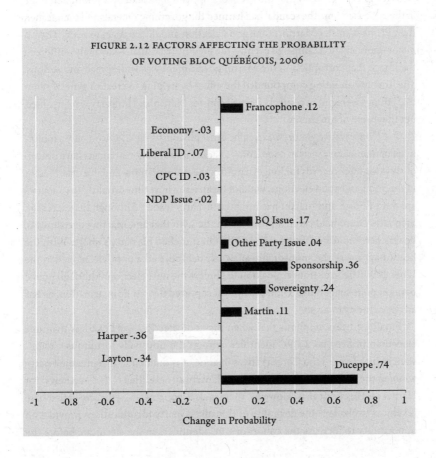

FIGURE 2.12 FACTORS AFFECTING THE PROBABILITY OF VOTING BLOC QUÉBÉCOIS, 2006

FLAWLESS CAMPAIGN, FRAGILE VICTORY

The 2006 federal election was a dramatic event that featured strong consequential campaign dynamics and the widely unexpected success of a party formed less than three years previously. To achieve its surprising victory, the new Conservative Party of Canada and its leader, Stephen Harper, benefited handsomely from two factors. First, they ran a flawless campaign. Recognizing the importance of valence issues, Harper and his colleagues emphasized a limited set of policies with broad appeal. Insofar as possible, divisive position issues such as abortion, immigration, and same-sex marriage were sidestepped, and party ideologues were tightly muzzled. As a result of their positive and well-executed campaign, the Conservatives were able to minimize the effects of Liberal efforts to brand them as right-wing extremists who would dismantle the health care system and other cherished public services.

Second, the Conservatives were lucky. The Gomery Commission Report in November 2005 ensured that the sponsorship scandal would be a prominent issue in the 2006 election. The scandal had harmed the governing Liberals and their leader, then Prime Minister Martin, in the 2004 election and did so again in 2006. Then, a major unanticipated campaign event—the income trust affair—strongly reinforced the image that corruption in the Martin government was widespread and serious. The Toronto shooting compounded the effect by helping to create a general sense that "things were out of control." Prime Minister Martin and his party were in office, but they were not in charge.

The Conservative victory was fragile. Most obviously, the CPC won only a minority of parliamentary seats in 2006, and Canadian minority governments have notoriously poor track records for longevity. Also, the sponsorship scandal, a major factor in the 2004 and 2006 elections, will not be an issue next time around. The Liberals are out of office and Martin has resigned as party leader. Although his successor, Stéphane Dion, held cabinet positions in the Chrétien and Martin governments, he was not implicated in the scandals that besmirched his party's image. With the heavy baggage of the sponsorship affair left behind, and a new "clean" leader, the Liberals will be in a stronger position to contest the next election. Although public opinion polls suggest that Dion has not yet captured the public imagination, he has an opportunity to do so.

Finally, it bears emphasis that when the 2006 election was held, less than one Canadian in five was a CPC identifier. Absent the unusually fortuitous circumstances that favored the Conservatives in 2006, it is difficult to imagine their party winning the next election with such a small partisan base. That is the "bad news" for Harper and his strategists. However, there is also "good news"—the size of that base is subject to change. The flexibility of Canadians' party identifications provides an opportunity to increase the cohort of CPC identifiers in the electorate before the next election. If the new Conservative government receives high marks for its performance in office, this will boost the number of CPC partisans. It will also bolster the image of Prime Minister Harper. With a larger group of identifiers and a more favorably received leader, the new Conservative Party will have a chance to retain, and perhaps to strengthen, its grip on power.

Notes

1   The data in Figure 2.1 were generated using a Bayesian state-space model for pooling time series data developed by Simon Jackman (2005).

2   The 2006 PSC survey was a nationwide pre-post 2006 Internet survey (pre-election N = 6116) conducted by YouGov, a major British survey research firm that also conducts research for the British Election Study.

3   More specifically, Johnston (1992) claimed that partisan volatility was more common on the Canadian Election Studies because of their failure to offer respondents the opportunity to answer "none of these" (i.e., nonpartisanship) when prompted with the standard,"Generally speaking do you usually think of yourself as a Liberal, Progressive Conservative, NDP" question. Traditionally, the CES question ended with "or what?" and this was thought to compel some nonpartisans to choose a party. The following question was utilized to measure partisan identification on the 2006 PSC study: "Thinking about *federal* politics, do you usually think of yourself as a Liberal, Conservative, NDP, Bloc Québécois, or what?"

4   Analyses are not shown, and comparisons made prior to 1983 utilize the CES.

5   For the multivariate analyses, respondents refusing to give their age were coded "45." Men were coded one on the gender variable, and women were coded zero. Income was an eight-category variable where a value of one indicates that the respondent had an income of less than $20,000, and a value of eight signifies that the respondent reported an income of over $100,000. Those refusing to give their income were coded four. The variable measuring government performance on the economy had a range from one to five, where respondents believing that the federal government had done a "very good job" in managing the economy coded the highest. Nonrespondents to this question were coded three. Party leader thermometers had a range from zero to 10, and respondents not evaluating a leader received the mean value given to the leader by other respondents in their region (values available from the authors upon request). For the position issue variables, scores of one on the variables signified favorability of closer relations between Canada and the United States, support for same-sex marriage, and support for lower taxes, and a score of -1 indicated opposition. Respondents who were unsure or did not know how to answer the question were coded zero. The sponsorship scandal variable was an index with a range of three to 15 created by the summation of three variables asking whether:

a) the scandal was an indication of widespread corruption in the Liberal Party; b) the scandal provided proof that the Liberal Party could not govern; and c) it was unfair to blame the entire Liberal Party for the scandal. Higher values on the index were given to respondents who believed that the Liberals were accountable for the scandal. In the analyses using respondents in Quebec only, those supporting sovereignty were coded two, those unsure were coded one, and those opposed were coded zero. The tactical voting variable was coded one if the respondent stated that they "really prefer[red]" a party other than the one they supported with their vote, and respondents voting sincerely were coded zero.

6   Probabilities were calculated using the STATA CLARIFY program (Tomz, Wittenberg, and King, 1999).

CHAPTER THREE

Too Close to Call

The 2004 Canadian Federal Election

anada's June 28, 2004, federal election was an exciting and, in some ways, a surprising contest. One major surprise was the election campaign itself. Rather than being the predictable, boring contest many commentators had anticipated, the campaign was a closely fought battle between the long-time governing Liberals and the new Conservative Party of Canada (CPC), formed only six months before the election was called. The election produced a Liberal victory, but the party won only a minority of parliamentary seats. How long the Liberals would be able to hold onto power was anyone's guess. A second surprise, at least for many observers, was turnout, which fell to the lowest level in history for a Canadian federal election. A third, potentially significant, surprise was the success of the separatist Bloc Québécois, accompanied by a resurgence of support for Quebec sovereignty in public opinion polls. When the election results were known, uncertainty became the watchword in Canadian politics.

At the beginning of 2004, everything seemed to be going the Liberals' way. In late autumn of 2003, former finance minister, Paul Martin, Jr., had replaced Jean Chrétien as Liberal leader and prime minister. Chrétien had led his party to three successive electoral victories, including the highly consequential 1993 contest that resulted in the virtual annihilation of the Progressive Conservative (PC) Party that had been the Liberals' principal rival in Canada's long-standing "two-party-plus" national party system (Epstein, 1964). Chrétien also had galvanized the alliance of federalist forces in the 1995 Quebec sovereignty referendum. Although the referendum proposal had been defeated by an extremely narrow margin (just over 1 per cent), support for sovereignty had gradually receded, and the separatist Parti Québécois (PQ) had been replaced as the provincial government of Quebec by the pro-Canada Liberals. Finally, the economy was buoyant. When Martin became prime minister, Canada's annual inflation rate was only 2.8 per cent, and its GDP was growing at an impressive 5.3 per cent. The unemployment rate was 7.6 per cent, not particularly high by Canadian standards, and it was trending downward. And exchange rates—always symbolically important for Canadians—showed the "loonie" (i.e., the Canadian dollar) was strengthening against the benchmark American dollar. As finance minister during much of the Chrétien era, new Liberal leader Paul Martin was well-positioned to claim credit for the good economic news.

Perhaps most important, when Martin surveyed the political landscape in early 2004, it appeared that his party did not have any serious rivals. After their devastating defeat in 1993, the Progressive Conservatives had never made a serious comeback. In their place were two regionally based parties, the neo-conservative Reform in the West, and the separatist Bloc Québécois (BQ) in Quebec. By its very nature, the BQ was a nonstarter as a federal party—its self-proclaimed mandate was to defend Quebec's interests in Ottawa while working to advance the cause of Quebec sovereignty. However, Reform did aspire to national power. To achieve its goal, the party needed a breakthrough in Ontario, where the Liberals enjoyed overwhelming superiority during the Chrétien years, winning an average of fully 98 per cent of that province's parliamentary seats in 1993, 1997, and 2000. The breakthrough would only happen if Reform could attract the numerically small, but politically consequential, minority of the Ontario electorate that continued to support the old-line Progressive Conservatives.

In its effort to "unite the right," Reform had rebranded itself as the Canadian Alliance before the 2000 election. When the right did not unite in that contest, the next move was to form yet another new party, the Conservative Party of Canada (CPC). Alliance leader, Stephen Harper, was chosen to lead the new party. Harper was a founding member of the Reform Party and had been elected to Parliament as a Reform MP in 1993. Although the birth of the new Conservative Party of Canada was accompanied by the formal dissolution of the Progressive Conservatives, some prominent PCs, including former Prime Minister Joe Clark, refused to go along. Clark denounced the new CPC as ideologically extreme, an unworthy successor to his party's historic tradition of "one-nation" Tory conservatism. Given what appeared to be continuing difficulties with the CPC's unification efforts, the Liberals could reasonably conclude that a 2004 election would be a ceremonial coronation of their new leader, Paul Martin.

Although elite-level ideological wrangling between the new CPC and diehard remnants of the old PC Party gave the Liberals cause for optimism, it bears emphasis that "left-right" ideological discourse normally has very limited resonance in Canadian federal elections. As discussed in earlier chapters, Canada's major national parties typically have competed by downplaying their ideological differences, while emphasizing their ability to "solve problems" and provide voters with a broad array of public services (Clarke et al., 1979, 1996). Problem-focused issues upon which virtually everyone agrees, such as lowering the unemployment rate or reducing hospital-care waiting times, typically dominate the electoral agenda. Political debate on these valence issues (Stokes, 1963, 1992) centers on which party and which leader is best able to "deliver the goods." Specific policies designed to solve problems of widespread concern are often avoided for fear of turning a potentially electorally advantageous valence issue into a divisive position issue that could lose a party votes. In a classic example, when asked by a reporter during the 1974 federal election campaign about how he would deal with rapidly rising prices, former Prime Minister Pierre Trudeau—noted for his athletic ability—replied he would "wrestle inflation to the ground." Many voters seemed to accept his response as a credible plan of action.

This is not to say that Canadian political parties cannot be placed along a left-right ideological continuum. Although keeping potentially divisive ideological topics and associated position issues out of the electoral arena has been the norm, the parties have differed on topics that collectively define what it means to be politically "left" or "right" in a mature democracy such as Canada. *Inter alia*, these topics include the extent of enthusiasm for redistributing wealth from richer to poorer groups, interest in expanding the number and size of welfare programs that collectively constitute Canada's social safety net, willingness to use military force as an instrument of foreign policy, and the desirable scope of government involvement in economy and society.

Coding the content of the parties' election platforms provides a useful way to summarize the evolution of their positions on a general left-right ideological continuum (Budge, 2001; Klingemann, 2006). Figure 3.1 presents these data for several parties for the 20 federal elections held between 1945 and 2006. The figure shows that the NDP has consistently and predictably been to the left of the Liberals and the Progressive Conservatives. Prior to 1979, the latter two parties were extremely close to the center of the scale, with the PCs actually being very slightly to the left of the Liberals on some occasions. Starting in the late 1970s and throughout the 1980s, under the leadership of Brian Mulroney, the PCs moved further to the right. After their disastrous performance in 1993, they retreated towards the middle of the

FIGURE 3.1 POSITIONS OF CANADIAN FEDERAL PARTIES
ON SUMMARY LEFT-RIGHT IDEOLOGICAL SCALE, 1945–2006

A. Positions of Federal Parties

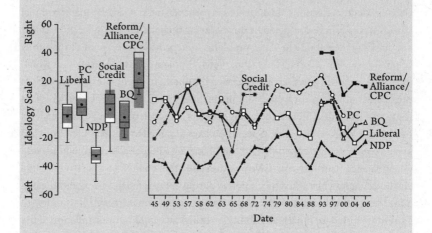

B. Average Ideological Distances between Parties, Old and New Party Systems

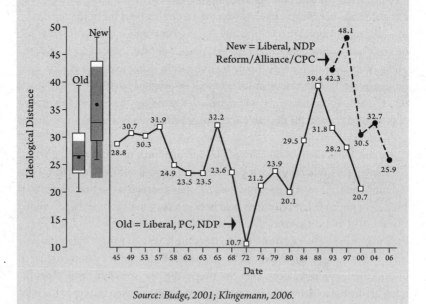

Source: Budge, 2001; Klingemann, 2006.

ideological spectrum. For their part, the Liberals have never strayed far from the center ground.

Figure 3.1 also illustrates why leading members of the old PC Party, such as former Prime Minister Joe Clark, were concerned about what the ideological proclivities of the new Conservative Party of Canada might be. Figure 3.1A shows that Reform and its successors, the Alliance and the CPC, consistently have been further to the right than the PCs. However—a point not noted by Clark and his colleagues—this distance has not been constant. As measured by summary left-right positions, the Alliance in 2000 and the CPC in 2004 and 2006, were not as extreme as Reform had been in 1993 and 1997. The result is that Canada's federal party system is now less ideologically polarized than in 1993 when Reform made its electoral breakthrough. In this regard, Figure 3.1B shows the absolute average (pair-wise) distances between parties in the old and new party systems (excluding the BQ). In 1993, 1997, and 2000, the average distances are always greater for parties in the new system (NDP, Liberals, Reform, Alliance, CPC) than for parties that were the charter members of the old system (NDP, Liberals, PCs). However, the average distance between the new system parties in 2000 and 2004 is not appreciably greater than it had been for the old system parties in several of the 15 elections held between 1945 and 1988. In fact, in 2006 the average distance for parties in the new system actually was less than it had been for seven of those earlier elections. This implies that the historic left-right ideological distance between competing parties had been restored. The new Conservative Party of Canada was to the right of center in the 2004 and 2006 elections, but the ideological distance between the CPC and its rivals was not especially extreme by historical standards.

However, it can be argued that the precise ideological positions of the parties did not matter much in 2004. The reason is that most Canadian voters espouse valence politics, i.e., they eschew ideological labels and focus their attention on the competing parties' demonstrated or anticipated performance in office and the character and competence of rival party leaders. For example, data from the 2004 Political Support in Canada (PSC) survey indicate that ideological labelling was very much the exception—only 31 per cent of the respondents reported that they used the labels "left" and "right" when they thought about parties and politics (Figure 3.2).[1] Moreover, if the new CPC was to do well in 2004, it would not be because a sizable minority of voters had adopted right-of-center ideological positions. Merely 3 per cent said they thought about politics and parties in left-right terms and placed themselves on the right, and an additional 8 per cent placed themselves on center-right. Nor did the PSC respondents think of themselves as politically "left"—only 14 per cent said they were on the left or center-left.

Clearly, the CPC could not rely on a newly minted cohort of ideologically motivated voters to propel it to power. Rather, the party could be successful only if two

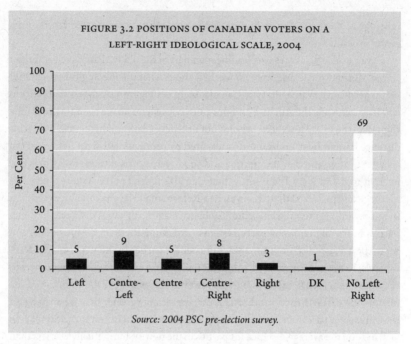

FIGURE 3.2 POSITIONS OF CANADIAN VOTERS ON A
LEFT-RIGHT IDEOLOGICAL SCALE, 2004

Source: 2004 PSC pre-election survey.

conditions were met. First, large numbers of people would have to lose confidence in the ability of the governing Liberals and their new leader to deliver the healthy economy and large assortment of public services that most Canadians demand (Kornberg and Clarke, 1992). Second, the CPC would have to convince voters that it was both willing and able to supply, not to curtail, those services. As events unfolded, the first of these conditions was soon satisfied when the character and competence of Prime Minister Martin and his party were called into serious question. The CPC's inability to satisfy the second condition became a key factor in determining the outcome of an unexpectedly exciting election campaign.

TO THE POLLS

Liberal plans for an uneventful "stroll to the polls" were abruptly overturned on February 10, 2004, when Auditor General Sheila Fraser released a report on $100 million in federal funds that had been spent to advertise the many good things the federal government was doing for Quebeckers. Repaying generous government patronage with acts of blatant corruption, prominent Quebec Liberals had simply pocketed their share of the money without performing any services for it. As one Liberal insider allegedly quipped: "It's one thing to get a contract for being a loyal party guy, but it's something else entirely not to do the work!" When the "Adscam" or sponsorship scandal broke, Liberal poll ratings plummeted, especially in Quebec where disaffected voters flooded to the BQ (see Figure 3.3). However, despite an avalanche of adverse publicity generated by the scandal, the Liberals maintained a lead over their rivals in national polls, and election planning continued.

The Liberals' next problem was created by their provincial counterparts in Ontario. In their successful 2003 election campaign, the Ontario Liberals had stolen a page from former US President George Bush, Sr.'s playbook and promised not to increase taxes. Then in May 2004, just days before the federal election was scheduled to be called, Liberal Premier Dalton McGuinty reneged and introduced substantial new levies to cover major revenue shortfalls in health care. Martin, wagering that widespread unhappiness with the Ontario Liberals would not affect feelings about his federal party, pressed ahead and called the election for June 28.

Martin had bet wrong. Party support in Canada can—and sometimes does— move in consequential ways during election campaigns (see Johnston et al., 1992; Blais et al., 2002). In the event, the media focused public attention on problems with the health system and the new Ontario tax, and Liberal support soon fell significantly. The chief beneficiary was the new Conservative Party, but the NDP also saw its vote intention share move upward. One week into the campaign, numerous ridings in Ontario, the cornerstone of Liberal success in the previous three federal

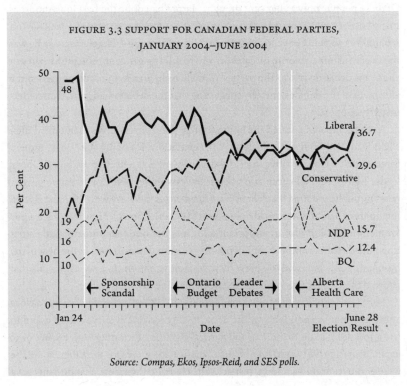

FIGURE 3.3 SUPPORT FOR CANADIAN FEDERAL PARTIES,
JANUARY 2004–JUNE 2004

Source: Compas, Ekos, Ipsos-Reid, and SES polls.

elections, were seemingly "up for grabs." With Ontario in play and Quebec opting strongly for the BQ, the 2004 election had turned into a race that would go right down to the wire.

At midpoint in the campaign several polls indicated that the CPC had pulled slightly ahead (Figure 3.3), and some media pundits proclaimed that a Conservative minority government was in the offing. Other, more cautious commentators recognized the uncertainty associated with pre-election polls and proclaimed that the contest was too close to call. Difficulties in forecasting the outcome are underscored by the PSC pre-election survey data; nearly one-third of those interviewed reported that they had not decided how they would vote. Moreover, nearly half of those who had made a decision said they might change their minds. Campaign events clearly could be influential.

The televised debates among the party leaders were in the class of potentially influential events. Reminiscent of loud-mouthed talk-show hosts, the leaders repeatedly tried to drown one another out with off-putting mixtures of accusations and denials. Although some observers concluded that CPC leader Harper had bested his rivals, this was clearly a relative judgment. The 2004 PSC post-election survey data indicate that only three people in five saw or heard part or all of the debates. Of these people, only 23 per cent thought Harper had done the best job. Almost as many (18 per cent) chose Martin, and 12 per cent opted for NDP leader Jack Layton. A plurality (30 per cent) chose BQ leader Gilles Duceppe—largely because he was the overwhelming favorite in Quebec, where fully 75 per cent thought he had outshone his debating rivals. The parties' trend lines in Figure 3.3 hardly moved in the aftermath of the debates, thereby suggesting that the debates had little, if any, effect on party support.

As the campaign entered the home stretch, the Conservatives maintained their slight lead, and even some analysts with reputations for being the "smart money" forecast that a Conservative minority government was a likely possibility. Liberal leader Martin fuelled speculation about the possibility of a Conservative government by publicly stating that "common sense dictates the party with the most elected members of parliament should hold power" (Dawson, 2004). How long such a government might last was an important question, but one that attracted little attention outside the common rooms of political science departments. In the heat of the moment, politicians and the press focused their attention on a series of polls that showed the Conservatives poised to knock the Liberals out of office.

Survey evidence suggests that many voters also thought the election was a close contest. When respondents in the 2004 PSC pre-election survey were asked to use a 100-point scale to indicate the parties' chances of winning with a score of 50 explicitly designated as an "even chance," the average scores for the Liberals and the Conservatives were 56 and 53, respectively. Hedging their bets, respondents gave both parties slightly better than "even money" odds. In contrast, the NDP's average score of 27 showed that they held "also ran" status in the minds of many voters. As discussed below, this perception would facilitate Liberal efforts to make tactical appeals to NDP supporters to switch to the Liberals to help defeat the Conservatives.

As the campaign entered its final phase, the Conservatives obliged their rivals by committing two acts of abject political stupidity. First, they accused Prime Minister Martin of being soft on child pornography. The result was an immediate public backlash, and Harper and his advisors were heavily criticized for engaging in "gutter politics." Then, Ralph Klein, Progressive Conservative premier of Alberta, told reporters that his government was considering a two-tier health care scheme that involved significant privatization. Health care was already a major issue in the campaign, and the Liberals quickly charged that Klein's statements proved that the Conservatives were indeed "right-wing nuts" who would destroy Canada's cherished system of universal equal-access medical care.

The Liberals then reinforced their message by "going negative" in a massive barrage in the media. Voters were told in no uncertain terms that Harper and his CPC colleagues harbored a "hidden agenda." In addition to unravelling health care and other important strands in the public service safety net, a Harper-led Conservative government, they argued, would pursue an intolerant social agenda that would ride roughshod over the rights of women, gays, lesbians, poor people, Native people, and various visible minorities. Harper was portrayed as being in league with American President George W. Bush, and it was intimated that Harper wanted to send Canadian troops to wartorn Iraq. Voters tempted to support the left-of-center NDP were encouraged to think tactically. By opting for their local Liberal candidate, they could help keep the extremist Conservatives out of office. The Liberals might be a second choice, but it was a choice that would thwart the policy mischief that would attend a CPC victory (cf. LeDuc, 2005).

In the weekend before the election, Martin travelled across the country inviting Canadians to join him in his crusade to keep the Conservative crazies at bay. The Conservative response was curiously tepid and very much "off message." Rather than maintaining a high national profile and continuing to hammer Martin and other Liberals great and small for their years of mismanagement, cronyism, and corruption, while assuring voters of his party's steadfast commitment to maintaining, indeed improving, the country's celebrated public services, Stephen Harper quietly retreated to his native Alberta. He remarked to reporters that he was glad the campaign was finally over. For him, it was.

On election day the national vote totals shows that 36.7 per cent voted Liberal, 29.6 per cent voted Conservative, and 15.7 per cent voted NDP. In Quebec the Bloc attracted 48.8 per cent of the vote, and the Liberals 33.9 per cent. These vote shares were a recipe for a minority government. Although the Liberals lost 39 ridings, they remained in power with 135 of 308 seats in Parliament, compared to 99 for the Conservatives, 54 for the BQ, and 19 for the NDP. For its part, the new Conservative Party had captured 21 more seats than the combined total for the Alliance and PCs in 2000, and made a limited breakthrough in Ontario by winning 24 of that province's 106 seats. However, the Conservative popular vote was fully 8.1 per cent less than what the Alliance and PCs had jointly achieved four years earlier. Equally disappointing for Harper and his colleagues, their party's vote share was 8 per cent less than its high point in the campaign polls only a few weeks earlier.

AT THE POLLS

What drove the vote? Recognizing that many voters lack ideological self-identifications and durable partisan attachments, Canadian political scientists often have emphasized the importance of short-term forces associated with party leader images and valence issues (e.g., Clarke et al., 1979, 1996). As noted earlier, unemployment and health care are classic examples of such issues. Virtually everyone agrees that low levels of joblessness and an effective, adequately funded health care system are "good things," and political debate focuses on who can best deliver them. Party leaders are evaluated in terms of their ability to address the social and economic problems that define the issue agenda during particular elections. By focusing public attention on valence issues and the qualities of their leaders, the national political parties are able to assemble or "broker" broad-based electoral coalitions that transcend the deep regional and ethnolinguistic cleavages that characterize Canadian society. The electorate's concerns with valence issues and the qualities of party leaders make brokerage politics possible.

In recent years, analysts have begun to re-evaluate the valence or brokerage politics model of electoral choice in light of the post-1993 party system that more closely mirrors these societal cleavages and includes at least one party, the Reform-Alliance-CPC, that has espoused a variety of right-of-center policy positions (Nevitte et al., 2000; Carty et al., 2000; Blais et al., 2002). Above, we have seen that the new post-1993 party system was initially more ideologically polarized than its predecessor. However, we have also seen that parties' ideological positions have dynamic qualities, with first the Alliance and then the CPC being substantially less extreme than Reform. Overall, by 2004 the new party system did not look terribly different in left-right terms from the one it had replaced.

We have also seen that a very large majority of Canadians report that they do not think of politics in abstract "left-right" terms. Although the failure of voters to employ ideological abstractions is hardly news to political scientists (see Converse, 1964), it may be that many Canadians now place more emphasis on specific position issues, such as women's reproductive rights, same-sex marriage, gun ownership, taxation-public services trade-offs, or Canada-US relations, than they did in earlier times. Voters take differing positions on these specific issues and, in turn, these positions map on to a more general ideological left-right continuum that academics, media elites, and politicians commonly use to organize their discussions of campaign issues. Below, we will consider the impact of such position issues on electoral choice in 2004. However, we first examine what the survey data tell us about two conditions that are often considered "fundamentals" undergirding the fortunes of governing parties.

FUNDAMENTALS

The Economy

Students of economic voting have long insisted that the economy is *the* fundamental of electoral politics (e.g., Lewis-Beck, 1988; Norpoth, Lewis-Beck, and Lafay, 1991). As observed above, Prime Minister Martin was the leader of a governing party that had been in office for 11 years when the 2004 election occurred. For much of that period Martin had been finance minister—in effect, he was Canada's "chief economic officer." Thus, it should have been easy for voters to assign credit or blame to the prime minister and his party for the state of the Canadian economy. Given these considerations and the fact that the economy was in good shape, Martin and his colleagues hoped to reap political profit from it. In fact, the 2004 PSC pre-election survey reveals that most Canadians thought the economy had done quite well over the past year and would continue to do so. Most of the survey respondents were cautiously optimistic, with only 28 per cent thinking economic conditions had deteriorated, and merely 12 per cent thinking they were about to get worse. Additionally, a majority believed that the Liberal government had performed credibly on the economy. Although only 4 per cent said the government had done a "very good job," fully 52 per cent said it had done a "good job" (see Figure 3.4). On the negative side, 35 per cent said a "poor job," and only 9 per cent said a "very poor job." These figures suggest that, to the extent that the economy would become an issue in 2004, the Liberals were correct to assume that they would benefit.

Partisanship

Party identification has long been an axial concept in theories of voting behavior. As discussed in Chapter Two, many Canadian voters have flexible partisan attachments, and they are willing to change their party identifications as they re-evaluate the performance of political parties and their leaders. However, at any point in time party identifications have significant effects on electoral choice, and a party that is disadvantaged in the size of its cohort of identifiers typically faces an uphill battle at the

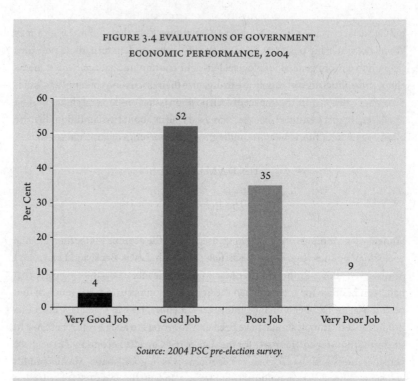

FIGURE 3.4 EVALUATIONS OF GOVERNMENT
ECONOMIC PERFORMANCE, 2004

Source: 2004 PSC pre-election survey.

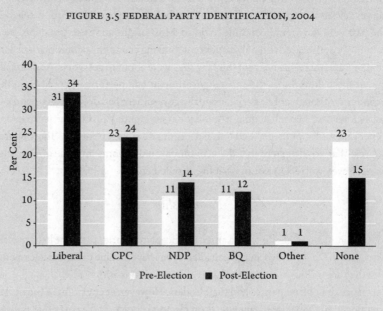

FIGURE 3.5 FEDERAL PARTY IDENTIFICATION, 2004

Source: 2004 PSC pre- and post-election surveys.

polls. In this regard, the Liberals had a sizable edge over their rivals in 2004. Although the percentage of Liberal identifiers in the PSC pre-election survey was down from what it had been in the 1993, 1997, and 2000 elections, the Liberals still had a substantial lead (31 per cent versus 23 per cent) over the new Conservative Party (see Figure 3.5). In Ontario, the bedrock of Liberal success throughout the Chrétien era, the Liberals had a 10 per cent lead (35 per cent versus 25 per cent) over the CPC. However, the Liberals trailed the Conservatives by a large margin in the Prairies (40 per cent versus 22 per cent) and a smaller one in British Columbia (29 per cent versus 23 per cent). As for the NDP, it did reasonably well in British Columbia, with a 23 per cent party identification share. However, the party's national share was only 11 per cent. The BQ's national figure was also 11 per cent, but this is misleading. In Quebec, the only province where the party competed, fully 46 per cent identified themselves as Blocquistes and only 28 per cent said they were Liberals.[2]

Figure 3.5 also shows the distribution of party identification in the 2004 post-election PSC survey. These numbers indicate that no party attracted substantial numbers of additional partisans during the campaign. However, the Liberals and NDP did best, increasing their cohorts by 3 per cent each. The CPC fared less well, boosting its number of identifiers by only 1 per cent. As a result, the CPC trailed the Liberals by fully 10 per cent (24 per cent versus 34 per cent). This sizable gap in party identifiers was not good news for the Conservatives, since partisanship is an important driver of how people vote. On election day the Conservatives' vote total was nearly 6 per cent above its share of party identifiers, but this was not sufficient to dislodge the Liberals from power. However, it does suggest that the Conservatives did have some important short-term forces working in their favor during the campaign.

ISSUES

The Sponsorship Scandal

The most readily identifiable of these anti-Liberal forces was the sponsorship scandal. As discussed above, the scandal had rained a torrent of adverse publicity on the Liberals in the run-up to the election call. The scandal was a quintessential valence issue. Not surprisingly, voters are massively opposed to corruption in government; indeed, it is effectively an operational definition of "bad government." Still, Martin and his associates had hoped that they could escape blame. The misdeeds in question had occurred before Martin became prime minister and he resolutely denied knowledge of or involvement in them.

However, the electorate thought otherwise. As illustrated in Figure 3.6, two-thirds of the PSC respondents thought Martin was lying, and three-fifths disagreed with the proposition that he had handled the scandal well. An equally large number agreed that the scandal proved that there was widespread corruption in the Liberal Party, and over three-quarters disagreed with the statement that the scandal was unimportant. The PSC respondents were less certain whether the Liberals should be forced from office because of the scandal. Two-thirds thought it was unfair to blame the whole party for what had happened, and a small majority (54 per cent) disagreed that the scandal proved that the Liberals were unfit to govern. Overall, a strong negative current of public opinion about the scandal was evident, but whether it would prove consequential remained to be seen.[3]

Same-Sex Marriage

Just as the blatant corruption associated with the sponsorship scandal was easily classified as a valence issue, same-sex marriage was an archetypical position issue. The latter issue had received widespread publicity in the run-up to the 2004 election. The spotlight of media attention continued to focus on the issue at various times during the campaign, typically when pro-same-sex-marriage advocates staged protests at CPC rallies where Harper was speaking.

Public opinion polls suggested that the issue divided the electorate quite evenly. The PSC survey tells the same story—40 per cent of the respondents favored such marriages, 40 per cent were opposed, and the remainder said that they were unsure or had no opinion. In addition, as Figure 3.7 shows, these opinions were correlated with decisions to support the CPC, NDP, or BQ. Thus, the percentage of voters supporting the Conservatives increased from 15 per cent among those supporting same-sex marriage, to 32 per cent among the "no opinion" group, to 49 per cent among those opposed. Support for the NDP shows exactly the opposite pattern, falling from 29 per cent, to 18 per cent, to 7 per cent as opinions on the issue shift from positive, to neutral, to negative. BQ voting mirrors the NDP pattern. Although these figures suggest the potential of same-sex marriage as an issue, it is noteworthy that less than one person in five said that the issue was "very important," and three in five considered it to be "not very important," or that they did not have an opinion on it. Later in this chapter multivariate statistical analyses are employed to gauge how the issue affected electoral choice in 2004.

Most Important Issues

To ascertain which issues mattered to voters, we asked the respondents in the 2004 PSC pre- and post-election surveys what they considered to be the most important issue in the election. Their responses provide strong evidence of the dominance of valence issues. In the pre-election survey, 44 per cent mentioned health care and 12 per cent cited another public service (see Figure 3.8). Another 17 per cent referred

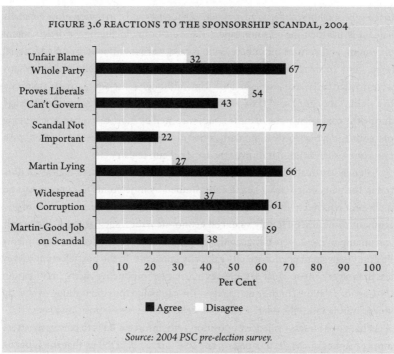

FIGURE 3.6 REACTIONS TO THE SPONSORSHIP SCANDAL, 2004

Source: 2004 PSC pre-election survey.

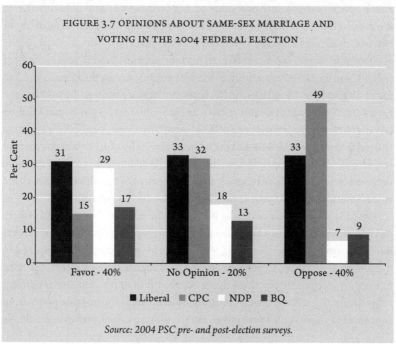

FIGURE 3.7 OPINIONS ABOUT SAME-SEX MARRIAGE AND
VOTING IN THE 2004 FEDERAL ELECTION

Source: 2004 PSC pre- and post-election surveys.

to the sponsorship scandal or government dishonesty and corruption more generally. Valence issues focusing on some aspect of the economy, including the deficit, unemployment, and various other economic issues, were mentioned by an additional 16 per cent. In sharp contrast, position issues on which the public and politicians were divided had much less resonance. Thus, although same-sex marriage, reproductive rights (abortion), and US-Canada relations all received considerable coverage during the campaign, none of these issues was cited by more than 1 per cent as being pre-eminent in the election. Similarly, small numbers chose other "hot button" position issues, such as immigration or the national gun registry.

Valence issues also dominated in the post-election survey. As Figure 3.8 illustrates, the percentage citing health care climbed by nine points to 53 per cent, and 11 per cent referred to the sponsorship scandal or the more general problem of government dishonesty. Heavily valenced economic issues, such as taxes, the deficit, and unemployment, were designated by 16 per cent of the post-election respondents. Position issues remained distinctly minority concerns. In the post-election survey, less than 3 per cent designated same-sex marriage, reproductive rights, immigration, US-Canada relations, or the gun registry. The campaign thus did nothing to change voters' minds about the relative importance of valence versus position issues.

What gives issues—valence or position—their force is links to parties in voters' minds (Stokes, 1963). In this regard, the PSC survey data tell us that the Liberals ended up with a sizable lead over other parties on the major issue of health care. In the pre-election survey, 29 per cent of those designating health care as most important had chosen the Liberals, 21 per cent the CPC, and 17 per cent, the NDP. In the post-election survey, 39 per cent favored the Liberals, and 18 and 26 per cent favored the CPC and the NDP, respectively. In the post-election survey the Liberals also had a lead, albeit somewhat smaller, on the economy. In sharp contrast, but as expected, voters exercised about the sponsorship scandal or other acts of government dishonesty overwhelmingly opted for one of the opposition parties. Specifically, 48 per cent favored the CPC, and the NDP and the BQ were chosen by 16 per cent and 15 per cent, respectively. Only 15 per cent favored the Liberals. In addition, the Conservatives did very well on position issues, receiving the endorsement of over three-fifths of all the voters mentioning issues such as same-sex marriage or the gun registry.

Figure 3.9 shows which parties the PSC respondents believed were closest to them on various important issues. Comparing data from the pre- and post-election surveys, it is evident that the Liberals and the NDP both made gains during the campaign. In the pre-election survey, 20 per cent favored the Liberals and 15 per cent, the NDP. In the post-election survey, these figures increased to 29 per cent and 21 per cent, respectively. In contrast, the CPC share moved upwards by only one point, from 23 per cent to 24 per cent. The message, then, is that the Conservatives were initially

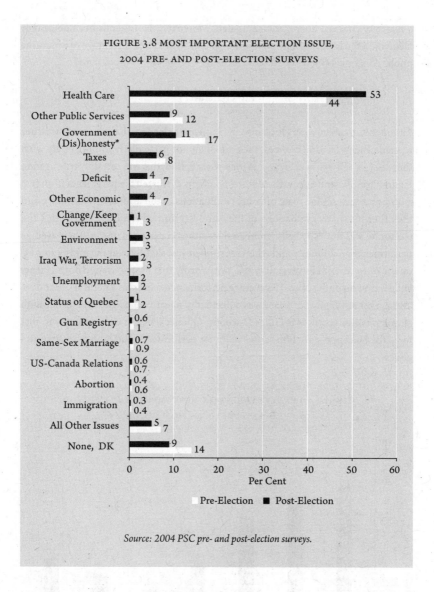

FIGURE 3.8 MOST IMPORTANT ELECTION ISSUE,
2004 PRE- AND POST-ELECTION SURVEYS

Source: 2004 PSC pre- and post-election surveys.

ahead of the Liberals on important issues, but they lost their lead as the campaign progressed.

As just indicated, the "big beast" was health care. A central feature of the Liberals' campaign strategy involved admonishing people to vote Liberal to protect health care programs from being gutted by a Harper-led CPC government. The survey data testify that the strategy worked. Health care, already a salient issue, became a majority concern during the campaign. Moreover, the Liberals became heavily favored on the issue, thereby positioning themselves to take advantage of mounting public concern about it.

Party Leaders

Although Canadian voters look closely at the party leaders in their search for cues to guide their electoral choices, they are often not particularly impressed by what they see (e.g., Clarke et al., 1996). With one exception, this was certainly true in 2004. Figure 3.10A illustrates how the PSC respondents evaluated the party leaders on two 0–10-point scales. One scale measures evaluations of the leaders' performance and the other measures evaluations of their honesty and ethics. It is evident that the electorate was not especially impressed by either Harper or Layton. Their average performance and honesty and ethics scores were just slightly over the mid-points (5) on the 0–10 scales. However, it is also noteworthy that Martin trailed both Harper and Layton on both scales. His average performance score was a neutral 5.0, and his average honesty/ethnics score was a decidedly negative 4.4. The one leader with strong positive scores was Gilles Duceppe. Quebeckers, the only voters who mattered for Duceppe, gave him scores of 6.3 for performance and 6.5 for honesty and ethics.

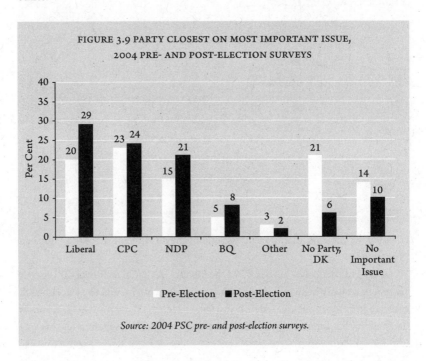

FIGURE 3.9 PARTY CLOSEST ON MOST IMPORTANT ISSUE, 2004 PRE- AND POST-ELECTION SURVEYS

Source: 2004 PSC pre- and post-election surveys.

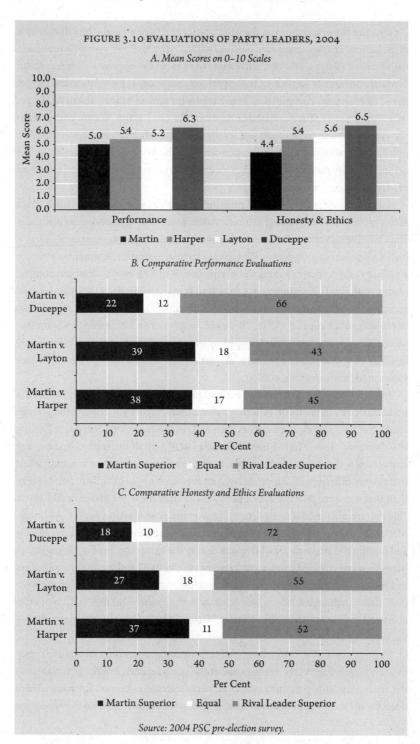

FIGURE 3.10 EVALUATIONS OF PARTY LEADERS, 2004

A. Mean Scores on 0–10 Scales

B. Comparative Performance Evaluations

C. Comparative Honesty and Ethics Evaluations

Source: 2004 PSC pre-election survey.

Two additional points about the performance and honesty and ethics dimensions of the leaders' images are in order. First, as anticipated by his lower average scores, large majorities of PSC respondents ranked one or more of the opposition leaders ahead of Martin on both dimensions. On the performance scale, 45 per cent ranked Harper ahead of Martin as compared to 38 per cent who ranked Martin ahead of Harper (see Figure 3.10B). The comparable numbers for the Layton-Martin comparison are 43 per cent and 39 per cent, and for the Duceppe-Martin comparison (Quebec only), they are 66 per cent and 22 per cent. On the honesty and ethics scale, the comparisons are more lopsided. Like Duceppe, Harper and Layton are ranked ahead of Martin by huge margins (see Figure 3.10C).

A second point is that Martin's scores on the performance and honesty and ethics scales are related very strongly to how voters reacted to the sponsorship scandal. Thus, his average score on the honesty and ethics scale increases steadily from a low of 2.0 points among people who made extremely negative judgments about the scandal to fully 7.5 points among those who dismissed it as "much ado about nothing" (data not shown). The summary correlation (r) is -.58. Similarly, Martin's average score on the performance scale moves steadily upward from 3.0 to 7.2 as reactions to the scandal change (r = -.51). These very impressive relationships indicate that Martin's image was seriously damaged by the scandal. And, as we will see shortly, this was a big deal in 2004 because, as usual, leader images mattered greatly when voters made their electoral choices.

The fact that none of the leaders except Duceppe was enthusiastically received is underscored by data on voters' feelings about them. Figure 3.11 displays the average scores the PSC survey respondents gave each of the leaders on 100-point "feeling thermometer" scales. In the rest of Canada (ROC), all of the leaders had average scores below the neutral point on the scale in the pre-election survey. In Quebec things were different; Duceppe received an average score of 58, fully 17 points more than that accorded Martin and 14 points more than those for Harper and Layton. This pattern also held among Quebeckers in the post-election survey. Although Martin, Harper, and Layton failed to generate strong positive reactions, Martin and Layton did make modest advances during the campaign. As Figure 3.11 shows, Martin's score climbed from 49 to 52 points in the ROC and from 41 to 48 points in Quebec. Layton's pattern was similar. However, feelings about Harper were essentially unchanged, falling by 1 point in both Quebec and the ROC. Not especially well-received before the election, Harper failed to ignite enthusiasm during the campaign.

Multivariate statistical analyses enable us to determine which factors are important for explaining voters' feelings about the party leaders. Predictor variables in the analysis include party identification; party selected as best on the issue a voter deems most important; evaluations of government performance on the economy;

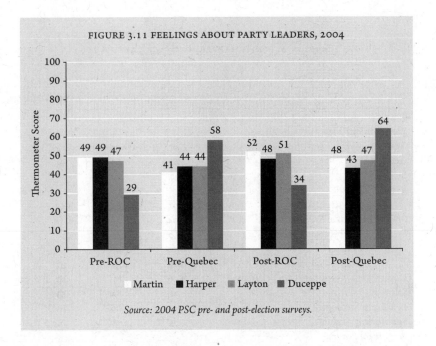

FIGURE 3.11 FEELINGS ABOUT PARTY LEADERS, 2004

Source: 2004 PSC pre- and post-election surveys.

reactions to the sponsorship scandal; position on the summary left-right ideology scale, with those denying that they think in left-right positions scored at the middle of the scale; and position on same-sex marriage. Several sociodemographic variables (age, gender, income, and region-ethnicity) are also included. Since the dependent variables are the 0–100 point thermometer scales, we estimate the models using OLS regression (Long, 1997).[4]

Considering factors affecting feelings about Martin, the analysis indicates that, as one would anticipate, Liberal party identifiers and people who select the Liberals as closest to them on the most important issue accorded higher scores to the Liberal leader, as did people who judged that the governing Liberals had done a good job in managing the economy (see Table 3.1). Older people also tended to accord higher scores to Martin, while NDP identifiers and residents of British Columbia gave him lower scores. Opinions about same-sex marriage and left-right ideological positions were not significant, but reactions to the sponsorship scandal had very large effects. The coefficient for this variable (-4.75) indicates that, other things held constant, voters who held very negative opinions about the scandal had Martin thermometer scores that were fully 33 points lower than those who minimized the seriousness of the affair.

The Harper and Layton analyses are also revealing. In Harper's case, party identification and choice of party as closest on most important issue had predictable and highly significant effects. With other factors held constant, being a CPC identifier

TABLE 3.1 PREDICTORS OF FEELINGS ABOUT
PAUL MARTIN, STEPHEN HARPER, AND JACK LAYTON, 2004

PARTY LEADER

	MARTIN	HARPER	LAYTON
Predictor Variables			
Age	.07*	-.02 -	.13***
Gender	-.81	-1.66	.92
Income	-.17	-.24	-.25
Region/Ethnicity:			
Atlantic	1.62	.63	2.43
Quebec-French	-1.04	2.69	-1.48
Quebec-Non-French	.50	-3.43	5.36
Prairies	-.30	.42	-.36
British Columbia	-3.29*	4.59*	-1.97
Government Performance on Economy	3.26***	.81	1.22
Same-Sex Marriage	.26	-1.86***	.53
Left-Right Ideology	.44	5.06***	-3.65***
Sponsorship Scandal	-4.75***	1.78***	.11
Party Identification:			
Liberal	4.82***	-3.07*	-.08
Conservative	-2.45	7.39***	-3.16*
NDP	1.15	-6.61**	11.50**
Bloc Québécois	-1.72	-8.98***	-.29
Other Party	4.02	-15.44**	11.89*
Party Best Important Issue:			
Liberal	8.83***	-4.72**	2.58
Conservative	-1.12	15.64***	-.09
NDP	-12.41***	-1.42	18.83***
Bloc Québécois	1.62	.63	2.43
Constant	43.05	32.63	59.74
Adjusted R^2	.43	.52	.34

*** $p \leq .001$; ** $p \leq .01$; * $p \leq .05$; one-tailed test.

Note: OLS regression analyses of feelings about party leaders, 2004 PSC pre-post panel survey.

raised feelings about Harper by seven points, and selecting the party as closest on an important issue raised them by nearly 16 points. However, in addition to these effects, opinions about same-sex marriage and left-right ideology both had significant impacts on feelings about the Conservative leader. Strong opinions about same-sex marriage caused feelings about Harper to change by 11 points, and moving from the left to the right (or vice versa) on the left-right ideology scale caused feelings about him to change by 20 points. The latter figure is impressive, but one needs to remember that only three voters in 10 actually thought of themselves in left-right terms. Feelings about Harper were largely impervious to other factors, the one exception being that British Columbians tended to like him more than did residents of other regions.

Feelings about Layton were driven by many of the same forces just discussed. Party identification and party closest on most important issue had very significant effects, such that being an NDP identifier raised Layton's thermometer score by nearly 12 points, and selecting the NDP on an important issue did so by nearly 19 points. In addition, younger voters were more favorably disposed towards Layton. Left-right ideology also mattered, having the capacity to move feelings about the NDP leader by nearly 15 points on the 100-point scale. However, as in Harper's case, only a small minority of people held the kinds of left-of-center ideological positions that would boost their feelings about him. In the next section of this chapter, we analyze how feelings about the leaders and other forces affected the choices voters made in 2004.

ELECTORAL CHOICES IN 2004

As discussed in earlier chapters, political scientists have developed a variety of different explanations of why people vote as they do. Here, we test the efficacy of several of these models in the context of the 2004 Canadian federal election. Table 3.2 summarizes the performance of competing models of Liberal, Conservative, and NDP voting for all of Canada. As measured by R^2 statistics and their ability to correctly predict voting behavior, demographic variables (age, gender, income, and region/ethnicity) have only very weak effects. This is a general finding, one that we see repeated in analyses of voting in several other elections in Canada and the United States. Evaluations of government economic performance and position issues (here same-sex marriage) also have quite weak effects, although opinions about same-sex marriage do have a larger impact on CPC than on NDP and, especially, Liberal voting. In contrast, the sponsorship scandal—a valence issue—has stronger effects on Liberal voting than on CPC or NDP voting.

As is the case in analyses of voting in other elections, core variables in the valence politics model of electoral choice perform relatively well. These variables are party identification, party best on most important issue, and party leader images. For Liberal and CPC voting, party leader images have the largest R^2s and the best classification performance, and for NDP voting, party best on most important issue does

TABLE 3.2 SUMMARY OF PERFORMANCE OF RIVAL MODELS
OF VOTING IN THE 2004 FEDERAL ELECTION (ALL CANADA)

A. Liberal Voting

	MCFADDEN R^2	MCKELVEY R^2	PER CENT CORRECTLY CLASSIFIED	AIC†
Rival Models				
Demographics	.05	.09	67.7	1341.29
Government Economic Performance	.10	.18	69.9	1261.86
Position Issues	.00	.01	67.7	1395.26
Sponsorship Scandal	.21	.34	76.7	1104.99
Federal Party Identification	.27	.42	79.9	1025.15
Party Best Important Issues	.37	.49	84.5	893.52
Party Leader Images	.38	.64	83.4	877.03
Valence Politics	.56	.76	88.8	635.86
Composite Model	.61	.79	89.9	599.05

B. Conservative Voting

	MCFADDEN R^2	MCKELVEY R^2	PER CENT CORRECTLY CLASSIFIED	AIC†
Rival Models				
Demographics	.11	.23	69.9	1243.73
Government Economic Performance	.06	.10	69.3	1304.35
Position Issues	.18	.35	72.7	1139.62
Sponsorship Scandal	.09	.15	67.7	1266.48
Federal Party Identification	.34	.47	83.1	918.39
Party Best Important Issues	.44	.55	87.8	786.90
Party Leader Images	.59	.82	87.5	576.10
Valence Politics	.68	.85	91.8	472.16
Composite Model	.70	.86	92.4	469.91

C. NDP Voting

	MCFADDEN R^2	MCKELVEY R^2	PER CENT CORRECTLY CLASSIFIED	AIC†
Rival Models				
Demographics	.06	.16	81.3	993.49
Government Economic Performance	.00	.00	81.5	1064.98
Position Issues	.12	.20	83.0	942.84
Sponsorship Scandal	.00	.00	81.5	1066.70
Federal Party Identification	.20	.26	85.7	860.19
Party Best Important Issues	.41	.47	89.4	640.57
Party Leader Images	.38	.59	85.8	670.85
Valence Politics	.53	.65	90.3	526.74
Composite Model	.58	.71	91.8	505.70

†—Akaike Information Criterion (AIC)—smaller values indicate better model performance.

slightly better than leader images. A valence politics model that includes all of these variables performs even better, with larger R^2s and more voters correctly classified. Regarding the latter and indicative of the explanatory power of the valence politics model, Table 3.2 shows that this model can correctly classify nearly 89 per cent of Liberal voters and slightly over 90 per cent of CPC and NDP voters. However, Table 3.2 also indicates that the valence politics model does not have the playing field entirely to itself. A composite model that includes the variables from the valence politics model, as well as all of the variables from other models, performs slightly better than the pure valence model. The composite model has the largest R^2s, the largest per cent correctly classified, and the lowest Akaike Information Criterion (AIC) value. The conclusion is that several models could make significant contributions to explaining why voters behaved as they did in 2004. Again, this is a finding that parallels results for voting in other elections considered in this volume.

Table 3.3 presents information concerning the performance of different variables in the composite models of Liberal, CPC, and NDP voting. Core variables in the valence politics model have a variety of highly statistically significant and properly signed effects. For example, as anticipated, having a Liberal identification enhances the likelihood of voting for that party, and identifying with any other party decreases that likelihood. Similarly, selecting the Liberals as best on the most important issue raises the probability of voting Liberal, and selecting any other party lowers it. Party leader images work exactly the same way, i.e., positive feelings about Martin increase the likelihood of voting Liberal and positive feelings about Harper or Layton decrease it. Patterns of effects of the valence politics variables on CPC and NDP voting are basically analogous. There is one noteworthy exception—holding a Conservative identification did not boost the probability of a CPC vote in 2004. Liberal, NDP, and BQ identifiers all were less likely to vote Conservative than were nonidentifiers, but CPC identifiers were not more likely to do so. Voting CPC in 2004 was not about being a Conservative identifier.

Table 3.3 reports other noteworthy findings as well. In line with the hopes of Liberal strategists, positive evaluations of the government's economic performance significantly increased the probability of a Liberal vote. However, as discussed below, the size of this effect was not particularly large. Same-sex marriage also had a significant effect on Liberal voting, but the effect was negative; other things being equal, people favoring such marriages were less likely to cast a Liberal ballot. As anticipated, the sponsorship scandal worked the same way, i.e., as judgments about the behavior of Martin and his party became increasingly negative, the probability of voting Liberal decreased.

Tactical voting was also a significant factor. Again, as the Liberals hoped, people who thought tactically were significantly more likely to vote Liberal and significantly less likely to vote NDP than were people who did not entertain tactical voting

TABLE 3.3 COMPOSITE MODELS OF LIBERAL, CONSERVATIVE,
AND NDP VOTING IN THE 2004 FEDERAL ELECTION, CANADA

	VOTE		
	LIBERAL	CPC	NDP
Predictor Variables			
Age	.00	.00	-.00
Gender	-.00	.23	-.18
Income	.09*	.04	-.11*
Region/Ethnicity:			
Atlantic	.06	.04	.19
Quebec-French	-.07	-1.75***	-.44
Quebec-Non-French	.41	-.15	-.13
Prairies	-.30	.42	-.36
British Columbia	-.62*	.59	.41
Government Performance on Economy	.25*	-.18	-.11
Same-Sex Marriage	-.14*	-.01	.08
Left-Right Ideology	.12	-.13	-.00
Party Identification:			
Liberal	.75**	-.69*	.09
Conservative	-.93**	.10	-.24
NDP	-1.08**	-1.70**	1.09**
Bloc Québécois	-2.45***	-1.49*	-.26
Other Party	-2.18*	.00	-3.83***
Party Best Important Issue:			
Liberal	1.05***	.13	-1.11**
Conservative	-1.32***	1.70***	-.85*
NDP	-1.26***	-.06	1.48***
Bloc Québécois	-2.20***	-2.44*	-2.81*
Sponsorship Scandal	-.19*	.11	.05
Leader Images:			
Martin	.06***	-.04***	-.02**
Harper	-.03***	.09***	-.02*
Layton	-.02**	-.04***	.07***
Duceppe	.00	-.00	-.01*
Tactical Voting	0.97***	-.19	-2.28***
Constant	-3.09***	-1.88	-2.41*
McFadden R^2	.61	.70	.58
McKelvey R^2	.79	.86	.71
Per Cent Correctly Classified	89.9	92.4	91.8
AIC†	599.05	469.91	505.70

*** p < .001; ** p < .01; * p < .05; one-tailed test.
Note: Binomial logit analyses of Liberal, Conservative, and NDP voting.

†—Akaike Information Criterion (AIC)—smaller values indicate better model performance.

considerations. As also anticipated, tactical thinking did not affect CPC voting. Finally, a few demographic variables were influential, with Quebec francophones being significantly less likely to vote CPC, and British Columbians significantly less likely to vote Liberal. Other things equal, higher-income earners were more prone to vote Liberal and lower-income earners were more likely to vote NDP. Despite campaign rhetoric about the new CPC being a party for wealthy Canadians, income level was not associated with Conservative voting.

The results in Table 3.3 tell us which variables had significant effects, but they do not tell us how large their effects were. For this purpose, we follow the procedure discussed in the previous chapter of manipulating the values of various significant predictor variables from their lowest to their highest levels, while holding other predictors at their means or other plausible values.[5] The results of this exercise show that leader images had very large effects on Liberal, CPC, and NDP voting in 2004. Thus, as feelings about Paul Martin are varied from their lowest to their highest values, the probability of voting Liberal increases by 70 points (see Table 3.4). The comparable effect for feelings about Stephen Harper on CPC voting are an enormous 94 points, and while the impact of feelings about Jack Layton on NDP voting are not quite as large, they are still an impressive 66 points. Feelings about rival party leaders are also influential, decreasing the likelihood of voting for a particular party. For example, increasingly positive feelings about Stephen Harper could reduce the probability of casting a Liberal ballot by 37 points, and increasingly positive feelings about Paul Martin or Jack Layton could reduce the probability of voting CPC by 41 and 42 points, respectively.

There are other noteworthy findings. Choosing a party as closest on an issue selected as most important had sizable effects. For example, Table 3.4 shows that choosing the Liberals rather than the CPC on most important issue increased the likelihood of a Liberal ballot by 31 points (19-[-12]). Similarly, selecting the CPC rather than the NDP enhanced the likelihood of voting Conservative by 31 points (25-[-6]), and selecting the NDP rather than the Liberals increased the chance of voting NDP by 25 points (20-[-5]). Tactical voting was influential too; thinking tactically increased the probability of voting Liberal by 34 points. Although this is a very sizable effect, the Liberals' problem in 2004 was that only approximately one voter in 10 reported that they behaved tactically. Regarding the sponsorship scandal, as evaluations of the affair became increasingly harsh, they lowered the likelihood of voting Liberal by 13 points. This is a relatively small effect, but as discussed earlier, the scandal did have a large indirect impact by influencing feelings about Liberal leader, Paul Martin. As for same-sex marriage, changing views of the issue could move the probability of Liberal voting, but only by nine points. Similarly, as judgments about government performance on the economy moved from negative to positive, the probability of opting for the Liberals increased by only 10 points.

TABLE 3.4 EFFECTS OF SIGNIFICANT PREDICTORS ON
PROBABILITY OF LIBERAL, CONSERVATIVE, AND NDP VOTING
IN THE 2004 FEDERAL ELECTION, CANADA

	VOTE		
	LIBERAL	CPC	NDP
Predictor Variables			
Age	X	X	X
Gender	X	X	X
Income	.07	X	-.04
Region/Ethnicity:			
Atlantic	X	X	X
Quebec-French	X	-.10	X
Quebec-Non-French	X	X	X
Prairies	X	X	X
British Columbia	-.06	X	X
Government Performance on Economy	.10	X	X
Same-Sex Marriage	-.09	X	X
Left-Right Ideology	X	X	X
Party Identification:			
Liberal	.13	-.17	X
Conservative	-.10	X	X
NDP	-.11	-.13	.09
Bloc Québécois	-.16	X	X
Other Party	-.14	X	-.05
Party Best Important Issue:			
Liberal	.19	X	-.05
Conservative	-.12	.25	-.04
NDP	-.12	-.06	.20
Bloc Québécois	-.12	-.07	-.07
Sponsorship Scandal	-.13	X	X
Leader Images:			
Martin	**.70**	**-.41**	-.14
Harper	-.37	**.94**	-.09
Layton	-.23	-.42	**.66**
Duceppe	X	X	-.05
Tactical Voting	.34	X	-.06

X—not a significant predictor.

Note: Boldface numbers indicate three largest changes in voting probability.

This latter finding underscores the difficulty Martin and his party had in capitalizing on the healthy economy in 2004.

Table 3.5 presents the results of analyzing composite models of Bloc Québécois voting in Quebec. As noted earlier, support for the BQ had surged in the wake of the sponsorship scandal, and the party gained nearly 50 per cent of the vote. And, indeed, the scandal did have a large impact on BQ support. As the right-hand column in Table 3.5 shows, as evaluations of the scandal became increasingly negative, the likelihood of voting BQ increased by 40 points. However, as large as this effect was, it was hardly the whole story. Feelings about party leaders had very strong effects. Indeed, as feelings about BQ leader, Gilles Duceppe, moved from negative to positive, the likelihood of voting BQ increased by a huge amount, 88 points. Effects associated with feelings about the other party leaders were also decidedly nontrivial, with changing feelings about Martin, Harper, and Layton being able to move the probability of a BQ ballot by 54, 43, and 52 points, respectively. The Harper effect is noteworthy because it is positive; other things equal, people who liked Harper were actually more likely to support the BQ. This seemingly perverse effect hints at the potential for the CPC to siphon votes away from the Bloc. As discussed in the previous chapter, this is exactly what occurred in 2006.

There are other stories in Table 3.5. One of them is that party preference on important issues mattered. And, as in the analyses of voting in the ROC, the effects were large. Thus, moving from the CPC to the BQ on most important issue increased the likelihood of a BQ vote by 78 points (30−[-48]). The effect of moving from the NDP to the Bloc was nearly as large, 68 points (30−[-38]). Party identification was in the picture, too; being a BQ identifier enhanced the probability of supporting the party by 26 points.

Finally, attitudes towards Quebec sovereignty made a predictable appearance. Since the late 1960s, sovereignty has been *the* key position issue in Quebec politics, reshaping first the provincial party system and then its federal counterpart. As noted above, the sponsorship scandal was widely viewed by Quebeckers as "a slap in the face," and it had inflamed pro-sovereignty sentiments in the winter and early spring of 2004. Indicative of the public mood, at the time of the 2004 election, 46 per cent of the PSC respondents said that they would vote "yes" in a future sovereignty referendum. And, as one would anticipate, moving from anti- to pro-sovereignty increased the likelihood of voting BQ, with the size of the effect being 24 points (see Table 3.5). The total effect of attitudes towards sovereignty was greater than this figure would suggest. As observed above, feelings about the BQ leader, Gilles Duceppe, and BQ partisanship have strong effects on BQ voting, and these two variables, in turn, were strongly correlated (r's = +.52 and +.53, respectively), with positions on the sovereignty issue. Voting in Quebec in 2004 was not only about sovereignty, but, reinvigorated by the sponsorship scandal, the sovereignty issue was in play in a way it had not been for several years.

TABLE 3.5 COMPOSITE MODEL OF BLOC QUÉBÉCOIS VOTING
IN THE 2004 FEDERAL ELECTION

	VOTE	CHANGE IN PROBABILITY
Predictor Variables		
Age	.01	X
Gender	.34	X
Income	-.19*	-.28
Quebec-French	1.21	X
Government Performance on Economy	.13	X
Same-Sex Marriage	.26	X
Left-Right Ideology	-.32	X
Quebec Sovereignty	.57**	.24
Party Identification:		
Liberal	-.34	X
Conservative	.02	X
NDP	-.01	X
Bloc Québécois	1.14*	.26
Party Best Important Issue:		
Liberal	-.48	X
Conservative	-2.63***	-.48
NDP	-1.95**	-.38
Bloc Québécois	1.78***	.30
Sponsorship Scandal	.29*	.40
Leader Images:		
Martin	-.03*	-.54
Harper	.02*	.43
Layton	-.03*	-.52
Duceppe	.06***	.88
Tactical Voting	.52	X
Constant	-3.76	X
McFadden R^2	.67	
McKelvey R^2	.83	
Per Cent Correctly Classified	91.8	
AIC†219.62		

X—not a significant predictor.
*** p < .001; ** p < .01; * p < .05; one-tailed test.

Note: Binomial logit analyses of Liberal and BQ voting. Boldface numbers indicate three largest changes in voting probability.

†—Akaike Information Criterion (AIC)—smaller values indicate better
model performance.

CONCLUSION: CRACKING THE MOLD

The 1993 federal election dramatically "broke the mold" of Canada's long-lived national party system. The old "two-party-plus" system (Epstein, 1964) had featured competition between the Liberals and the Progressive Conservatives, with occasional swells of support for smaller parties such as the NDP and Social Credit. The Liberals typically emerged victorious, but the Conservatives occasionally would prevail. In 1993 and thereafter, the party system had one large party, the Liberals, competing regionally with the Reform/Alliance in the West, the NDP in Ontario, the Bloc Québécois in Quebec, and the rump of the old Progressive Conservative Party in the Maritimes. Liberal election victories in 1993, 1997, and 2000 suggested that a new "one-party-plus" system had been established, and that it would be very difficult for any opposition party to dislodge the Liberals. However, this conclusion turned out to be premature. In 2004 the new Conservative Party of Canada demonstrated that the Liberals were vulnerable. The CPC could not unseat the Liberals, but, by forcing them into minority government status, the Conservatives "cracked the mold" of the new party system. By so doing, they established the conditions necessary to drive the Liberals from power in Ottawa. As discussed in the previous chapter, they accomplished this in 2006.

Formed less than a year before the 2004 election, the CPC was greatly aided by the sponsorship scandal. The scandal broke only a few months after Paul Martin had become Liberal leader. Although he had been finance minister during a lengthy period of increasing economic prosperity, evidence presented in this chapter indicates that his image suffered substantial damage because of the scandal. Many voters were learning about Martin precisely when he was being accused of facilitating the misappropriation of 100 million dollars of public money. Since party leader images—a major component of the valence model of electoral choice—are extremely influential determinants of voting behavior, the scandal's negative impact on Martin's image was a major reason why the Liberals struggled throughout the 2004 campaign and ultimately were able to secure only a minority government.

Yet the Liberals *did* prevail. A valence issue, health care, was the key. Health care quickly became a major issue in the election, and its importance increased as the campaign progressed. The Liberals recognized that this was an issue that they could use to advantage against the new CPC. Since the CPC and its leader, Stephen Harper, had never held power, they had no record of successfully managing important public programs. This made it relatively easy for the Liberals to frighten voters with accusations that Harper and his colleagues were right-wing fanatics bent on eviscerating health care and other cherished public services. Data presented above indicate that the success of the Liberal attack was not due to their use of the adjective "right wing" per se. Most Canadian voters do not think about politics in terms of "left" and "right," and there is only a small electoral market for explicit ideological appeals. What mattered to most people was not that Harper was "right wing," but rather that he would attack, not defend and improve, health care. Off-the-cuff comments about privatization of health programs by the Progressive Conservative premier of Alberta, Ralph Klein, lent seeming credibility to the Liberals' accusations. The dominance of the health care issue gave the Liberals enough—just enough—to cling to power.

In the wake of the election, it was abundantly evident that the Conservatives had to establish themselves in the public mind as a pragmatic center-right party. To this end, they had to learn to play the brokerage politics game with its heavy emphasis on valence issues and credible leadership. The problem for Harper was that playing the brokerage politics game risked alienating his Western base of economic and social small "c" conservatives. At a minimum, he had to convince the ideological hardcore in his party that winning trumps ideology, one major implication of which was to stay resolutely "on message" during election campaigns. Only 18 months later, Harper accomplished his goal. Muzzling the ideological hardcore who had frightened valence-oriented voters in 2004, he ran a very well-organized, tightly focused campaign and, as luck would have it, he benefited from unforeseen events. Exploiting a mixture of discipline and good fortune, Harper led the CPC to victory in the 2006 election.

Notes

1 The 2004 PSC study was supported by US National Science Foundation (NSF) grants to Kornberg (#0420401) and Kornberg and Scotto (#0422569). The study consisted of a national pre- and post-election panel survey conducted via the TNS-Canadian Facts RDD CATI system. A post-election, self-completion, mail-back survey was also administered. Weights were developed and used to account for household size, gender, age, region, panel attrition, and a Quebec oversample. Sample sizes were 2,495 and 1,361 for the pre- and post-election RDD surveys, and 1,058 mail-back questionnaires were returned.

2 A party identification question-wording experiment was conducted. A random half-sample of the 2004 PSC survey respondents were asked a version of the party identification question that ends with "or what," and the other random half received a version that ends with "or none of these" (see Johnston, 1992). A single partisan identification variable was generated using data generated by the two versions of the question.

3 For the battery of questions tapping reactions to the sponsorship scandal, respondents were first asked whether they had heard of the scandal. Over 80 per cent indicated that they were aware of it. Those aware of the scandal were asked whether they agreed or disagreed with the following statements: a) "Prime Minister Paul Martin has done a good job in dealing with the scandal"; b) "The scandal proves

that there is widespread corruption in the Liberal Party"; c) "Paul Martin is lying when he says he didn't know about the scandal before becoming Prime Minister"; d) "Despite all the press coverage, the scandal really is not very important"; e) "The scandal shows that the Liberal Party cannot govern the country effectively"; and f) "It is unfair to blame the entire Liberal Party for the scandal." For each question, answers indicating the respondent believed that the scandal was a sign of corruption on the part of the prime minister or the Liberal Party were coded one, and those disagreeing with such an assessment were coded -1 (those not having a position or who were unsure or unaware of the scandal were coded zero). An additive index was created using the sum of the respondents' scores on the questions. Those with scores of -5 or -6 were recoded to -3; scores of -4 and -3 were recoded to -2; and scores of -2 or -1 were recoded to -1. Respondents who had not heard of the scandal or had neutral assessments were coded zero. Scores of one or two were recoded to a score of one; scores of three or four were recoded to a score of two; and scores of five or six were recoded to a score of three. Negative scores indicate that the respondent did not hold either the Liberal Party and/or Prime Minister Martin accountable for the scandal, and positive scores indicated that the respondent assigned at least some culpability to the prime minister and/or his party.

4   In the multivariate analyses that follow, age is a continuous variable with those refusing to state their age given the value 45. Gender is coded one if the respondent was a man and zero if the respondent was a woman. Income is an eight-category variable that ranges from one through eight. The median score of four is assigned if the respondent refused to indicate their income. The "government per-formance on the economy" variable is a five-category variable ranging from zero through four and based on respondents' answers to the question: "Would you say the federal government has done a very good job, a good job, a poor job, or a very poor job in handling the economy?" Respondents who did not know or refused to answer the question were coded two, and higher scores indicate a more positive evaluation. The same-sex marriage variable is respondents' support (coded one) or opposition (coded -1) on the issue times intensity of support or opposition, measured by a variable ranging from one (not important or don't know) to three (very important). Respondents who did not have a position on the issue were coded zero. The left-right ideology variable ranged from one to five, with respondents answering that they were left coded one, center-left coded two, center-right coded four, and right coded five. Those saying that they were in the center or did not think in left-right terms were coded three.

5   Probabilities were calculated using the STATA CLARIFY program (Tomz, Wittenberg, and King, 1999).

CHAPTER FOUR

Red Voters, Blue Voters

The 2004 American Presidential Election

Other than Abraham Lincoln and Franklin Roosevelt, no American president's identity was changed so quickly and dramatically from peacetime to wartime president by a single event as was George W. Bush's. The impact of the transforming events—the Confederates firing on Fort Sumpter, the Japanese attack on Pearl Harbor, and Al-Qaeda's attacks on New York and Washington—undoubtedly were heightened because they occurred on American territory. Other presidents, of course, had had both their public and personal lives changed by war and its aftermath. For example, Woodrow Wilson only reluctantly took the United States into World War I to "make the world safe for democracy." His subsequent failure to get the Senate to endorse US membership in the League of Nations, the international organization of which he was also the principal architect, precipitated the debilitating illness that would lead to his death. In addition, both Harry Truman and Lyndon Johnson decided not to seek re-election because of mounting public criticism of their leadership as wartime presidents during the Korean and Vietnamese conflicts. In contrast, George W. Bush's decision to not only run but also to run hard for re-election on the basis of his leadership on the "War on Terror" can be characterized as affirming one-third of the old saw that "some are born great, some achieve greatness, and others have greatness thrust upon them."

This chapter is concerned with why, three years after the worst attack on American soil since Pearl Harbor, in the wake of an economic recession, and with American troops mired in protracted conflicts in Iraq and Afghanistan, George W. Bush accomplished what his father had not—re-election to the most powerful political office in the world. We begin by analyzing the ebbs and flows in Bush's support during his first term, and then consider the advantages and disadvantages he and his opponent, Massachusetts Senator John Kerry, had going into the 2004 campaign. As we will see, before the campaign each candidate could count on the support of about 30 per cent of the electorate who were identified with the respective parties. Although strong partisans almost always vote for their party's presidential candidate in a particular election, it is also important to recognize that partisan attachments are not immutable, and a variety of forces affect electoral choice. Thus, after documenting the long- and short-term dynamics of partisanship in the run-up to the 2004 election, we consider several factors that may have led voters to make the choices they did. We next assess the power of competing explanations of presidential voting in 2004. The conclusion reconsiders why Bush, despite the many difficulties facing him, was re-elected.

THE DYNAMICS OF "W's" APPROVAL RATINGS

Even a simple "ocular analysis" of Gallup and other polls shows that President Bush was on a public opinion roller coaster during his first term. As Figure 4.1 illustrates, his job approval ratings increased dramatically following 9/11, with another, much smaller, increase occurring when the Iraq War began in March 2003. These visual impressions are confirmed by a time series analysis of the Gallup monthly presidential approval series for the period starting with Bush's inauguration in January 2001. The analysis uses an error-correction model (e.g., Hendry, 1995) to investigate long- and short-run factors affecting how the public rated the president. In this model, party identification and economic conditions are designated as key long-term forces affecting the evolution of presidential approval. Over the long haul, approval ratings are controlled by the balance of Republican and Democratic party identifiers in the electorate—what is known as "macropartisanship"—and public expectations about the future of the national economy (see Erikson, MacKuen, and Stimson, 2002).[1] Movements in macropartisanship and economic expectations also influence presidential approval in the short-run, as do various "shocks" to public opinion, such as those generated by international crises and wars, terrorist attacks, scandals, and natural disasters. The model is specified as follows:

$$(1\text{-}L)PRESAP_t = B_0 - A_1^*(PRESAP_{t\text{-}1} - C_1^*MACROP_{t\text{-}1} - C_2^*NATEXP_{t\text{-}1}) +$$
$$B_1^*(1\text{-}L)MACROP_{t\text{-}1} + B_2^*(1\text{-}L)NATEXP_{t\text{-}1} + \Sigma B_{3\text{-}k}^*SHOCKS_{t\text{-}i} + \varepsilon_t + \theta\varepsilon_{t\text{-}1} \text{ where:}$$

$PRESAP_t$ = presidential approval in month t;

$MACROP_t$ = the balance of Republican and Democratic party identifiers at time t;

$NATEXP_t$ = national economic expectations at time t;

$SHOCKS_t$ = various shocks operating at time t-i;

ε_t = stochastic error at time t, $\sim N(0,\sigma^2)$;

L = backshift operator;

$A_1, B_0\text{-}B_k, C_1, C_2, \theta$ = model parameters.

Estimating model parameters confirms that 9/11 had a huge effect. It boosted Bush's approval by over 24 points in September 2001 and by nearly 14 points more in the following month (see Table 4.1). 9/11's impact then diminished gradually but steadily, with the adjustment parameter (A_1 in the model) indicating the influence of the attack (and all other shocks) eroded at slightly over 6 per cent per month.[2] The initiation of hostilities with Iraq in March 2003 also helped the president, prompting a

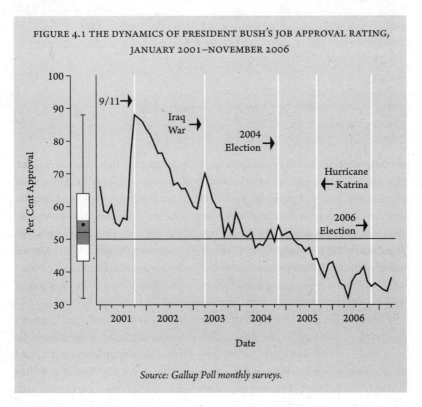

FIGURE 4.1 THE DYNAMICS OF PRESIDENT BUSH'S JOB APPROVAL RATING, JANUARY 2001–NOVEMBER 2006

Source: Gallup Poll monthly surveys.

TABLE 4.1 FACTORS AFFECTING THE DYNAMICS OF PRESIDENTIAL
APPROVAL, JANUARY 2001–MAY 2006

	B	s.e.
PREDICTOR VARIABLES		
Δ National Economic Expectations (t)	0.10**	0.03
Δ Macropartisanship (t)	0.69***	0.16
Approval-Macropartisanship- Economic Expectations ECM (t-1)	-0.06***	0.11
9/11 (t)	24.27***	2.11
9/11 (t-1)	13.55***	2.17
Iraq War Begins (t)	8.88***	1.82
Saddam Hussein Captured (t)	2.36	1.90
Iraq War Δ(Log Cumulative Casualties (t-2))	-0.80*	0.37
Hurricane Katrina (t)	-2.34a	1.76
First-Order Moving Average	-0.65***	0.12
Constant	-14.13***	4.75

Adjusted R^2 = .79
Durbin Watson Residual Autocorrelaton Test, d = 2.03, p = .90
Breusch-Godfrey Residual Autocorrelation Test, $\chi(12)$ = 9.81, p = .111
Jarque-Bera Normality Test, $\chi(1)$ = 0.59, p = .74
Arch 1 Test, $\chi(1)$ = 0.28, p = .60
White Heteroskedasticity Test, $\chi(19)$ = 17.36, p = .57
N = 65

*** p < .001; ** p < .01; * p < .05; a p < .10; one-tailed test.

temporary nine-point rally in his approval rating. In contrast, the capture of Saddam Hussein had a much smaller, statistically insignificant impact of less than three points. Casualties in Iraq had a gradual, predictably negative effect—the 1,262 American deaths from the start of the war in March 2003 to the eve of the election in November 2004 caused Bush's approval to decline by some 10 per cent. Thus, although Bush's popularity initially benefited greatly after 9/11 as Americans rallied to a self-styled wartime president, the huge boost generated by the horrific attacks eventually evaporated, with news of mounting casualties in wartorn Iraq driving down his standing with the electorate as the 2004 election approached.

Data from the American National Election Study (ANES) testify that Iraq was a potentially serious problem for the president as he campaigned for re-election. In the 2004 ANES pre-election survey, nearly three-fifths of the respondents (57 per cent) disapproved of his handling of the war, with fully 49 per cent saying that they "strongly disapproved." In this regard, there is a kind of perverse parallel between

Bush, Sr.'s position in 1992 and his son's in 2004. Bush the elder's public standing benefited hugely from the 1991 Gulf War against Iraq from which the victorious United States forces quickly withdrew. However, his popularity then diminished slowly, but profoundly, because of mounting public discomfort with a recessionary economy (e.g., Clarke, Rapkin, and Stewart, 1994).[3]

In contrast, our time series analysis of "W's" approval shows that his standing with the voters was only marginally affected (by slightly less than two points overall) by the downturn in economic expectations that ensued in the wake of 9/11. However, his popularity suffered because of his decision to remain in Iraq after capturing Baghdad. As the situation in Iraq spiralled downward, so did his approval rating. As the 2004 election approached, it appeared that Iraq might well have the same negative consequences on his re-election prospects as the economic downturn had for his father a decade earlier. Given poll evidence indicating his weakened position, commentators conjectured that if "W" won in 2004, it would be because he mobilized the Republican partisan base, especially the "Christian Right" (e.g., Rozell, 2004). Accordingly, we next consider the nature of Americans' partisan attachments and their impact on the electoral prospects of both Bush and his Democratic challenger, Senator John Kerry.

PARTISANSHIP: THE MOVING MOVER

As noted earlier, the questions of whether and for whom people will vote in free competitive elections has long agitated and frequently confounded not only candidates for public office but literally small armies of campaign "specialists"—pollsters, public relations experts, speech writers, and fundraisers. And, perhaps not surprisingly, initial attempts to address these two questions through systematic research were undertaken in the United States. The first major voting studies were conducted by political sociologists at Columbia University in the 1940s (Berelson, Lazarsfeld, and McPhee, 1954; Lazarsfeld, Berelson, and Gaudet, 1948). Subsequently, researchers at the University of Michigan carried out a series of investigations in the 1950s and the early 1960s that were the basis of two groundbreaking books, *The American Voter* (1960) and *Elections and the Political Order* (1966).

The "Michigan" model of voting behavior, theoretically rooted in mid-twentieth-century social psychology, attempted to go beyond the static social determinism of the Columbia school by acknowledging the importance of both long- and short-term influences on voters' decisions. "Issue orientations" and "candidate orientations" were designated as principal short-term forces, and a new concept, party identification, was used to summarize long-term forces. According to Campbell et al. (1960), party identification was a positive affective orientation towards a party grounded in feelings of oneness with it. Crucially, party identifications were durable. Much as people form lasting bonds with regional, religious, or ethnic groups, they were said to forge enduring attachments with political parties. Voters not only develop social identities as, for example, Southerners, Catholics, or Irish-Americans, but they also acquire political identities as Republicans or Democrats. Just as is the case for social identifications, party identifications are typically products of primary group social-ization processes occurring during childhood and adolescence.

In the 1960s and 1970s, the case for the theoretical importance of the Michigan concept of party identification was bolstered by studies that demonstrated its seeming stability within and across generations (e.g., Jennings and Niemi, 1974). Additionally, as hypothesized, analyses of election survey data indicated that party identifications had direct effects on the vote, and seemed also to function as "percep-tual screens" through which candidates and issues were viewed and evaluated. The obvious fact that candidates were transitory players on the political stage, coupled with evidence that most voters lack coherent political belief systems and have low levels of political knowledge and issue concern, made partisanship almost by default the principal explanatory weapon in the theorectical arsenal developed by students of American voting behavior (e.g., Stokes, 1963; Converse, 1964; see also Converse and Markus, 1979; Kelley and Mirer, 1974).

The strength of the relationship between party identification and voting behavior impressed Campbell and his colleagues in the 1950s and 1960s, and Figure 4.2 shows the pattern has remained essentially unchanged since then. In 14 ANES national surveys conducted between 1952 and 2004, the percentage of Democratic identifiers voting for "their" party's presidential candidate has ranged from a low of 58 per cent in 1972 to a high of 89 per cent in 1964 and 2004 (see Figure 4.2A). In sharp contrast, the percentage of Republican identifiers opting for a Democrat has never exceeded 27 per cent.

A comparable pattern obtains for voting for Republican presidential candidates. The number of Republican identifiers voting for a Republican has varied between 70 and 96 per cent, and the percentage of Democratic identifiers doing so is always much lower, between 5 and 41 per cent (see Figure 4.2B). In 2004, fully 91 per cent of Republican identifiers voted for President Bush, as compared to 9 per cent of Democratic identifiers. Over all of the ANES surveys, 77 per cent of Democratic identifiers have voted for a Democratic presidential candidate, and 87 per cent of Republican identifiers have chosen a Republican candidate. Together, these two groups account for nearly three-quarters of all voters in presidential elections held over the past half-century.[4]

Yet, there is another part to the story. With the advantage of several decades of ANES data, it is clear that party identification has sizable aggregate- and individ-ual-level dynamics that were not apparent to early researchers. In the early 1950s there were many more Democratic than Republican identifiers (47 per cent versus

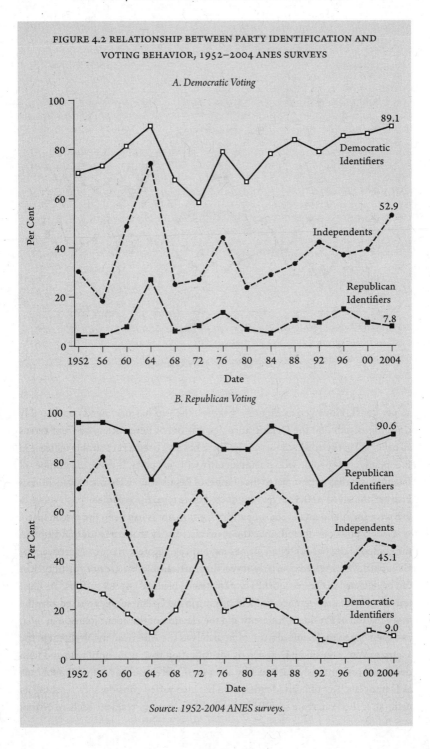

FIGURE 4.2 RELATIONSHIP BETWEEN PARTY IDENTIFICATION AND
VOTING BEHAVIOR, 1952–2004 ANES SURVEYS

A. Democratic Voting

B. Republican Voting

Source: 1952-2004 ANES surveys.

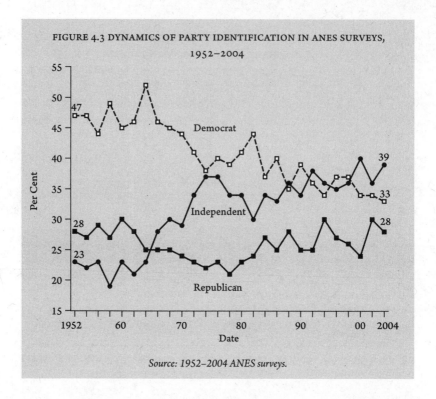

FIGURE 4.3 DYNAMICS OF PARTY IDENTIFICATION IN ANES SURVEYS, 1952–2004

Source: 1952–2004 ANES surveys.

28 per cent). However, as Figure 4.3 shows, the gap has narrowed considerably since then, such that the Democratic edge was only 5 per cent (33 per cent versus 28 per cent) in the 2004 ANES survey. There has also been a very sizable increase in Independents—people who do not identify with any party. Indeed, the number of Independents has outnumbered the number of Republican or Democratic identifiers in five of the seven ANES surveys conducted since 1992. Approximately two voters in five were Independents in 2004, nearly twice as many as had been the case in 1952.

Gallup polls conducted since the 1950s also testify that party identification in the United States has exhibited major long-term aggregate dynamics. Moreover, the Gallup data, aggregated quarterly, reveal that partisanship has greater volatility than can be detected in the infrequently administered (biennial) ANES surveys.[5] As illustrated in Figure 4.4, Democratic identification in the Gallup surveys peaked after the assassination of President Kennedy and the election of President Johnson in 1964, and then began to decline almost immediately as the American involvement in the Vietnam War intensified. Democratic identification rose again until 1980 and then decreased precipitously, such that by 2004 there were nearly as many Republicans as Democrats. Republican identification has also varied considerably, reaching its nadir after the Watergate scandal and the resignation of President Richard Nixon.

The Republican partisan share then rose sharply during the two Reagan presidencies, fell substantially during the Clinton years, and then rose again during Bush, Jr.'s first term.

Impressive dynamics also characterize the cohort of Independents in the Gallup surveys. The percentage of Independents rose sharply during the Vietnam War and continued to climb until the mid-1970s, declined somewhat, and then began to rise again in the mid-1980s (see Figure 4.4). When the Iraq War began in March 2003, Independents constituted nearly two-fifths of the electorate and outnumbered Democrats and Republicans. Although the Independent cohort declined somewhat in the run-up to the 2004 election, it continued to be the largest group in the electorate.

Additional evidence of substantial aggregate partisan dynamics is provided by the National Annenberg Election Study (NAES) data (Romer et al., 2006). The NAES survey was in the field virtually every day between October 2003 and November 2004, and interviewed over 80,000 people.[6] Accordingly, one can group these data to produce reasonably large weekly national samples. Trends in party

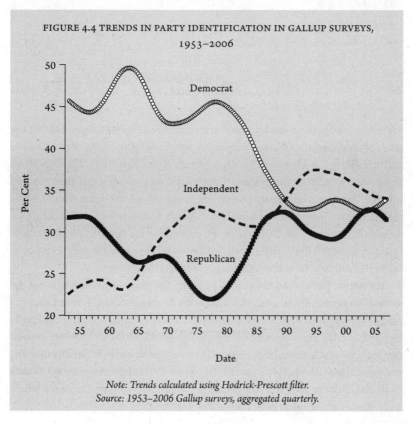

FIGURE 4.4 TRENDS IN PARTY IDENTIFICATION IN GALLUP SURVEYS, 1953–2006

Note: Trends calculated using Hodrick-Prescott filter.
Source: 1953–2006 Gallup surveys, aggregated quarterly.

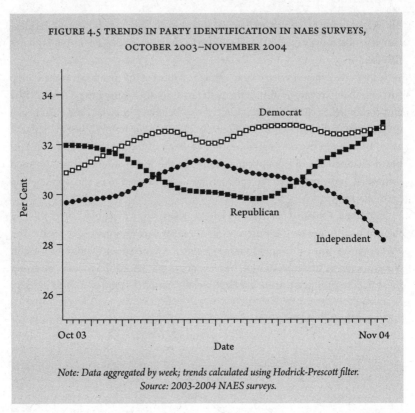

FIGURE 4.5 TRENDS IN PARTY IDENTIFICATION IN NAES SURVEYS,
OCTOBER 2003–NOVEMBER 2004

Note: Data aggregated by week; trends calculated using Hodrick-Prescott filter.
Source: 2003-2004 NAES surveys.

identification for these weekly samples are not dramatic, but they reveal that the
share of Independents followed a distinctly curvilinear path, rising until mid-2004
and then falling steadily as election day approached (see Figure 4.5). The Republican
share was a virtual mirror image—it declined until mid-2004 and then trended
upward. The Democratic group also increased slightly over the entire year, such that
the number of Democrats and Republicans was virtually identical on Election Day.
Overall, then, the NAES data indicate the presence of modest, but possibly consequential, aggregate dynamics in partisanship, with a net swing of nearly four points
in the Republicans' favor during the year preceding the election.

The ANES, Gallup, and NAES data all testify that party identification is not the
storied "unmoved mover" made famous by the Michigan model. Nor is it simply a
case of slowly paced electoral replacement, with older groups of voters gradually
being replaced by new ones with different party identifications, or once-in-a-genera-
tion realignments in the balance of partisan forces occasioned by politically cataclysmic events (see Campbell et al., 1966). The quarterly Gallup and weekly NAES data
emphasize that the pace of change is too rapid for those scenarios to be the whole
story. Rather, some voters must *change* their partisanship.

The conjecture that partisanship in the United States has an individual-level dynamic is supported by data from multiwave panel surveys. Here, we illustrate the general pattern using data from the 2000–02–04 ANES panel and the 2004 NAES pre-post election panel (see Chapter 6). The ANES data reveal that only a minority (29 per cent) were perfectly stable identifiers—persons who identified with the same party at the same level of intensity over a four-year period (see Figure 4.6). An additional 21 per cent did not identify with a party and maintained that position during the four years. The remainder—half the sample—changed either the intensity or the direction of their partisanship. Specifically, 17 per cent, although remaining loyal to a party, became *more or less* strongly identified with it. More impressive, fully 29 per cent moved from being Independents to being identifiers or vice versa, and 4 per cent changed the direction of their identification one or more times. The story told by the shorter 2004 NAES panel is similar—nearly a quarter of those interviewed reported a directional change in party identification and, all told, less than half said their partisan attachments were unchanged in direction and intensity.

In sum, party identification does not possess the aggregate- or individual-level stability claimed for it when the Michigan model was the reigning paradigm in electoral studies. Over the past half-century, there have been impressive movements in

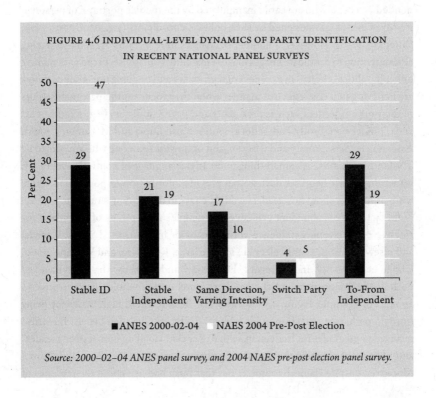

FIGURE 4.6 INDIVIDUAL-LEVEL DYNAMICS OF PARTY IDENTIFICATION IN RECENT NATIONAL PANEL SURVEYS

Source: 2000–02–04 ANES panel survey, and 2004 NAES pre-post election panel survey.

aggregate partisanship; the shares of Democratic and Republican identifiers have waxed and waned, at times fairly precipitously. Also, although there have always been some people who have stood apart from the parties, the cohort of Independents is now much bigger than it used to be. And, although the size of its partisan base has fluctuated over time, the Democratic Party has suffered the greatest net loss of identifiers. In the 1950s there were almost twice as many Democrats as Republicans. The two groups are now much more similar in size. Finally, the individual-level dynamics demonstrated in the ANES and NAES panels testify that in any given election cycle an impressively large group of voters may alter the intensity or direction of their partisanship. Short-term forces related to voters' issue concerns and candidate images have the potential to influence not only voting behavior but also partisan attachments.

CANDIDATE IMAGES: CUES FOR LEADERSHIP

An important contribution of the Michigan model was its emphasis on candidate images as significant short-term forces on electoral choice. Some observers have concluded that the importance of candidate images proves that voters are simple-minded "suckers" who are easily manipulated by the media's portrayal of personality-based campaigns designed by slick political consultants (e.g., McGinnis, 1969; Patterson, 1980). However, a number of analysts have recently argued that paying close attention to candidate images makes eminently good sense. Faced with making difficult political choices in a context of high stakes and ongoing uncertainty, voters are behaving in a cost-effective manner when they focus on the personality traits of top political leaders such as presidents and prime ministers (e.g., Clarke et al., 2004; Sniderman, Brody, and Tetlock, 1991; see also Lupia and McCubbins, 1998). Assessing leaders' probity and wisdom, and opting for someone who appears to be a "safe pair of hands," is a smart thing to do. In the language of political psychology, leader images are heuristic devices that provide information-impoverished voters with useful cues about how leaders would behave in demanding situations.

In fact, there is abundant evidence that people's perceptions of candidates for elective office strongly influence voting behavior in the United States, Canada, and elsewhere (e.g., Campbell et al., 1960; Clarke, Kornberg, and Wearing, 2000; Clarke et al., 2004). In this regard, Figures 4.7 and 4.8 show that the images of both of the major presidential candidates were, on the whole, quite positive in 2004.[7] For example, Figure 4.7 indicates that Bush received high marks for being "moral," perhaps a reflection of his widely advertised Christian beliefs. Bush also received good grades for leadership, with 63 per cent labelling him "a strong leader" and 71 per cent rejecting the unflattering characterization that he was "indecisive." Moreover, despite claims by some critics that Bush had lied about the presence of

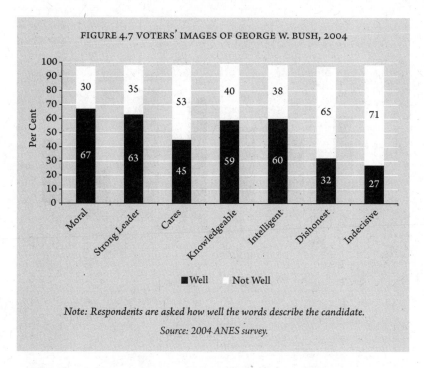

FIGURE 4.7 VOTERS' IMAGES OF GEORGE W. BUSH, 2004

Note: Respondents are asked how well the words describe the candidate.

Source: 2004 ANES survey.

"weapons of mass destruction" in Iraq, two-thirds of the ANES respondents rejected the adjective "dishonest" as an appropriate description. Also, despite his periodic malapropisms and frequent difficulties with the basic rules of English grammar, 60 and 59 per cent, respectively, agreed that the descriptors "intelligent" and "knowledgeable" fit him well. Bush's biggest failing, despite his frequent claim to being a compassionate conservative, was that a majority of the public was not especially impressed. Slightly over half agreed that the phrase "cares for people like me" did not describe the president well.

Kerry's demeanor, his oratorical skill, and his long career in the Senate undoubtedly contributed to the large majorities of ANES respondents who judged that his strongest qualities were being "knowledgeable" and "intelligent" (see Figure 4.8). Slightly more respondents regarded Kerry rather than Bush as caring (54 per cent versus 45 per cent), and slightly more rejected the label "dishonest" (67 per cent versus 65 per cent). The principal knocks against Kerry, perhaps reflecting his infamous "I voted for it before I voted against it" statement explaining his position on the Iraq War, as well as efforts of Republican spinmeisters to portray him as "weak" and "vacillating," concerned leadership. A sizable minority of those interviewed regarded Kerry as "indecisive" (45 per cent) and almost as many (44 per cent) rejected the characterization of him as a strong leader.

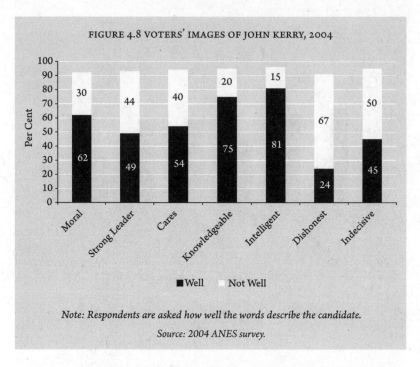

FIGURE 4.8 VOTERS' IMAGES OF JOHN KERRY, 2004

Note: Respondents are asked how well the words describe the candidate.

Source: 2004 ANES survey.

If beauty really is in the eye of the beholder, so also are presidential images. Table 4.2 indicates that Democratic identifiers typically had more favorable images of their candidate than did their Republican counterparts, whereas Independent images were in the middle. For example, nearly three-quarters of Democrats rejected the "indecisive" labelling of the senator as a canard, whereas almost as many Republicans felt it was quite appropriate, as did a smaller majority of Independents. Similarly, 86 per cent of Democrats judged that Kerry *was* a strong leader, as did 55 per cent of Independents, but only 13 per cent of Republicans. Republicans also begged to differ with the senator's strong suits—that he "really cares," is "knowledgeable," and is "intelligent." Almost three-quarters disagreed with the "really cares" label; 38 per cent disagreed with the "knowledgeable" designation; and 27 per cent disagreed with the "intelligence" one.

Democrats were equally unimpressed with the president's most advertised positive qualities. For example, 43 per cent judged that Bush could not make up his mind; 50 per cent believed he was dishonest; 50 per cent were unimpressed with his morality; 61 per cent felt he was *not* a strong leader; and some 6 out of 10 of Democratic identifiers judged President Bush was neither knowledgeable nor intelligent. They also took sharp issue with the compassionate conservative label Bush had appropriated in his first run for the presidency; fully 83 per cent of Democrats believed "he *did not* care" about people like them.

TABLE 4.2 PRESIDENTIAL CANDIDATE TRAITS BY PARTY IDENTIFICATION, 2004 (PERCENTAGES AGREEING THAT WORD MENTIONED DESCRIBES CANDIDATE "EXTREMELY WELL" OR "QUITE WELL")

A. *George W. Bush*

TRAIT	REPUBLICAN	INDEPENDENT	DEMOCRAT	EVERYONE
Moral	97	65	50	69
Strong Leader	96	61	39	64
Really Cares	88	39	17	46
Knowledgeable	90	55	39	60
Intelligent	91	56	40	61
Dishonest	9	36	50	33
Indecisive	11	30	43	28

B. *John Kerry*

TRAIT	REPUBLICAN	INDEPENDENT	DEMOCRAT	EVERYONE
Moral	38	69	91	67
Strong Leader	13	55	86	53
Really Cares	27	56	87	58
Knowledgeable	62	80	92	79
Intelligent	73	84	94	84
Dishonest	46	22	12	26
Indecisive	73	46	26	47

Note: All differences among party identification groups are statistically significant, p < .001.

Although Bush might not have been especially upset about learning so many Democrats felt that way about him, more problematic for his re-election prospects would be that 61 per cent of Independents also felt that way. He might also have felt slighted that although both he and the senator were graduates of Yale and Harvard, almost half of the Independents believed that Bush was neither knowledgeable (45 per cent) nor intelligent (44 per cent), whereas only 20 per cent and 16 per cent accepted these negative characterizations of his opponent, Senator Kerry.

Despite the several positive traits attributed to him by both Democrats and Independents, Senator Kerry was viewed by almost half the public as "indecisive." Almost as many believed he was not a "strong leader." These are not the kinds of qualities people normally look for in a "wartime president." Conversely, despite his less than scintillating prosecution of the Iraq War and the claims of his Democratic opponent that largely because of this, America's prestige in the world had sunk to an all-time low, President Bush came off well, precisely in terms of the two qualities of leadership, strength and decisiveness, on which Kerry was judged most negatively.

Overall, the two leaders had very similar global ratings. Across the seven character traits, Kerry's average positive rating was 64.6 per cent, and Bush's was just slightly less, 62.1 per cent. Neither Bush nor Kerry had a decisive candidate image edge.

POSITION ISSUES AND VALENCE ISSUES

Over the past half-century, variations on the Michigan model have been used by many researchers to explain voting behavior in the United States and other mature democracies. However, this model does not have the field to itself. Soon after Campbell et al. (1960) published the canonical statement of the Michigan model, there was a strong challenge to its supremacy by the "Rochester" or spatial modelling school. The spatial modelling approach is grounded in rational choice theories of human behavior. It received its impetus from Anthony Downs's 1957 seminal study of the logic of inter-party competition in which he proposed that voters try to maximize their utilities by comparing the positions of competing parties in a uni- or multidimensional issue space with their own positions in that space. By selecting the party that is closest to them, voters maximize their expected utility. For their part, parties attempt to position themselves in the same space so as to maximize public support. They do so by adjusting their issue positions in light of the distribution of voter positions in the space. The spatial modelling approach has generated a large theoretical literature and numerous empirical analyses (see Merrill and Grofman, 1999; Adams, Merrill, and Grofman, 2005).

Variations of Downs's initial formulation have continued to attract investigators despite the powerful critique offered by Donald Stokes (1963, 1992). Stokes agreed with Downs about the relevance of issues for electoral choice. However, he distinguished between two types of issues—position issues and valence issues. Stokes noted that Downsian position issues provide at least two locations along an "issue continuum" on which voters can locate themselves. Current debates regarding abortion and same-sex marriage provide good examples of position issues. Some people argue that abortion on demand is a woman's inalienable right, whereas others contend that abortion should be allowed only in certain circumstances, and still others claim that abortion should never be permitted. Similarly, people take different positions on same-sex marriage; some think gays and lesbians should be allowed to wed, and others think such marriages should be forbidden. Yet another good current example of a position issue is immigration. Some people argue that stringent measures should be taken to limit immigration of all kinds, others want to forbid only illegal immigration, and still others advocate an "open door" policy for legal and illegal immigrants alike.

Unlike position issues, valence issues concern conditions on which virtually all voters are in agreement. As discussed in earlier chapters, the economy is a classic example. Virtually everyone favors high rates of economic growth and low rates of inflation and unemployment. Health care, education, the environment, terrorism, and corruption and crime also provide good examples. Overwhelming majorities of people strongly favor adequate health care, widespread affordable educational opportunities, and a clean environment. Equally, almost everyone is strongly opposed to terrorism, corruption, crime, and other threats to personal and national security. Stokes argued that valence issues typically dominate the issue agenda in the United States and other mature democracies. For valence issues, political debate concerns which party or leader is most competent to design and implement policies that can achieve consensual goals. "Who can?" and "How?" not "What?" are the motivating questions in a "Stokesian" world of valence politics.

POSITION ISSUES

To operationalize key features of a spatial model of electoral choice, we employed eight seven-point issue scales and a seven-point "liberal-conservative" ideology scale.[8] Table 4.3 shows the average absolute distances between the 2004 ANES respondents and the presidential candidates on these scales. In five cases, the differences in these distances are statistically significant. Four of these significant differences—for government services, women's roles, abortion, and diplomacy versus force—although small—favor John Kerry. Only one, level of defense spending, favors George Bush. Across the eight scales, the average absolute distances between voters and Kerry is 1.7 points, and for Bush, it is 1.9 points. To the extent that the voters adhere to a utility maximizing model, these data suggest that the president was at a slight disadvantage, and, as we shall see, such Downsian-type logic matters.

TABLE 4.3 ABSOLUTE DISTANCES BETWEEN VOTERS AND CANDIDATES ON SEVEN-POINT POSITION ISSUE AND IDEOLOGY SCALES

	Distance From:			
	BUSH	KERRY	t	P
Policy-Ideology Scale				
More v. Fewer Government Services	1.98	1.79	2.36	.019
Decrease v. Increase Defense Spending	1.67	1.79	-1.96	.051
Government Provide Jobs v. People on Own	2.00	1.91	1.03	.302
Government Help Blacks v. Blacks Help Selves	1.87	1.82	0.59	.555
Women Equal Roles v. Women in Home	1.99	1.36	9.78	.000
Use Diplomacy v. Use Force	2.36	1.87	5.24	.000
Abortion on Demand v. Ban on Abortions	1.33	1.05	4.65	.000
Liberal v. Conservative	1.97	2.07	-1.04	.296

VALENCE ISSUES

Economic Evaluations

As observed, the health of the economy is a prototypical valence issue. Conventional wisdom holds that governments may get too little credit for a good economy and too much blame for a poor one (e.g., Bloom and Price, 1975). That said, widespread perceptions of economic malaise almost always result in a withdrawal of public support for an administration, and voters are quite willing to "throw the rascals out" when they believe the economy has been mismanaged. As noted earlier, an excellent recent example of the adverse political consequences attendant upon a sluggish economy occurred when former president, George Bush, Sr., lionized for leading the United States to a swift victory over Iraq in the Gulf War, was soundly defeated by Bill Clinton in the 1992 presidential election (e.g., Clarke, Rapkin, and Stewart, 1994).

The 2004 ANES survey data indicate that three years after 9/11 public perceptions of national economic conditions were decidedly mixed.[9] When asked about the condition of the national economy "in the country as a whole over the past year," 45 per cent said it was worse, almost twice as many as the 24 per cent who said it was better, while slightly over 30 per cent said that it was the same (see Figure 4.9). Despite this, in response to a question on how they *personally* had fared during the past year, fully 43 per cent replied that they were in better shape, as opposed to the 32 per cent who complained their personal condition had worsened and the 25 per cent who said it was unchanged.

Similarly mixed judgments characterize responses about how personal and national economic conditions would fare over the next year. Again, the ANES respondents were considerably more sanguine about their own prospects than they were about those for the national economy. More generally, however, the ratio of positive to negative responses was much higher for *prospective* judgments about both national and personal economic conditions than it was for *retrospective* evaluations regarding how the economy and one's personal circumstances had fared in the past. Still, the modal answer about future national and personal economic conditions was "the same." In the wake of a lingering recession, the latter response can hardly be interpreted as an expression of unbridled economic optimism.

When considering the possible political impact of economic evaluations, the mixed tenor of those evaluations suggests a note of caution. Certainly, widespread negativity about what had transpired in the past suggests that there was an opportunity for Kerry on the economy. Equally, however, such pessimistic appraisals may have been counterbalanced by greater, if tempered, optimism about the future. In his acceptance speech at the 2004 Democratic national convention, Kerry had tried to capitalize on unhappiness about how the economy had fared during Bush II's

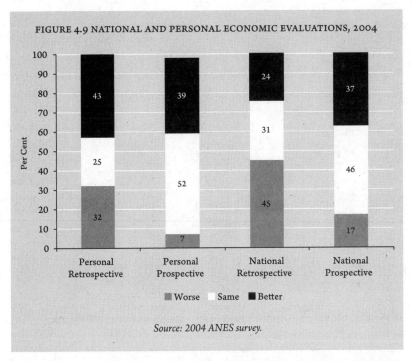

FIGURE 4.9 NATIONAL AND PERSONAL ECONOMIC EVALUATIONS, 2004

Source: 2004 ANES survey.

administration by declaring, "Help is on the way!" But, what did he have in mind? Kerry's ambiguity about how to improve the economy, coupled with a modest economic revival and relative optimism about its future prospects, may have encouraged sizable numbers of voters to stay the course with a known quantity—Bush and the Republicans.

Performance on Important Issues

The 2004 ANES respondents were asked to evaluate President Bush's performance on four valence issues: the budget deficit, the economy generally, terrorism, and foreign relations generally.[10] Judgments varied across these issues areas, but many voters were dissatisfied. Specifically, only one-third and two-fifths, respectively, approved of how he had handled the deficit and the overall economy (see Figure 4.10A). A majority also gave the president a failing grade on foreign relations. Only when it came to combating terrorism did a majority (55 per cent) judge his efforts favorably.

There is additional evidence in the 2004 ANES survey that the latter issue was important for Bush. Respondents were asked to indicate what they thought was the "most important issue facing the United States over the last four years." Consistent with Stokes's argument that valence issues tend to dominate national electoral

FIGURE 4.10 VALENCE ISSUES AND PRESIDENTIAL PERFORMANCE, 2004

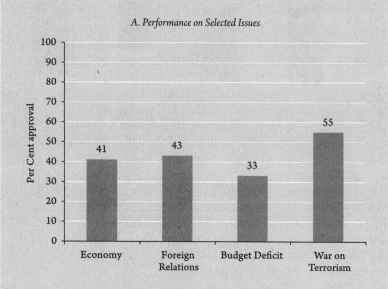

A. Performance on Selected Issues

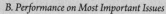

B. Performance on Most Important Issues

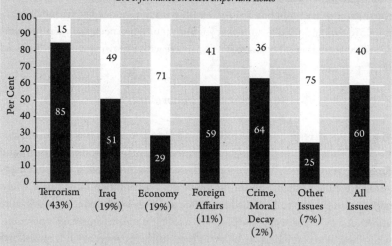

Note: Numbers in parentheses are percentages of respondents citing issue as most important.

Source: 2004 ANES survey.

politics, a large majority of the answers to this "most important issue" question clearly involve valence rather than position issues. Fully 43 per cent cited terrorism and 19 per cent mention the economy, and an additional 2 per cent referred to crime or moral decay (see Figure 4.10B). Nor is it the case that all of the 19 per cent of the "Iraq" answers were positional, with respondents arguing that the United States should or should not have gone to war. Rather, for some people the Iraq issue had to do with how well the administration was prosecuting a war that they endorsed. In contrast to valence issues, widely publicized position issues, such as same-sex marriage, abortion, and immigration, were seldom cited as "most important."

Figure 4.10B also shows voters' judgments of government performance on the issues they designated as most important.[11] Performance assessments varied widely across various issues. For example, despite President Bush's persistent claims that the economy was enjoying a strong recovery, only a *minority* who listed the economy as their most important issue (29 per cent) thought that the administration had done a good job managing it. Similarly, notwithstanding the president's relentless cheerleading about the progress made on the war in Iraq, only a bare majority (51 per cent) whose most important issue was Iraq agreed that the war was going well. In contrast, nearly 60 per cent of those who regarded foreign policy generally as their most important issue gave the administration a favorable grade, as did the 64 per cent concerned with crime and moral decay. However, only relatively small numbers of voters were concerned with these latter two issues.

Much more helpful for President Bush was that negatives on Iraq and the economy were more than compensated for by the 43 per cent of the electorate for whom terrorism was the most important issue. Fully *85 per cent* of these people believed President Bush and his colleagues were doing a good or very good job in combating terrorists. This huge number made it possible for the administration to have an overall three-to-two favorable margin on performance on "most important issues." The kudos transcended partisan boundaries. In addition to receiving almost universally positive ratings from Republican identifiers, the administration was lauded by over a third of Democratic identifiers and well over half of Independents. As we will see below, favorable approval ratings provided the president with an important advantage in his campaign for re-election.

RIVAL MODELS OF ELECTORAL CHOICE

Over the past several decades, a variety of competing explanations of electoral choice have been advanced. Following earlier discussions, these explanations may be grouped in terms of the following sets of explanatory variables: a) demographics; b) economic evaluations; c) party identification; d) valence issues and government performance; e) position issues; and f) candidate images. Here, we compare the performance of rival models of voting behavior in the 2004 presidential election that include these explanatory variables, and a more general composite model that includes all of them.

We employ several factors in evaluating model performance: the statistical significance of predictor variables, goodness of fit (as measured by estimated R^2 statistics and ability to correctly classify voters' electoral choices), and explanatory power discounted by the number of parameters estimated. For the latter purpose, we employ the Akaike Information Criterion (AIC) (see Burnham and Anderson, 2002).[12] Since the dependent variable is dichotomous (coded one for a Bush vote and zero for a Kerry vote), binomial logistic regression is used to estimate model parameters (Long, 1997).

Socio-Demographics

The first model estimates the probability of voting for Bush as a function of sociodemographic characteristics and religiosity using the specification:

$$\text{VoteBush} = f(\beta_0 + \beta_{1\text{-}3}\text{Region} + \beta_{4\text{-}6}\text{Race-Ethnicity} + \beta_7\text{Gender} + \beta_8\text{Education}$$
$$+ \beta_{9\text{-}11}\text{Religion} + \beta_{12}\text{Religiosity} + \beta_{13}\text{Religiosity*Protestant})$$

In this model, possible effects of region are assessed using three 0–1 dichotomous variables for residence in the Southern, north-central, and Western regions (residence in the Northeast is the reference category). Similarly, the impact of race-ethnicity is assessed using dichotomous variables designating membership in African American, Hispanic, and other nonwhite race-ethnicity groups ("white" is the reference category). Education is measured as a seven-category variable ranging from having a grade 8 education or less to holding an advanced degree. Three religion variables distinguish Protestants, Catholics, and those subscribing to another faith (i.e., Jewish, Muslim, Eastern Orthodox, etc.) from voters saying that they do not have any religious beliefs. Religiosity is a factor score constructed from an analysis of respondents' reported beliefs about the literal truth of the Bible, frequency of prayer, and frequency of church attendance.[13] In keeping with conjectures that intensely religious Protestants were especially likely to support President Bush, a Protestant x religiosity interaction variable is also included in the model.

Table 4.4A presents the results of estimating the parameters in this model. Some parameters are statistically significant, with their signs indicating that men, higher income persons, more intensely religious people and, especially, more intensely religious Protestants were more likely to vote for Bush than Kerry. African Americans and Hispanics were more likely than whites to support Kerry. However, the explanatory power of the model leaves much to be desired. The McFadden and McKelvey

TABLE 4.4 RIVAL MODELS OF VOTING FOR GEORGE W. BUSH IN THE 2004
PRESIDENTIAL ELECTION

A.	Demographics		B	S.E.
	Age		-0.01	.01
	Gender		0.56***	.17
	Income		0.05**	.02
	Race:	African American	-3.09***	.36
		Hispanic	-1.06***	.35
		Other Non-White	0.12	.38
	Region:	North Central	-0.10	.24
		South	0.08	.25
		West	-0.11	.25
	Religion:	Catholic	-0.43	.28
		Protestant	-0.13	.27
		Other	-0.27	.27
	Religiosity		0.49***	.13
	Religiosity x Protestant		0.63**	.25
	Constant		-0.72*	.42

McFadden R^2 = .17, McKelvey R^2 = .21
Per Cent Correctly Classified = 65.9, AIC = 972.54

B.	Party Identification	B	S.E.
	Republican	3.04***	.28
	Democratic	-2.14***	.26
	Constant	-0.30**	.13

McFadden R^2 = .44, McKelvey R^2 = .59
Per Cent Correctly Classified = 81.6, AIC = 617.65

C.	Economic Evaluations	B	S.E.
	National & Personal Retrospective	1.38***	.11
	National & Personal Prospective	0.53***	.09
	Constant	-0.14	.08

McFadden R^2 = .24, McKelvey R^2 = .40
Per Cent Correctly Classified = 76.1, AIC = 835.53

D.	Bush Administration Performance	B	S.E.
	Performance	1.80***	.12
	Constant	-0.26*	.13

McFadden R^2 = .65, McKelvey R^2 = .78
Per Cent Correctly Classified = 89.7, AIC = 389.65

E.	Position Issues	B	S.E.
	Kerry New Deal	-2.60***	.29
	Kerry Women	-1.06***	.16
	Bush Base	1.93***	.22
	Bush New Deal	2.09***	.23
	Constant	0.04	.16

McFadden R^2 = .69, McKelvey R^2 = .90
Per Cent Correctly Classified = 91.4, AIC = 347.66

F.	Candidate Images	B	S.E.
	Kerry Traits	-2.07***	.22
	Bush Traits	2.58***	.23
	Constant	-0.07	.15

McFadden R^2 = .69, McKelvey R^2 = .86
Per Cent Correctly Classified = 93.6, AIC = 337.96

*** $p < .001$; ** $p < .01$; * $p < .05$; one-tailed test.
†—Akaike Information Criterion (AIC)—smaller values indicate better model performance.

estimated R^2s are only .17 and .21, respectively, and the percentage of correctly classified voters is 65.9 per cent, only about 16 per cent more than would be predicted by naively guessing that everyone was in the modal category of the dependent variable (i.e., they voted for Bush).

Omitting the religiosity and religiosity x Protestant variables weakens the model further. Although the parameter for the Protestant variable is significant and positive, indicating that Protestants were more likely than others to support Bush, the McFadden and McKelvey R^2s drop to .13 and .17, respectively. The percentage correctly classified is only 5.4 per cent above the mode-guess baseline. A model using only religious affiliation, religiosity, and the Protestant times religiosity interaction term fares poorly as well, with weak R^2s, and a very mediocre classification rate. Clearly, sociodemographic characteristics and religiosity cannot explain voting in the 2004 presidential election.

Partisanship

The second model investigates if party identification *by itself* can predict presidential voting. The model is:

$$\text{VoteBush} = f(\beta_0 + \beta_1 \text{Republican Identification} + \beta_2 \text{Democratic Identification})$$

We consider as party identifiers only as those who say that they are Republicans or Democrats in response to the first question in the standard ANES party identification battery (see Miller, 1991). To this end, we construct two 0–1 dummy variables to indicate if a respondent is a Democrat or a Republican (Independents are the reference category). Separating Republicans from Democrats in this way avoids the need to assume that partisanship is unidimensional (e.g., Petrocik, 1974; Weisberg, 1980). It also provides insight into whether partisanship had asymmetric effects on voting in the 2004 election.

Estimating the parameters in this pure party identification model (see Table 4.4B) shows that both the Republican and Democratic dummy variables have statistically significant effects on presidential voting. As expected, Republicans are more likely, and Democrats are less likely, than Independents to cast their ballots for President Bush. Unlike sociodemographic variables, the impact of partisanship on voting is decidedly nontrivial—the McFadden and McKelvey R^2s are .44 and .59, respectively, and the model correctly classifies nearly 82 per cent of the voters. This is a 30 per cent improvement on the naive mode-guessing model. The party identification model therefore suggests that although partisan attachments may not have the impressive stability assumed by Campbell et al. (1960), they are strongly related with voting behavior at a particular point in time.

Economic Evaluations

As noted above, economic evaluations are the canonical basis for judging a president's performance. Accordingly, the next model considered investigates the extent to which economic judgments influenced the choice between Bush and Kerry. Based on results of an explanatory factor analysis of national and personal economic evaluations over retrospective and prospective time horizons, we specify a voting model with two independent variables.[14] One of these variables measures judgments about the course of the national economy and personal finances over the past year. The second independent variable captures judgments about how the national economy and personal finances will evolve over the coming year. In equation form, the model is:

$$\text{VoteBush} = f(\beta_0 + \beta_1 \text{Retrospective Economic Evaluations} + \beta_2 \text{Prospective Economic Evaluations})$$

Above, we observed that unease about the state of the national economy represented an opportunity for Kerry if he could represent himself as an agent for change and people recognized the need for change. However, as discussed above, not everyone was dissatisfied with economic conditions. Indeed, substantial minorities were optimistic about the future. Those people might well have believed that they had good reason to stick with the incumbent president. Empirically, Table 4.4C shows that both retrospective and prospective economic judgments mattered. As anticipated, voters who had positive recollections about past economic conditions and who were optimistic about the future were more likely to vote for the president. However, the overall effects of economic evaluations are not especially impressive; the McFadden R^2 is .24, the McKelvey R^2 is .40, and 76 per cent of the voters are correctly classified.

Although economic evaluations exert statistically significant effects when they are the only predictors, the economic voting model has only mediocre explanatory power. This leads us to conclude that Kerry was unable to make a desultory economy a decisive factor in voting decisions in 2004. However, unlike Al Gore's failure to utilize a strong economy as a stepping stone to the presidency in 2000, Kerry may be able to excuse his failure to make economic concerns into a winning issue. In 2004 the issue agenda was very different from what it had been four years earlier, with the "new issues" of terrorism and the Iraq War jostling with the economy and other traditional issues for attention during the campaign. Consonant with this interpretation, retrospective and prospective economic evaluations are statistically insignificant in the composite model of presidential voting that we consider below.

Assessments of Administration Performance

The next model addresses Stokes's (1963, 1992) argument that voters' evaluations of a president's performance on valence issues typically drive their electoral choices. Assessments of the Bush administration's performance are measured using answers to questions inviting respondents to evaluate Bush's performance in four issue areas commonly assumed to be important yardsticks for judging how well the president was doing. These are controlling the deficit, presiding over economic prosperity, combating terrorism, and competently handling foreign policy. Also employed are answers to two questions asking respondents to evaluate the overall performance of the government in Washington and how that government was performing on the issue thought to be most important.[15] The administration performance model is:

$$\text{VoteBush} = f(\beta_0 + \beta_1 \text{Adminstration Performance})$$

Although extremely parsimonious, the administration performance model performs very well. As Table 4.4D shows, the performance variable has a strong, statistically significant, and properly signed (positive) effect. The fit of the model is very good, with the McFadden and McKelvey R^2s being .65 and .78, respectively. Perhaps more intuitively indicative of the power of the model is the fact that it correctly classifies nearly 90 per cent of the votes.

Position Issues

As discussed above, the 2004 ANES survey asked respondents to place themselves and the presidential candidates on several seven-point issue position scales. These data provide the basis for investigating the explanatory power of a Downsian-type spatial model of electoral choice. To reduce the number of explanatory variables to a manageable number, we performed exploratory factor analyses of the variables measuring the absolute distances between respondents and the two candidates. In both instances, these analyses yielded two factors.[16]

In Kerry's case, issues concerning government involvement in the economy, defense spending, and diplomacy versus the use of military force dominate the first factor. This dimension also taps respondents' perceptions of the distance between their own and Kerry's position on a general "liberal-conservative" scale. It thereby identifies a cluster of issues that have been recurrent central features of American political discourse since the Great Depression. We label this factor the "Kerry New Deal" dimension, and factor scores for this dimension capture perceived distances between respondents and Kerry on it. The second Kerry factor is dominated by variables measuring the absolute distance between him and respondents on the abortion and women's rights questions. This second factor thereby taps important aspects of what is called the "Post-Modern" issue agenda that has become a part of American political debate since the social upheavals of the 1960s and 1970s (e.g., White, 1973).[17]

An exploratory factor analysis of voters' placement of themselves and President Bush on various position issues yields similar, but not identical, results. Loading on the first factor is the variable measuring the absolute distance between Bush and respondents on the general liberal-conservative scale, as well as variables tapping absolute distances on abortion, women's rights, defense spending, and diplomacy versus military action. Taken together, these are a distinctive complex of issues that observers have identified as major concerns motivating the president's core constituency. In contrast, the New Deal-type government spending issues were relegated to a second factor in the Bush analysis. Given these results, we label the first factor "Bush Base" and the second, "Bush New Deal."[18]

The results of the preceding factor analyses lead us to specify the issue position model:

$$\text{VoteBush} = f(\beta_0 + \beta_1 \text{BushBase} + \beta_2 \text{BushNewDeal} + \beta_3 \text{KerryNewDeal} + \beta_4 \text{KerryPost-Modern})$$

The values of the independent variables are the factor scores extracted from the two exploratory factor analyses just described.

A logit analysis of the issue position model demonstrates that it performs very well—indeed, marginally better than the administration performance model considered above. Coefficients for the four independent variables are statistically significant and properly signed, such that the Bush Base and Bush New Deal variables are positively associated with a vote for the president, and the Kerry New Deal and Kerry Post-Modern variables are negatively associated with such a vote (see Table 4.4E). The fit of the model is impressive, with estimated R^2 statistics equally .69 (McFadden) and .90 (McKelvey). Fully 91.4 per cent of the voters are correctly classified. These are impressive numbers, and they suggest that a Downsian-type spatial model may make an important contribution to explaining presidential voting in 2004.

Candidate Images

There are good reasons to believe that candidates' public images significantly influence voters' decisions. Modern American presidential campaigns are heavily candidate-centered and major candidates are on "24/7" display months before the election occurs. Bush (in 2000) and Kerry (in 2004) had to wage heavily financed and widely publicized campaigns for the hearts and minds of voters in their parties' primary elections. Moreover, in 2004 Bush was inevitably highly salient as an incumbent president. As for Kerry, from the moment he had the nomination locked up in early spring he was surrounded by hordes of reporters who followed his every move because he was the de facto Democratic candidate. As the 2004 election approached, the rush of campaign events placed the candidates in an ongoing storm of media scrutiny. Voters thus had manifold opportunities to form images of the competing candidates. As noted above, political psychologists argue that candidate images provide voters with important cues for making decisions in a world fraught with risk and uncertainty.

To determine the influence of candidate images in 2004, we first performed exploratory factor analyses of each candidate's traits presented above in Figures 4.7 and 4.8. These analyses indicate that the ANES respondents organized both Bush and Kerry's traits along a single dimension.[19] We thereby test the ability of candidate traits to predict presidential preference using two factor-score variables that summarize voters' perceptions of the traits of Kerry and Bush, respectively. The model may be summarized as:

$$\text{VoteBush} = f(\beta_0 + \beta_1 \text{BushTraits} + \beta_2 \text{KerryTraits})$$

Estimating model parameters suggests that candidate traits have very strong effects on voting behavior in presidential elections. As expected, positive perceptions of Bush's traits increased the probability of voting for him, and positive perceptions of Kerry's traits lessened that probability (see Table 4.4F). The explanatory power of the model is indicated by the very substantial McFadden and McKelvey R^2s (.69 and .86, respectively), and that the percentage of correctly classified voters is fully 93.6 per cent. Viewed slightly differently, the latter statistic tells us that the behavior of nearly 19 voters in 20 would be forecast by knowledge of how voters perceived the traits of the rival candidates.

Comparative Model Performance

The performance of the six models in Table 4.4 varies widely. Models featuring sociodemographic characteristics and economic evaluations had some statistically significant predictors but left the behavior of many voters incorrectly classified. The party identification model did somewhat better in the latter respect, but fell well short of the performance of the administration performance, position issue, and candidate image models. All parameters in the latter three models were statistically significant and correctly signed, and all three models did excellent jobs in classifying voters' behavior. The superiority of these three models is also indicated by their better (smaller) AIC values. The AIC is a model comparison statistic that takes into account

TABLE 4.5 COMPOSITE MODEL OF FACTORS AFFECTING VOTING
FOR GEORGE W. BUSH IN THE 2004 PRESIDENTIAL ELECTION

	B	S.E.
Predictor Variables		
Bush Administration Performance:		
Administration Performance	0.76***	.21
Leader Images:		
Bush Traits	1.16***	.34
Kerry Traits	-0.79**	.31
Position Issues:		
Bush Base	1.12***	.33
Bush New Deal	1.04***	.32
Kerry New Deal	-1.54***	.37
Kerry Post-modern	-0.80***	.25
Party Identification:		
Republican	-0.12	.54
Democrat	-1.46**	.53
Economic Evaluations:		
National & Personal Retrospective	-0.03	.28
National & Personal Prospective	-0.09	.25
Demographics:		
Age	-0.01	.01
Gender	-0.35	.46
Income	-0.00	.04
Race: African American	-1.41*	.70
Hispanic	-1.10	.85
Other	1.72*	.86
Region:		
North Central	0.83	.68
South	1.39*	.69
West	0.55	.67
Religion		
Catholic	0.94	.79
Protestant	-0.19	.70
Other	1.30	.79
Religiosity	-0.95**	.39
Religiosity x Protestant	1.64**	.62
Constant	0.06	1.11

McFadden R^2 = .83, McKelvey R^2 = .93
Per Cent Correctly Classified = 95.7, AIC† = 238.90
N = 787

*** $p < .001$; ** $p < .01$; * $p < .05$; one-tailed test.
†—Akaike Information Criterion (AIC)—smaller values indicate better model performance.

the number of parameters a model requires to provide a given level of explanatory power (e.g., Burnham and Anderson, 2002). Rank-ordering the three models by their AIC values indicates that the candidate image model performs best, followed by the position issue and administration performance models in that order.

Another way of investigating comparative model performance involves assessing contributions to explaining voting behavior controlling for the contributions made by other models. To this end, we include all variables in the several models of interest in one composite specification. Parameter estimates for this composite model (see Table 4.5) buttress the results of estimating the individual models by showing that all candidate image, position issue, and administration performance coefficients are statistically significant and correctly signed. Variables from other models perform less well, and the coefficients for Republican Party identification and both retrospective and prospective economic evaluations fail to achieve significance. Similarly, several of the sociodemographic characteristics do not have significant effects and, of those that do, only religiosity and the religiosity x Protestant interaction term are significant beyond the minimal .05 level.

The composite model has a related story to tell as well. Note that this model has better overall fit statistics than any of the individual models. The composite model's McFadden and McKelvey R^2s are .83 and .93, respectively, and it is able to correctly classify nearly 96 per cent of the voters correctly. Moreover, despite its much richer parameterization, the composite model has the best (smallest) AIC value, 238.90. These statistics are consistent with the idea that multiple competing theoretical models have unique contributions to make in explaining presidential voting behavior in 2004.

How large are these contributions? Since logit coefficients such as those in Table 4.5 are difficult to interpret, we answer this question by calculating changes in the probability of voting for President Bush rather than Senator Kerry as the values of various predictor variables change while all other predictors are held constant at their means or other plausible values.[20] Figure 4.11 displays the change in the probability of voting for Bush rather than Kerry when the value of a variable of interest is changed from its minimum to its maximum value.

These figures show that judgments of the Bush administration's performance; the absolute distance between respondents' issue positions and those they ascribed to Bush on what we call the "Bush Base" and "Bush New Deal" dimensions; and favorable images of him all had major positive effects on the probability of casting a ballot for the president. Indeed, the average change in probability of supporting Bush for "minimum-to-maximum" changes in these four variables is 83 points. The only other predictor variable with a comparable positive effect on Bush voting is Protestant fundamentalism, but the total effect is less than 20 per cent because of the negatively signed fundamentalism variable. Figure 4.11 also shows that the greatest

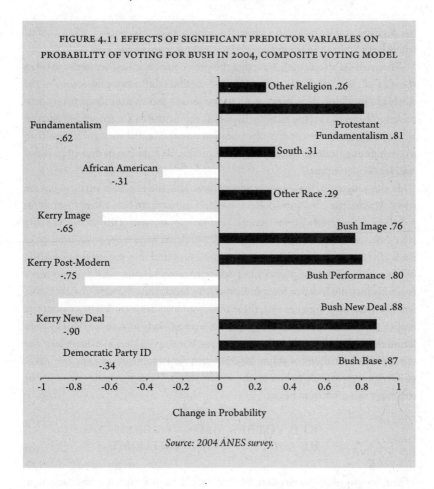

FIGURE 4.11 EFFECTS OF SIGNIFICANT PREDICTOR VARIABLES ON PROBABILITY OF VOTING FOR BUSH IN 2004, COMPOSITE VOTING MODEL

Change in Probability

Source: 2004 ANES survey.

negative effects on the likelihood of a Bush vote were proximity to Kerry on what we have termed "Kerry New Deal" and "post-modern" position issues, favorable images of Kerry and, perhaps surprisingly, religiosity per se. Democratic party identification and race (African American) also eroded the probability of a Bush vote—by 34 per cent in the case of the former and 31 per cent in the latter.

In sum, the preceding analyses indicate that three sets of variables had major effects on presidential voting behavior in 2004. Two of these, performance evaluations and candidate traits, are key elements in the valence politics model described in Chapter One. As Stokes (1963, 1992) argued, voters' judgments about the proven and likely performance of presidential candidates do much to drive electoral choices. However, in 2004, at least, Stokes does not have the field to himself. Rather, as Downs (1957) and subsequent generations of spatial modellers have claimed, perceived distances between voters and candidates on salient position issues strongly influence the decisions voters make. In a sense, the 2004 presidential election was a contest where both Stokes and Downs could claim success for their theories.

The analyses also demonstrate that the performance of another key variable in theories of electoral choice differs from what Stokes and other proponents of the Michigan model would expect. Both in the longer and shorter terms party identification lacks the serene stability hypothesized by the Michigan school. Also, in 2004 the direct effects of party identification on presidential voting were less than overwhelming. Indeed, in the composite model, Republican partisanship is not statistically significant.

In our judgment, these results do not mean that the effects of partisanship are trivial. Rather, the effects are indirect, as voters use partisan cues to help them form judgments about candidates and issues. For example, analyses of the 2004 ANES data (not shown in tabular form) indicate that Republicans had a more positive image of Bush. They were closer to him on positional issues, and they judged the condition of the economy and the president's performance on various valence issues more favorably than did Independents and, especially, Democrats. However, as just noted, when partisanship together with these other variables are included in a composite model, the results show that Independents were as likely to vote for Bush as were Republicans. For that matter, Democratic partisanship had less of a direct negative effect on the probability of voting for Bush than did factors such as a positive image of Kerry and proximity to him on the several issues. We return to this point in our summary and discussion below.

RED VOTERS, BLUE VOTERS: THE 2004 ELECTION OUTCOME

When, shortly after the election, Bush stated, "I earned capital in the campaign, political capital, and now I intend to use it," he had good reason to crow. As the first wartime president since Richard Nixon, he had accomplished something that other Republicans (Eisenhower, 1956; Nixon, 1972; and Reagan, 1984) who had also won notable re-election victories, had not. That is, he also led his party to victory in both houses of Congress. Moreover, he had done it despite widespread public concern about the condition of the economy, huge budget and trade deficits, and mounting criticism of his handling of the war in Iraq, a conflict he had started. Yet, still, he was re-elected.

All of these relationships occurred within and were influenced by the much broader context of the campaign itself. Foremost among these campaign factors, we would contend, was partisanship. As we have seen, Democratic and Republican identifiers see the political world differently so that partisanship had strong indirect effects on other major factors. The great majority of Republican identifiers viewed Bush and his performance as president much more favorably than did their Democratic counterparts. This was also the case with both valence and positional issues. The Independents fell almost consistently somewhere in between their two camps.

However, it is important to note that when Republicans liked Bush, they really liked him! For example, on ideology and for four of seven important issue perceptions, Republican identifiers generally felt closer to Bush than Democratic identifiers felt to Kerry. And as noted above, there were more Republican identifiers in the 2004 election than there were four years earlier. Moreover, many of them lived in the South, which is larger and still growing in population, rather than in the Northeast, which is smaller and has lost population over the years. As Michael Nelson (2005: 5) astutely observes, the Republicans have been the big winners in the exchange of partisan bases between their party, whose previous stronghold was the Northeast, and the Democrats for whom the South used to be the "solid." No more. And as Nelson further notes: "Sweeping the South's 153 electoral votes now puts the Republican presidential nominee well over halfway to victory, an advantage over when the South was solidly Democratic, but had only 120–125 electoral votes."

Three other factors added to the advantage Bush derived from what may be termed this "structural factor" that helped to divide the country into "red" (Republican) and "blue" (Democratic) states. The first was that not only a substantial number of Independents viewed Bush's overall performance in office favorably, but so did about one-third of the Democratic identifiers. Second, by a large margin, the valence issue that the public judged most important was terrorism. Many Independents and Democrats joined Republicans in lauding the president for his work on this issue. The third advantage was that the president's image as a strong leader who could "make up his mind" fit well with his claim he would take all necessary action to combat terrorists. Again, large numbers of Independents and Democrats agreed with Republicans that Bush exhibited strength as a leader. Moreover, they also agreed with Republican charges that Kerry was "wishy-washy" and "irresolute." In sum, the image and issue factors that greatly increased the probability of a Bush vote transcended partisan divisions in the electorate.

In this regard, it is important to recall the distinction Converse (1964) drew between elite and mass perceptions of politics. Bush's "cowboy" image, his malapropisms, and his ongoing battle with basic English grammar, as well as his tax cuts for the wealthy, his decision to invade Iraq, and his responsibility for the supposedly low levels of esteem in which America was held by the international community may have appalled editorial writers at the New York Times and Washington Post, as well as thousands of faculty members in colleges and universities throughout the country. However, these negative views of him were not shared by millions of average Americans, as anyone who monitored even a small sample of daily radio call-in programs or Internet blogs would have realized. In addition to Republican stalwarts whose view of Bush was overwhelmingly favorable, millions of other voters whose perspective on the president was considerably more objective still liked him just fine. And, if Europeans, or for that matter, some Canadians did not like him or America, so what?

That said, it is well to remember Key's (1966) famous admonition that "voters are not fools." In this regard, although many Americans gave Bush high marks for his leadership in the war on terror, they were simultaneously much less charitable about his handling of the economy and Iraq. They also judged that the president was less caring, less knowledgeable, and less intelligent than his opponent. However, they also had serious doubts about Senator Kerry.

We would argue that in 2004, as in 2000, George W. Bush was fortunate in his opponent. Although Kerry's support in the polls exceeded 50 per cent after the Democratic convention in early August, it dropped back into the 40s a few weeks later, and never reached the 50 per cent mark afterwards. One may ask why. A major reason according to many election post-mortems was that the senator conducted a less than exemplary campaign. In contrast, the Republican campaign directed by Karl Rove and Ken Mehlman was a well-organized, disciplined, everyone-on-the-same-page effort that made few, if any, major mistakes. There were repeated reports of discord within the senator's camp, of his unhappiness with his organizers and advisors and, in turn, their anger and frustration not only with him, but also with his wife, who allegedly had to be reminded that her husband was the candidate, not her (Thomas, 2004). Reporters following Kerry on the campaign trail also noted that he was often rambling, verbose, and off message (McFaetters, 2004). He was particularly ineffective in failing to take advantage of many people's concerns about the economy. In this regard, he was faulted for not giving his vice presidential running mate, Senator John Edwards, free rein to connect with voters using his popular "two Americas" stump speech. Edwards, who was a far more dynamic speaker and campaigner than Kerry, was shunted off to the "boondocks," rather than being scheduled to address large audiences in key battleground states.

Perhaps most perplexing was why Kerry did not respond to his Swift Boat attackers. Why did he not take the offensive and challenge the president to a debate about military service to the nation? Kerry, after all, had volunteered for especially hazardous service in Vietnam and had been wounded and decorated for valor, whereas the president had avoided service in Vietnam by securing an appointment in the Texas Air National Guard. However, the senator said not a word in his own defense, and it took others such as Republican Senator John McCain to dismiss charges against Kerry as baseless and scurrilous. There were other questions. For example, why did Kerry volunteer for hazardous combat, serve with distinction, but then return to the United States and vehemently denounce the war? Was his statement about voting for the Iraq War before he voted against it another illustration of a tendency to change opinions capriciously? Perhaps Kerry really could not make up his mind on crucial issues, as his Republican detractors claimed.

There may also have been yet another factor which might have been difficult for average Americans to articulate, but which may have led them to doubt whether the senator was really presidential material. We would contend that what they were feeling was that Kerry lacked authenticity in his attempts to connect with average voters by professing his love for NASCAR races and being photographed in hunting clothes with a shotgun slung over his shoulder. These efforts may have brought to the minds of many voters similar scenes from past elections, such as the aristocratic Bush, Sr.'s claim in 1992 that he "just loved pork rinds" and found supermarket scanners fascinating. Others might remember the 1988 Democratic presidential candidate, Michael Dukakis, trying to show his support for the military by being photographed popping out of a tank with an oversized helmet on his head. Such crude attempts at image-making risk striking voters as profoundly phony. Thus, it is not surprising that of the two candidates—both from very elite backgrounds—George W. Bush came off as the more genuine article. Many Americans may have concluded that the real Kerry was not the one photographed in a hunting outfit, but the one photographed windsailing at an exclusive Cape Cod resort. In contrast, the photo of the president with a chainsaw clearing bush on his ranch *was* the real Bush. And, at the end of the day, it seems to us that millions of Americans, even many of those who voted for the senator, are more about clearing their property than they are about windsailing off Hyannis Port. Although "opportunity knocked" for Kerry in 2004, his difficulties in projecting an image of authenticity and strength helped to give the president the number of "red voters" he needed for victory.

Notes

1 Public expectations about the future of the economy are measured by the aggregate response to the following question on the Michigan Survey of Consumers: "Looking ahead, which would you say is more likely—that in the country as a whole, we'll have continuous good times during the next 5 years or so, or that we will have periods of widespread unemployment or depression, or what?" The variable is the percentage expecting good times minus the percentage expecting unemployment and depression.

2 The adjustment parameter (-0.06) in the error correction model indicates the rate at which shocks to the system erode in each month after they occur.

3   The 1991 Gulf War was modelled as having a gradual temporary (pulse-decay) impact on presidential approval. Even large effects such as those associated with this war eventually disappear, with the rate of erosion governed by the adjustment parameter. For details, see Clarke, Rapkin, and Stewart (1994).

4   Following Miller (1991: 558), we draw the boundary between identifiers and nonidentifiers by considering partisans to be only those who identified themselves as Republicans or Democrats when asked the first branch of the standard ANES survey question on party identification (e.g., "Generally speaking, do you think of yourself as a Republican, a Democrat, an Independent, or what?").

5   The standard question wording for the Gallup polls is: "In politics, as of today, do you consider yourself a Republican, a Democrat, or an Independent?" The ANES question usually elicits a higher percentage of respondents who declare themselves Independents, but the ANES and Gallup series fluctuate in tandem with one another (e.g., Clarke and Suzuki, 1994).

6   The NAES question for ascertaining partisan identification differs slightly from the ANES question. It reads: "Generally speaking, do you usually think of yourself as a Republican, a Democrat, an Independent, or *something else*?"

7   For nearly three decades, ANES interviewers have asked respondents to think about each party's presidential candidate and subsequently asked whether they thought a series of traits described the candidates extremely well, quite well, not too well, or not well at all. These responses were assigned values of five, four, two, and one, respectively. Those not responding or not knowing how to evaluate a certain trait were assigned a value of three.

8   The only exception to the standard seven-point ANES Likert scales used to measure the respondent and candidates' locations on positional issues with two extremes is made for the abortion question. The respondent is asked to take one of the following four positions on abortion as their own and ascribe a position to the presidential candidates: a) By law, abortion should never be permitted; b) The law should permit abortion only in case of rape, incest, or when the woman's life is in danger; c) The law should permit abortion for reasons other than rape, incest, or danger to the woman's life, but only after the need for the abortion has been clearly established; and d) By law, a woman should always be able to obtain an abortion as a matter of personal choice. When we model the issue space, we multiply the absolute distance between the respondent and the candidates on the abortion issue by 7/4 to match the seven-point scale used for the other policy questions.

9   Recent ANES studies all ask respondents to assess whether their personal and the national economic situation in the past year ("retrospections") and in the next year ("prospections") got/would get better or worse. In most years, respondents were given the opportunity to answer whether performance was/would be much or somewhat better/worse. For all four questions, we coded the responses

as follows: 5 = much better; 4 = somewhat better; 3 = same, don't know, or refused; 2 = somewhat worse; and 1 = much worse.

10 On the 2004 ANES, respondents were asked if they approved or disapproved of the way George W. Bush handled the four issues, followed by a question asking if they approved/disapproved strongly or not strongly. Responses were assigned the following values: 5 = approve strongly; 4 = approve not strongly; 3 = don't know or refusal to answer the question; 2 = disapprove not strongly; and 1 = disapprove strongly.

11 As part of the Comparative Study of Electoral Systems project (CSES), ANES respondents were asked if they thought the "Government in Washington" had done a "very good job," a "good job," a "bad job," or a "very bad job" on an open-ended question asking the respondent to name the most important issue facing the nation and another question probing how well the overall performance of the federal government had been. Responses were assigned the following values: 5 = very good job; 4 = good job; 3 = don't know or refusal to answer the question; 2 = bad job; and 1 = very bad job.

12 The value for the AIC equals -2 times the log-likelihood for the model plus 2 times the number of parameters specified. Lower AIC values signify better models. Parsimonious models are advantaged because the number of parameters increases the value of the AIC. For the differences between the McFadden and McKelvey R^2, see Long and Freese (2001).

13 Respondents were asked whether: a) they thought the Bible was the word of God and should be taken literally (assigned a value of three); b) they thought the Bible was the word of God but open to interpretation (assigned a value of two); or c) the Bible was written by humans and was not the word of God (assigned a value of one). Respondents who did not provide a valid answer to the question were given a value of one on this variable. The frequency of church attendance was coded: 5 = at least weekly; 4 = almost weekly; 3 = once or twice a month; 2 = a few times a year; and 1 = never or did not answer the question. Frequency of prayer was coded: 5 = several times a day; 4 = once a day; 3 = a few times a week; 2 = once a week or less; and 1 = never or did not answer the question. The religiosity scale was the respondents' factor scores extracted after a principal components analysis (PCA) of the three variables, an analysis that yielded a single factor with an eigenvalue (λ) of 1.9, with each of the three indicator variables containing loadings greater than .75.

14 A principal components analysis of the four questions assessing respondents' economic evaluations yielded a two-factor solution. The retrospective questions had rotated loadings greater than .80 on the first dimension ($\lambda = 1.8$), and the prospective questions had rotated loadings greater than .70 on the second dimension ($\lambda = .89$).

15 The administration performance variable is the factor score obtained on a single dimension ($\lambda = 1.7$) from a principal components analysis (PCA) of the following two variables, both having loadings

greater than .90: a) the sum of the variables asking the respondent to evaluate the job the government in Washington was doing overall and what the respondent judged to be their most important issue; and b) the factor score obtained on a single dimension ($\lambda = 3.0$) from a primary PCA of the four variables that measured the respondents' evaluations of George W. Bush. The loadings for the variables included this analysis were all greater than .80.

16 Variables tapping the dimensionality of the distance between each candidate and the respondent were analyzed separately. The question asking respondents to locate themselves and the candidates on a scale measuring the trade-off between environmental protection and job creation failed to produce strong loadings on the two dimensions of issue space extracted for either Bush or Kerry and was omitted from the PCAs used to estimate the issue space between the respondents and the two candidates.

17 After verimax rotation, the absolute issue distances between Kerry and the respondents loading on the Kerry New Deal ($\lambda = 3.3$) factor all had loadings above .60, and the absolute issue differences loading on the Kerry Post-Modern ($\lambda = 1.0$) had loadings above .70.

18 After verimax rotation, the traits loading on Bush Base ($\lambda = 3.4$) all had loadings above .50, and the issues loading on Bush New Deal ($\lambda = 1.0$) all had loadings above .60.

19 To make the following scores extracted from the PCA easily interpretable, we reversed the ordering of negatively worded traits ("dishonest" and "can't make up his mind"), giving the "extremely well" response a value of one, a "well" response a value of two, et cetera. The loadings on Bush's trait factor ($\lambda = 4.0$) ranged from .49 to .84, and the loadings on Kerry's trait factor ($\lambda = 3.6$) ranged from .56 to .81. The negatively worded traits had the lowest loadings, suggesting that the question wording may have contributed to a substantial portion of the unexplained variance for these indicators.

20 In the analyses where the impact of a specific dichotomous variable was not being ascertained, we assumed that the respondent was white, female, Independent, secular, and from the Northeast.

CHAPTER FIVE

Doing Politics His Way

The 2000 American Presidential Election

It was Winston Churchill, Britain's great leader during World War II, who is alleged to have observed that throughout history certain leaders have had a genius for snatching defeat from the jaws of victory. It would not be surprising if on January 20, 2001, thousands of unhappy Democrats, watching George W. Bush take the oath of office as president of the United States, might have ascribed that attribute to their party's erstwhile candidate, Albert A. Gore, Jr.

To many political leaders and average citizens alike in the United States and elsewhere, the 2000 presidential election appeared to be one that the Democratic candidates, Vice President Albert Gore and his running mate, Connecticut Senator Joseph Lieberman, could not possibly lose. As a new millennium dawned, the country was at peace and, fuelled by a combination of cheap energy, low interest rates, and technological innovation, the economy was experiencing robust growth. Reacting with giddy exuberance to the computer-driven "dot-com" boom, investors had pushed the stock market to record levels. Inflation and unemployment—twin evils that had stalked voters' pocketbooks throughout much of the 1970s and 1980s—were faded memories. As a result of the economic boom, not only was there no longer a budget deficit but it was rumoured that the Federal Reserve chairman, Dr. Alan Greenspan, was concerned that if the budget surpluses continued to mount, policy-makers might be tempted to pay off the national debt—not a good idea in his view. Finally, a major fear of the late 1990s, that the world's computing facilities would implode when the calendar ticked over to the year 2000, had proved to be groundless. The much ballyhooed "Y2K" bug was a no-show.

Not that the country was problem-free. On the domestic front, health costs had continued to climb and millions of Americans still had no health insurance. Critics also charged that the country was drowning in a flood of illegal aliens because the government could not or would not control immigration. The public school system was another target, with critics characterizing it as a morass of corruption and ineptitude that was failing to provide American children with the high quality education they would need to compete effectively in the global economy of the twenty-first century. In addition, its status as the world's only superpower notwithstanding, the United States was encountering serious problems in the international arena. Defying the best efforts of departing President Clinton, the decades-long conflict between Israel and the Palestinians not only remained unresolved but had actually intensified. American embassies in sub-Saharan Africa and the Middle East had been attacked. Special Forces soldiers had been killed in Somalia, and the destroyer USS *Cole* had suffered a major terrorist attack while in a Middle Eastern port. In addition, Iraq's leader Saddam Hussein was a continuing irritant despite a US-led economic embargo and constraints placed on Iraqi military action by "no-fly" zones in the northern and southern parts of the country.

These and other problems notwithstanding, the situation as Democrats gathered in Los Angeles for their convention appeared extremely promising, not only for retaining control of the presidency but also for breaking the tenuous control Republicans had on Congress. The Democratic presidential and vice presidential aspirants were seasoned serious professionals who had earned the respect of political friends and foes alike. In addition to their outstanding credentials, Gore and Lieberman had reputations as good family men and staunch adherents to their respective religions. In short, they were individuals with the "right stuff" to perpetuate Democratic control of the White House.

In contrast, there were a number of questions raised about their Republican opponents. The Republican vice presidential candidate, Dick Cheney, was respected for his history of demonstrated competence in public life. He had become Gerald Ford's chief of staff when he was only 34, and he had served a number of terms as congressman from Wyoming. Then, he had been secretary of defense during the first Gulf War, as well as a successful chief executive of the giant Halliburton Corporation, before being tapped by George W. Bush to be his vice presidential running mate. Although there was no questioning Cheney's ability and résumé, there was his relatively advanced age and, more important, his history of serious cardiac problems. Could he withstand the rigors of a long presidential campaign and the stress of returning to public life at the highest levels should the Republicans recapture the presidency?

As for the Republican presidential candidate himself, which George W. Bush would the country be getting if he were to become president? Some observers feared it would be the George Bush who, by his own admission, was at best an indifferent college student with a less than scintillating record in business and a reputation for being a heavy drinker until his early middle age. In contrast, it might be the successful two-term Texas governor with a passionate interest in public education, a self-designated "compassionate conservative" who was committed to faith-based initiatives to better the lives of the less fortunate. This George Bush seemed devoid of ideological rigidity as reflected in his ability to reach out to and work harmoniously and productively with his Democratic legislative opponents in Texas. In the event, questions about Bush's competence and character would matter a great deal, because he became president after losing the popular vote by a narrow margin (539,000 ballots), but winning a majority in the electoral college. However, the outcome of the election was not known until long after voters had trekked to the polls. Indeed, it would take fully 36 days after Election Day before Bush was in effect "elected" president by the 5–4 Supreme Court decision to stop the recount in Florida where only a few hundred highly contested ballots separated the Republican and Democratic presidential candidates. Then the real George W. Bush stepped onto the world stage. In this chapter, we consider the set of forces that produced this widely unexpected, highly unusual, election outcome.

FUNDAMENTALS:
PARTY IDENTIFICATION AND VALENCE ISSUES

Eight years of peace and prosperity seemingly put Vice President Al Gore and his running mate, Senator Joe Lieberman, in what might be termed the "cat-bird" seat in their campaign for the country's highest office. Quite simply, the Democrats had what political scientists call "the fundamentals" right (Johnston, Hagen, and Jamieson, 2004; Gelman and King, 1993; Wlezien, 2001). One of these fundamentals was party identification. As discussed in earlier chapters, partisanship might not be an "unmoved mover" in the field of psychological forces affecting voting behavior but, at any point in time, it had significant direct and indirect forces on electoral choice. In this regard, although the historically large Democratic lead in party identification had eroded over time, this long-term trend was overlaid by countervailing shorter-term movements during the Clinton years. In the run-up to the 2000 election, the American National Election Study (ANES) pre-election survey revealed that 34 per cent identified themselves as Democrats, and only 23 per cent as Republicans. The story told by monthly Gallup polls conducted over the year preceding the election was similar. The Democratic share of identifiers averaged 34 per cent, and the Republican share averaged 30 per cent. The Democrats' lead in party identifiers clearly favored the Gore-Lieberman ticket.

Partisanship was not the Democrats' only advantage. Economic conditions are often characterized as another important fundamental. As observed above, the American economy was booming in the late 1990s. The public reacted with predictable enthusiasm, something that a multitude of "economic voting" studies said should benefit an incumbent administration (e.g., Lewis-Beck, 1988; Clarke et al., 2004). Specifically, Figure 5.1 shows that 39 per cent of the ANES respondents said the national economy had improved during the year before the election, and a further 44 per cent said it had stayed the same.[1] In the context of the "roaring '90s," we interpret the latter number as a positive response—voters expected that the "good times" would continue to roll. Less than one person in five said the economy had deteriorated over the last year. ANES respondents were similarly positive about how their personal financial circumstances had evolved over the last year, and many also were optimistic about their future and that of the country as a whole.

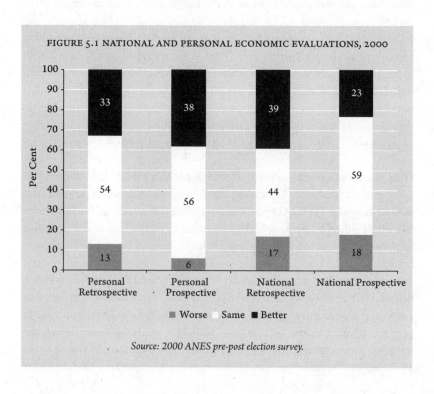

FIGURE 5.1 NATIONAL AND PERSONAL ECONOMIC EVALUATIONS, 2000

Source: 2000 ANES pre-post election survey.

There are other indications that voters were "bullish" on the economy. For example, fully 70 per cent of those participating in the 2000 ANES survey said the economy had improved during the Clinton years, and only 6 per cent said it had worsened (see Figure 5.2).[2] ANES respondents also were favorably impressed with the reduction in the budget deficit, with 59 per cent offering a positive appraisal, and only 16 per cent, a negative one. A smaller, but still substantial, 57 per cent gave President Clinton himself a favorable evaluation for his stewardship of the economy and only 3 per cent gave him an unfavorable one (see Figure 5.3).[3] Numbers like these were guaranteed to make Democratic political consultants smile.

Figures 5.2 and 5.3 also suggest that the economy was very much the Democrats' strong suit in the suite of voters' government performance evaluations. Judgments about trends in personal and national security were less sanguine. Thus, evaluations of trends in the crime rate were, on balance, favorable, but the percentages of positive responses were much lower than those for the economy. Responses about national security were quite evenly balanced, with negative judgments slightly outweighing positive ones. And, although it is not typically considered to be a "fundamental" factor affecting voting decisions, the administration's biggest perceived failing was seen to be an absence of moral leadership. President Clinton's scandalous affair with White House intern Monica Lewinsky, and continuing questions about his

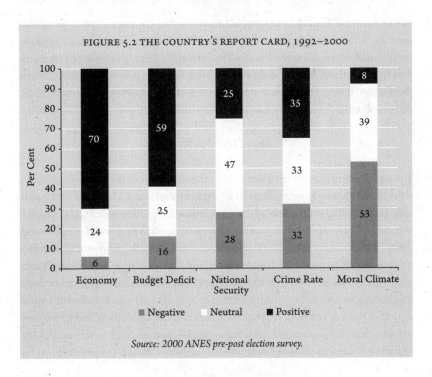

FIGURE 5.2 THE COUNTRY'S REPORT CARD, 1992–2000

Source: 2000 ANES pre-post election survey.

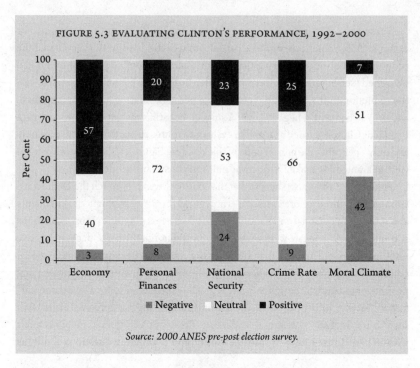

FIGURE 5.3 EVALUATING CLINTON'S PERFORMANCE, 1992–2000

Source: 2000 ANES pre-post election survey.

murky financial dealings and troubled marriage had left their imprint on public opinion. In the ANES survey, only 8 per cent of those interviewed made a positive judgment about trends in the country's moral climate since Clinton took office, and fully 53 per cent thought it had deteriorated (see Figure 5.2). Similarly, less than one person in 10 thought the president had performed well in setting a high moral tone, and over four in 10 thought he had performed badly (see Figure 5.3).

Important Problems

The positive response of the electorate to the condition of the economy and the potential for reaping benefits from this situation by the Gore-Lieberman camp is also reflected in public perceptions of the most important problems facing the country in 2000 and judgments about how the administration had performed in addressing them.[4] The economy was "a dog that (almost) didn't bark." Suggestive of widespread public satisfaction, economic conditions of any kind were cited as most important problems by only 16 per cent of the ANES respondents (see Table 5.1), and of those mentioning an economic problem, a majority (53 per cent) gave the administration a grade of good or fair. Almost as many (15 per cent) cited education, and 60 per cent of these people also assessed the administration's performance in this area as fair or better. A combined 26 per cent cited social issues: health (10 per cent); elder

TABLE 5.1 MOST IMPORTANT PROBLEM FACING THE COUNTRY AND
GOVERNMENT PERFORMANCE, 2000

	PER CENT MENTIONING	GOVERNMENT PERFORMANCE			
		GOOD	FAIR	POOR	DK
Most Important Issue					
Health	10	8	43	49	0
Education	15	8	52	39	2
Elder Care	8	10	49	39	3
Other Social Issues	8	7	39	51	3
Economy	16	11	42	42	5
Defense	4	9	40	46	6
Foreign Affairs	6	36	45	18	2
Terrorism	0.7	17	67	17	0
Race	1	11	44	33	11
Abortion, Women's Issues	1	0	9	91	0
Crime	10	2	56	41	1
Moral Decay	6	2	14	82	2
Clinton Morality	0.3	0	0	100	0
Government Functioning	4	11	30	59	0
Immigration	0.6	0	0	100	0
Environment	2	0	50	44	6
Miscellaneous Other	5	4	34	60	2
DK, None	3	–	–	–	–
Total		9	41	44	6

Party Best Most Important Issue
All Issue Mentions:
Republican = 21%
Democrat = 25%
No Difference, DK = 53%

N = 905 (random half-sample)
Source: 2000 ANES pre-post election survey.

care (8 per cent); and other social issues (8 per cent), with majorities making positive assessments of the government's performance in the first two areas, but only 46 per cent assigning it similar grades on other social issues.[5] A total of 10 per cent cited the related issues of defense and foreign affairs, with a large majority of respondents making positive assessments of the administration's handling of the latter area while a near majority gave them a similar grade on defense.

Only two other problems were cited by more than 5 per cent of the public: crime by 10 per cent with a 58 per cent positive response; national moral decay by 6 per cent with fully 82 per cent giving the Clinton administration a grade of poor. Terrorism and immigration, issues that became major concerns in the 2004 and 2006 elections, were almost invisible in 2000, being mentioned by only slightly over 1 per cent of the ANES respondents. The president's personal morality was condemned by all who cited it, but again suggestive of its limited potential as an election issue, the president's moral turpitude was referenced by less than 1 per cent of those interviewed. Considering all issues, 50 per cent judged the administration's performance on important issues as fair or good, 44 per cent judged it as poor, and 6 per cent were unsure. Thus, even when invited to cite important national problems, half of the electorate was unwilling to judge President Clinton and his colleagues harshly. With partisan and economic fundamentals in place, and at least an even split on performance across all salient problems, Messrs. Gore and Lieberman seemed poised for victory.

As "the most powerful vice president in American history" for eight years, a claim that had been made for him from virtually his first few months in office, Al Gore could plausibly, and justifiably, claim credit for contributing to the positive perceptions the electorate generally accorded the Clinton-Gore administration.[6] Moreover, he had been successful in resisting any attempts the Republicans might have made to paint him with the same moral brush with which Clinton had been tarred. As noted above, he seemed of the "right stuff," both morally and otherwise, to be president. He had been a dutiful son and brother, a Harvard graduate, a faithful husband and devoted father, and a politically successful Tennessee congressman and senator before assuming the vice presidency. He had not attempted to avoid military service in Vietnam as had both Clinton and Bush and, although widely ridiculed for his alleged claim of "inventing the Internet" (he insisted he never made it), he was recognized as an authority on leading-edge technology and an enthusiastic supporter of environmental protection. Also, he had proven to be a skilled and forceful debater, having easily bested a number of political "heavyweights," including Ross Perot on a wide-ranging TV debate on free trade; former congressman and cabinet secretary, Jack Kemp, in the 1996 vice presidential debate; and former Senator Bill Bradley, briefly his opponent in the primaries for his party's 2000 presidential nomination.

Finally, Gore was given credit by many observers for having made an astute strategic decision in selecting Joe Lieberman as his running mate. Senator Lieberman was often called every conservative's favorite liberal, especially after he rose in the Senate to denounce Clinton's conduct in the Lewinsky affair. Conservatives' comfort with Lieberman was enhanced by his advocacy of school vouchers and welfare reform, and his sharp criticism of the culture of sex and violence he insisted was virtually omnipresent on television and in movies. Lieberman's Orthodox Judaism was seen as an additional plus since his presence on the ticket might significantly enhance Democratic prospects of carrying Florida and Pennsylvania, two battleground states with large Jewish populations. Since Lieberman was a strong defender of Israel, he might even improve the ticket's prospects in some of the so-called red states with large numbers of Evangelical Protestants, arguably Israel's strongest supporters in the United States apart from Jewish voters (Fingerhut, 2002).

Despite these several presumed pluses, public enthusiasm for Gore, as reflected in a large series of public opinion polls conducted between January and November 2000, was less than stellar. As Figure 5.4 shows, Gore's vote intention shares were in the mid-40 per cent range in February, rose briefly to the mid-50s in March, and then stayed below 50 per cent until the Democratic National Convention. The convention provided the vice president with a very large boost, lifting his support well above 50 per cent until the latter part of September when it began to erode. Immediately after the first presidential debate on October 3, Gore's support climbed above 50 in some polls but, as Figure 5.4 illustrates, the underlying trend was downward. Only in the final few days before the election did polls show him regaining the support of half of the electorate. His ultimate "razor-thin" plurality of the popular vote (48.4 for Gore versus 47.9 per cent for Bush) confirmed that Gore was, at best, just barely the people's choice.

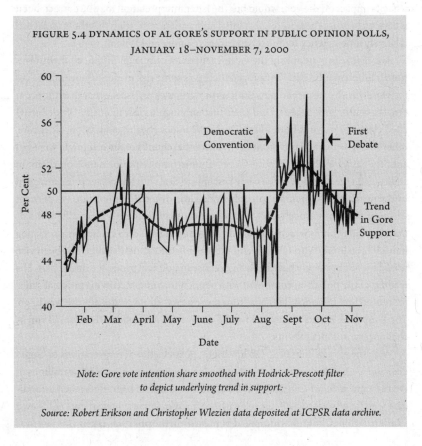

FIGURE 5.4 DYNAMICS OF AL GORE'S SUPPORT IN PUBLIC OPINION POLLS, JANUARY 18–NOVEMBER 7, 2000

Note: Gore vote intention share smoothed with Hodrick-Prescott filter to depict underlying trend in support.

Source: Robert Erikson and Christopher Wlezien data deposited at ICPSR data archive.

The obvious question is why? We may speculate that one reason the positive perceptions of the Clinton-Gore administration held by much of the public did not seem to translate into greater electoral support for the Gore-Lieberman candidacy was that the vice president made a major error in not embracing President Clinton and his record in office more closely. Doing so would have enabled the Gore campaign to take greater advantage of the outgoing president's formidable skills as a campaigner, as well as the affection in which he was held by so much of the Democratic base, especially its African American component. Indeed, Clinton was broadly popular with much of the electorate in the run-up to the 2000 election. Consonant with the positive performance evaluations discussed above, his job approval rating in Gallup monthly polls averaged 60 per cent over the January-November period— well above the 53 per cent average rating for his three most recent predecessors (Bush, Sr., Reagan, and Carter). People in the Gore-Lieberman camp seemingly erred in distancing themselves from a popular president, either because his affair with Ms. Lewinsky was personally repugnant to them, or they vastly overestimated what its impact on the vote would be. The latter interpretation may be correct, but it is curious because there were substantial polling data indicating that the scandal had relatively little salience for most Americans (Sonner and Wilcox, 1999).

Another reason people in the Gore-Lieberman campaign distanced themselves from Clinton may be that they judged there was some risk in identifying themselves too closely with a former administration's performance on issues other than the economy. In this regard, Table 5.1 indicates that although a clear majority (57 per cent) cited classic bread-and-butter New Deal-style issues (health, education, elder care, other social issues, and the economy), substantial chunks of the electorate were not entirely happy with the Clinton-Gore administration's performance on them. In addition, on the question of the party best able to deal with important problems cited by the public, the Democrats had only a small lead over the Republicans (25 per cent versus 21 per cent, respectively), with 53 per cent saying there was no difference, or that they didn't know which party could do better. Thus, Gore's caution in associating himself too closely with Clinton and the administration of which he had been vice president might merely have been an exercise in political prudence on his part. His reading of the poll data, combined with abundant confidence in his political skills, prompted him to conclude that a "four more years" strategy was not the way to go. The Gore-Lieberman ticket could make it on its own. In effect, they would run as challengers, not incumbents.

With the easy benefit of 20/20 hindsight, post-election interpretations of Gore's decision were sharply critical. Most of the "chattering classes," as well as millions of Democratic stalwarts, argued that Bush was fortunate in running against a candidate who failed to associate himself with the many positive achievements of his own administration. Clinton's widespread popularity in the polls was taken as *prima facie* evidence that he would have made the Democratic ticket an easy winner—had he been closely associated with it. Rejecting Clinton symbolically by selecting Lieberman, and literally failing to enthusiastically embrace the popular president

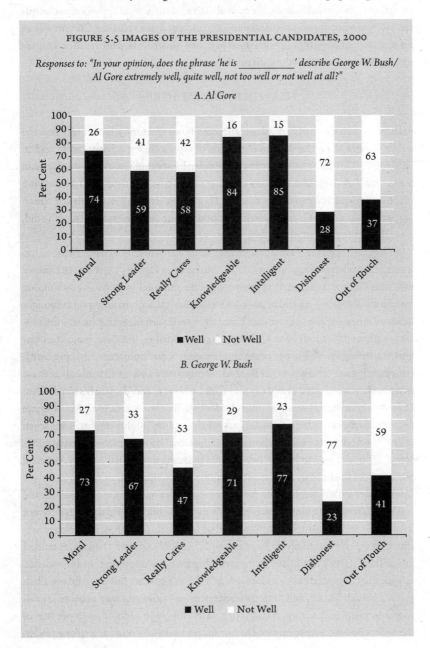

FIGURE 5.5 IMAGES OF THE PRESIDENTIAL CANDIDATES, 2000

Responses to: "In your opinion, does the phrase 'he is _____' describe George W. Bush/ Al Gore extremely well, quite well, not too well or not well at all?"

A. Al Gore

B. George W. Bush

at the Democratic convention, Gore did not take advantage of the "valence politics boost" of peace and prosperity that had kept Clinton's poll numbers high, despite the Lewinsky affair. Peace and prosperity are classic valence issues—these are "good things" everybody wants, and Clinton had delivered them to an appreciative electorate. Many Democrats and political pundits concluded that spurning Clinton was an act of abject political stupidity on Gore's part, one for which he paid in full on January 20, 2001, when Bush took the oath of office.

CANDIDATE IMAGES

Another reason Gore may not have attracted more electoral support was that the public did not share the disdain that some of Gore's closest advisors were said to have had for Governor Bush. Bush was regarded by some of Gore's inner circle as an intellectual lightweight, a rich boy coasting on his family's name and undeserving of the opportunity to run for his country's highest office—in Texas parlance, a man "all hat and no cattle." Gore may well have bought into such an assessment. If he did, it would eventually cost him dearly.

In fact, although Gore's image with the public was generally a positive one, so too was that of his Republican opponent.[7] As illustrated in Figure 5.5A, the ANES survey indicates Gore was regarded as knowledgeable and intelligent by overwhelming majorities of voters—84 and 85 per cent, respectively. Large majorities also thought he was a moral person (74 per cent), and disagreed with ideas that he was dishonest (72 per cent) or "out of touch" (63 per cent). Smaller, but clear, majorities saw him as a strong leader (59 per cent) and someone who "really cares" (58 per cent). However, Figure 5.5B shows that Bush also scored very well on virtually all of these criteria. He was regarded as equally moral, more honest, and, despite his much more limited political experience, a stronger leader than his Democratic rival. Also, despite frequent media caricatures of Bush as a syntax-mangling "goofus-doofus," over seven in 10 of the ANES respondents thought that the term "knowledgeable" applied either "very" or "quite" well to him. When it came to Bush's image, like Al Gore, political pundits were the ones who were out of touch with public opinion.

We observed in Chapter Four on the 2004 presidential election that Democratic and Republican party identifiers typically view the political world through different lenses. This was no less true four years earlier (see Table 5.2). Thus, on each personality trait (and occasionally by large margins), Republicans and Democrats tended to see their party's candidate more favorably than his opponent. Independents' assessments of both candidates consistently fell in between, but they did see Bush as more moral, honest, and a strong leader, whereas Gore was seen as more knowledgeable, intelligent, caring, and in touch. Interestingly, in addition to 67 per cent of the Independents, 47 per cent of *Democratic* partisans saw Bush as a strong leader, as opposed to the 55 per cent of Independents and only 27 per cent of Republicans who applied that label to the vice president.

As we will show later in this chapter, just as in 2004, leader images were a major determinant of the vote in the 2000 presidential election. In both 2000 and 2004, Bush was at little, if any, disadvantage when it came to image. In particular, on the important perception of who was the stronger leader, Bush had an advantage over his Democratic rivals in both elections. A key component of valence politics, we argue, is that leader images are important heuristic devices. Leader images provide cues to

TABLE 5.2 PRESIDENTIAL CANDIDATE TRAITS
BY PARTY IDENTIFICATION, 2000

(Percentages Agreeing that Word Mentioned Describes Candidate
"Extremely Well" or "Quite Well")

A.   George W. Bush

Trait	REPUBLICAN	INDEPENDENT	DEMOCRAT	EVERYONE
Moral	93	70	61	73
Strong Leader	93	67	47	67
Really Cares	80	47	25	47
Knowledgeable	87	73	58	71
Intelligent	93	79	63	77
Dishonest	7	23	35	23
Out of Touch	19	44	54	41

B.   Al Gore

Trait	REPUBLICAN	INDEPENDENT	DEMOCRAT	EVERYONE
Moral	58	68	91	74
Strong Leader	27	55	83	59
Really Cares	31	51	85	58
Knowledgeable	73	81	93	84
Intelligent	78	82	92	85
Dishonest	43	30	15	28
Out of Touch	47	41	26	37

Note: All differences among party identification groups are statistically significant, $p < .001$.

Source: 2000 ANES pre-post election survey.

voters who are "smart enough to know they are ignorant about what the future might bring," and seek safe harbor in strong political leadership.

Sighing and Smirking: The Presidential Debates

When considering how candidate traits played in the 2000 election, we argue that one reason Al Gore did not "clean up" on George W. Bush was that he did not derive the advantage he, his advisors, and many commentators anticipated he would receive from debating his Republican rival. Recall that the vice president had a well-earned reputation as a skilled, knowledgeable, and aggressive debater who, if given the opportunity, would expose Bush as a novice, an inexperienced ex-governor of a state with a historically weak chief executive. In a debate with Gore, Bush would be revealed as a candidate who was not in command of, or even able to speak knowledgeably about, either domestic or, especially, foreign policy problems. Plainly, Gore would show Bush to be the dummy he really was.

Three debates were held, the first taking place in Boston on October 3, 2000. Most of the post-debate expert "spin" commentary judged it a disaster for the vice president. To many TV viewers who tuned in to the first debate, Gore came across as the classic bully. To add to his misery, the widely watched *Saturday Night Live* comedy program ridiculed Gore for his antics, and in the process turned him into a joke. In a matter of hours after the program had aired, Gore had been transformed from the likely leader of the free world to a combination of schoolyard bully and Elmer Fudd (Smith and Voth, 2002).

Frantic attempts by his advisors to remedy the situation by presenting a quieter softer Al Gore attired in "earth-colored" clothing in the second debate did little to diminish the ridicule. Instead, it had the opposite effect, providing new grist for the comedians. Gore was said to have tried to have a personality transplant: transforming himself from a smirking brute to Mr. Rogers. Comedian and liberal Al Franken opined that the second debate only succeeded in "locking in perceptions from the first debate." Smith and Voth's (2002) study of the role of humor in the election concluded that SNL played a significant role in shaping public perceptions of the vice president during the remainder of the campaign.

It was not that Bush escaped unscathed from the comedic assault. His repeated malapropisms and the repetition of the phrase "fuzzy math" to respond to Gore's assault on his education, health care, and social security proposals were also skewered as much or more than the vice president's pledge to defend cherished social programs by placing them in a "locked box" (Shales, 2000). However, the costs to Gore's image rendered by the comedic mocking and exaggerations of his speech and behavior impaired his ability to project himself as a clearly superior leader. It was Gore, not Bush, who was the candidate with gravitas and a singular knowledge of both foreign and domestic policy. It was Gore who was the candidate with long experience in Congress, who had been a heartbeat away from the presidency for eight years, and whose claim to be the candidate best able to guide the nation rested on this background and experience. Thus, the damage to his image by his disastrous debate performance was far greater than for Bush, from whom little was expected.

Indeed, poll data suggest that Gore's frantic attempts to counteract being cast as a villainous cartoon character after the first debate, by appearing to become a different person in the second debate and still another after the third, seemed to make matters even worse. Although Gore's support in the polls was already trending downward before the first debate (see Figure 5.4; see also Johnston, Hagen, and Jamieson, 2004), the polls also indicate that he had a clear lead over Bush immediately after the first debate but was clearly trailing him after their third encounter (Holland, 2000). Although it is difficult to precisely calibrate debate effects net of other forces at work in the campaign, it strongly appears that the debates fostered perceptions of Gore that were the opposite of what he and his advisors had expected. Rather than brightening his image, the debates tarnished it at a critical juncture in the campaign. And, as we will show below, candidate images had powerful effects on whether voters opted for Gore or Bush.

POSITION ISSUES AND POLICY SPACES

Party identification, performance on heavily valenced issues such as the economy and national security, and leader images all significantly influenced voting behavior in the 2004 presidential election. However, position issues also exerted important effects. Readers will recall that position issues have a "pro-con" quality, with candidates and voters arraying themselves along dimensions of being in favor or against particular policies or policy trade-offs. Similar to its 2004 counterpart, the 2000 ANES survey asked respondents to position themselves and the presidential candidates on several such dimensions.[8] Overall means are presented in Figure 5.6 and individual-level differences are summarized in Table 5.3. The latter results indicate that the ANES respondents saw Gore as significantly closer to them on five issues—environmental protection versus jobs, environmental protection versus assistance to business, equal roles for women, abortion, and gun control. Bush was closer on two issues—government aid to African Americans and government provision of jobs. Bush was also significantly closer to voters on an overall liberal-conservative ideological scale. Not surprisingly, Republican identifiers were closer to Bush on this scale, and Democratic identifiers were closer to Gore. However, Democratic identifiers were not as distant from Bush as Republican identifiers were from Gore, and Independents were not notably closer to Gore than to Bush. Viewed globally, practically all of the differences on position issues tended to be quite small. Thus, Gore did

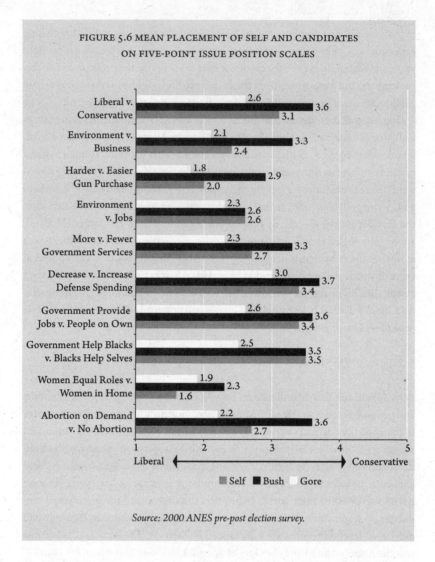

FIGURE 5.6 MEAN PLACEMENT OF SELF AND CANDIDATES
ON FIVE-POINT ISSUE POSITION SCALES

Source: 2000 ANES pre-post election survey.

not derive the significant benefit over his rival that might be anticipated from having been Number 2 in an eight-year administration where he had ample opportunity to learn the location of public opinion "sweet spots" on a range of contentious issues.

As discussed in Chapter Four, voters' party-issue proximities on several position issues were not orthogonal to one another in 2004. Rather, they tended to hang together to constitute an overarching architectonic of loosely constrained bidimensional policy spaces. Exploratory factor analyses indicate that this was also true in 2000, with proximities to both Bush and Gore being partially defined by a classic New Deal-Great Society dimension defined largely in terms of the scope of

TABLE 5.3 MEAN INDIVIDUAL-LEVEL ABSOLUTE DIFFERENCES IN
PROXIMITY TO AL GORE AND GEORGE W. BUSH ON POSITION ISSUES, 2000

	GORE	BUSH	t	P
More v. Fewer Government Services	1.14	1.08	1.28	.200
Decrease v. Increase Defense Spending	0.99	0.92	1.70	.089
Government Provide Jobs v. People on Own	1.40	**1.02**	7.08	.000
Government Help Blacks v. Blacks Help Selves	1.26	**1.03**	4.66	.000
Environment v. Jobs	**1.01**	1.16	-3.25	.001
Women Equal Roles v. Women in Home	**0.76**	1.02	-7.44	.000
Abortion on Demand v. No Abortion	**1.04**	1.12	-1.83	.068
Harder v. Easier Gun Purchase	**1.01**	1.17	-3.84	.000
Environment v. Business	**1.08**	1.28	-3.76	.000
Overall Liberal v. Conservative Scale	1.18	**1.07**	2.54	.011

Note: Boldface numbers indicate statistically significant difference in proximity between candidates and voters ($p < .05$, two-tailed test).

Source: 2000 ANES pre-election survey.

desirable government activity in various policy areas, such as job provision, assistance to African Americans, and extent of spending on government services (see Table 5.4).[9]

However, there is also a second policy dimension for both candidates. For Gore in 2000 (and for Kerry in 2004), this dimension is clearly defined in terms in women's roles in society and their freedom to make reproductive choices. For Bush, the second dimension is defined by women's roles and reproductive choice, but it also includes positions on gun control and voters' general liberal versus conservative self-definitions. As in our 2004 analyses, we designate this complex of issues as "Bush Base" to designate its motivating appeal to social conservatives. As the multivariate analyses below will reveal, dimensions defining the Gore and Bush policy spaces had sizable effects on the choices voters made in the 2000 presidential election.

RIVAL MODELS: ANALYZING ELECTORAL CHOICE

In the introduction to this book, we discussed several competing theoretical perspectives on electoral choice and rival models of voting behavior that are suggested by these perspectives. In Chapter Four, we investigated the ability of these models to explain voting behavior in the 2004 presidential election. Here, we use the ANES survey data to test the explanatory power of these models in the context of the 2000 presidential election. The models we consider are: a) demographics; b) economic evaluations; c) party identification; d) government performance; e) issue proximities; and f) candidate images. To maximize comparability and facilitate generalization,

TABLE 5.4 EXPLORATORY FACTOR ANALYSIS OF THE STRUCTURE
OF ISSUE PROXIMITY SPACE FOR BUSH AND GORE

	BUSH		GORE	
	F1	F2	F1	F2
Issue				
No Abortion v. Abortion on Demand	.13	**.67**	.22	**.53**
Women Equal Roles v. Women in Home	.11	**.58**	-.13	**.84**
Government Help Blacks v. Blacks Help Selves	**.60**	.05	**.68**	.06
Government Provide Jobs v. People on Own	**.66**	.01	**.69**	.04
Decrease v. Increase Defense Spending	**.62**	.17	**.64**	.10
More v. Fewer Government Services	**.64**	.23	**.66**	.19
Protect Environment v. Jobs	**.56**	.33	.43	.33
Protect Environment v. Business	**.54**	.39	**.53**	.33
More v. Less Stringent Gun Control	.08	**.68**	.33	.35
Liberal v. Conservative Position	.20	**.51**	**.59**	.10
Per Cent Item Variance Explained	30.7	10.5	31.2	10.5

Note: Boldface numbers are factor loadings greater that .50.

the measures of various predictor variables in the models are identical or very similar
to those employed in the analyses of voting in the 2004 presidential election (see
Chapter Four). In addition, as in the 2004 analyses, the dependent variable is a
dichotomy scored one if a survey respondent voted for the Republican candidate
(Bush) and zero if the respondent voted for the Democratic candidate (Gore).
Binomial logit (Long, 1997) is used to estimate model parameters.

Table 5.5 presents the results. Panel A shows that several of the demographic variables behaved as expected. Interpreting the results in terms of who voted for Gore,
the analysis shows that younger people, women, people with lower incomes, African
Americans, Hispanics, and persons of "other" religions all were more likely to vote for
the vice president than were older people, men, higher income people, and whites.
In contrast, Gore did less well than Bush among people who deemed themselves to
be very religious, particularly very religious Protestants.[10] All of these relationships
are consonant with conventional wisdom about the demographics of party support
in contemporary America.

However, what is most striking about the results is the overall weakness of the
relationships. The McFadden and McKelvey estimated R^2 statistics are only .16 and
.31, respectively, and the analysis misclassifies the behavior of 30 per cent of the voters.
In 2000, as in 2004, demographic characteristics are only very loosely articulated

with electoral choice. With few exceptions, demographic characteristics are very imperfect guides to how people voted.

Economic evaluations have even weaker effects. In 2000 voters' economic evaluations are structured in terms of two factors—judgments about the past and future of the national economy and judgments about one's past and future personal economic circumstances.[11] Table 5.5B shows that national, but not personal, economic evaluations have a significant impact on presidential voting. However, contrary to what one might anticipate, persons making positive evaluations were more, not less, likely to vote for George Bush. This relationship is perverse in terms of what the literature on economic voting leads one to expect about how a buoyant economy affects support for the standard-bearer of an incumbent party (cf. Nadeau and Lewis-Beck, 2001). The economic evaluations' voting behavior relationships are also very weak—the estimated R^2s are less than .10, and the percentage of voters correctly classified is less than 15 per cent greater than what one could do with a naive "mode-guessing" rule. The failure of the economic voting model in 2000 is consistent with our argument that Gore decoupled himself from the Clinton record in voters' minds, including the economic aspects of that record that might have helped him.

The third model of electoral choice that we consider is party identification.[12] Analyses indicate that partisanship presents no surprises. Relative to Independents (the reference category), Republican partisans favored Bush and Democratic partisans favored Gore (see Table 5.5C). In addition, compared to the demographic and economic models, the party identification model demonstrates its explanatory muscle. The McFadden and McKelvey R^2s are much larger (.40 and .55, respectively), and the percentage of voters correctly classified approaches 80 per cent, 30 per cent more than one would guess using the mode-guessing procedure. The statistical power of party identification is consistent with both social-psychological and revisionist rational choice conceptualizations that make partisanship a key factor in the skein of forces driving electoral choice (e.g., Campbell et al., 1960; Fiorina, 1981). However, as in other presidential elections, partisanship was not all that mattered in 2000.

Rather, panels D and E of Table 5.5 document that voters' evaluations of the performance of the Clinton administration and their proximities to the candidates on various position issues had strong effects on the choice between Bush and Gore. Concerning administration performance evaluations, exploratory factor analyses reveal that such evaluations are structured by two factors—economy-crime and moral climate-national security.[13] Both factors were influential; voters who gave the Clinton administration high grades for its performance were less likely to support Bush than were those who gave the administration lower grades (see Table 5.5D). The result for the moral climate-national security factor suggests that Gore was indeed correct to worry that public reaction to Clinton's moral failings would work

TABLE 5.5 RIVAL MODELS OF VOTING FOR GEORGE W. BUSH
IN THE 2000 PRESIDENTIAL ELECTION

A.	*Demographics*		B	S.E.
	Age		-0.01**	.00
	Gender		0.60***	.14
	Income		0.06**	.02
	Race:	African American	-3.37***	.37
		Hispanic	-0.93**	.35
		Other Non-White	0.57*	.31
	Region:	North Central	-0.23	.20
		South	0.42*	.21
		West	-0.30	.22
	Religion:	Catholic	0.05	.29
		Protestant	0.20	.27
		Other	-1.31**	.50
	Religiosity		0.36**	.14
	Religiosity x Protestant		0.34*	.18
	Constant		-0.11	.42

McFadden R^2 = .16, McKelvey R^2 = .31
Per Cent Correctly Classified = 70.0, AIC† = 1251.91

B.	*Economic Evaluations*	B	S.E.
	Personal	-0.11	.07
	National	-0.58***	.07
	Constant	-0.14	.08

McFadden R^2 = .05, McKelvey R^2 = .09
Per Cent Correctly Classified = 62.9, AIC = 1390.53

C.	*Party Identification*	B	S.E.
	Republican	2.30***	.24
	Democratic	-2.63***	.22
	Constant	0.17	.11

McFadden R^2 = .40, McKelvey R^2 = .55
Per Cent Correctly Classified = 79.6, AIC = 874.72

D.	*Clinton Administration Performance*	B	S.E.
	Economy, Crime	-1.42***	.11
	Moral Climate, National Security	-1.44***	.11
	Constant	-0.11	.08

McFadden R^2 = .35, McKelvey R^2 = .58
Per Cent Correctly Classified = 79.0, AIC = 946.48

E.	*Position Issues*	B	S.E.
	Gore New Deal	-1.59***	.14
	Gore Women's Issues	-0.86***	.10
	Bush Base	1.23***	.12
	Bush New Deal	1.39***	.13
	Constant	-0.23**	.09

McFadden R^2 = .44, McKelvey R^2 = .75
Per Cent Correctly Classified = 81.3, AIC = 821.63

TABLE 5.5 RIVAL MODELS OF VOTING FOR GEORGE W. BUSH
IN THE 2000 PRESIDENTIAL ELECTION

F. Candidate Images	B	S.E.
Gore Traits	-1.87***	.15
Bush Traits	2.20***	.16
Constant	-0.38***	.10

McFadden R^2 = .55, McKelvey R^2 = .79
Per Cent Correctly Classified = 87.5, AIC = 664.34

*** $p < .001$; ** $p < .01$; * $p < .05$; one-tailed test.

†—Akaike Information Criterion (AIC)—smaller values indicate better
model performance.

to erode his support. However, the result for the economy-crime factor indicates that distancing himself from the president came with a cost. The estimated R^2 statistics and correct classification statistics for the administration performance model are very similar to those for the partisanship model discussed above, thereby suggesting that the two models have approximately equal explanatory power.

The position issue model also works well. All four policy-space factors have the expected effects on the vote. Thus, people close to Bush on the "New Deal" and "Base" dimensions were more likely to choose him than were people who placed themselves further away (see Table 5.5E). Predictably, the Gore policy-space factors had the opposite effects; people close to Gore on the "New Deal" and "Women's Issues" dimensions were less likely to choose Bush. The position issue model correctly classifies slightly over 80 per cent of the voters, and it has very sizable estimated R^2s—.44 (McFadden) and .75 (McKelvey).

Although the administration performance and position issue models yield impressive results, the candidate image model fares even better. As in 2004, exploratory factor analyses of the candidate trait variables (see Figure 5.5 above) indicate that public images of the two presidential candidates could be effectively summarized by single factors. These factors have powerful effects. As shown in Table 5.5F, the factor score variables work as anticipated, with positive images of Bush boosting his support, whereas positive images of Gore lower it. However, the big story is the collective strength of these relationships. The candidate image model has larger estimated R^2 statistics than any of its rivals, and it can correctly classify the behavior of nearly 88 per cent of the voters.

The Akaike model selection criterion (Burnham and Anderson, 2002) provides further insight regarding the overall performance of the competing models of electoral choice. As discussed in Chapter Two, the Akaike Information Criterion

TABLE 5.6 COMPOSITE MODEL OF FACTORS AFFECTING VOTING FOR
GEORGE W. BUSH IN THE 2000 PRESIDENTIAL ELECTION

	B	S.E.
Predictor Variables		
Valence:		
Clinton Performance:		
Economy-Crime	-0.84***	.18
Moral Climate-National Security	-1.08***	.18
Leader Image:		
Bush Traits	1.33***	.20
Gore Traits	-0.99***	.20
Policy Spaces:		
Bush Base	0.85***	.20
Bush New Deal	0.60***	.20
Gore New Deal	-0.56***	.21
Gore Women	-0.46***	.16
Party Identification:		
Democrat	-1.74***	.33
Republican	1.36***	.36
Economic Evaluations:		
Personal–Retrospective & Prospective	0.27*	.15
National–Retrospective & Prospective	0.04	.16
Demographics:		
Age	0.00	.01
Gender	0.42	.29
Income	0.02	.04
Race:		
African American	-1.48**	.57
Hispanic	-0.59	.63
Other	-1.35*	.79
Region:		
North Central	-0.09	.39
South	0.19	.39
West	-0.58	.44
Religion:		
Catholic	-0.33	.55
Protestant	-0.70	.54
Other	-2.07**	.97
Religiosity	0.45*	.27
Religiosity x Protestant	-0.53	.36
Constant	0.54	.78

McFadden R^2 = .73
McKelvey R^2 = .90
Per Cent Correctly Classified = 91.8, λ = .83
AIC = 444.824
N = 1054

*** p < .001; ** p < .01; * p < .05; one-tailed test.

†—Akaike Information Criterion (AIC)—smaller values indicate better model
performance.

(AIC) helps one to compare the performance of competing models by taking into account the number of parameters used to achieve a given level of explanatory power. Comparing the AIC values (smaller values indicate better performance) indicates that the candidate image model wins the "tournament of models" (see Table 5.5). Position issues are in second place, followed by party identification and Clinton administration performance evaluations.[14] The economic evaluation and demographic models trail far behind and, despite using many more parameters, the latter actually surpasses the former. Viewed in terms of the larger arguments of this chapter, the AIC comparison buttresses the case that candidate images were crucial in 2000, and economic evaluations—a potential "ace" in Gore's hand—were largely neutralized.

Additional evidence regarding the relative power of the various competing models of electoral choice can be gathered by forming a composite model that contains all of the individual models. Estimating parameters for the composite model shows that candidate images, administration performance judgments, position issues, and party identification all had highly significant (p < .001) effects on voting in the 2000 presidential election (see Table 5.6). Although their levels of statistical significance are much less impressive, the effects of some of the demographics are noteworthy. Net of all other considerations, African Americans were less likely to vote for George Bush, as were persons of "other" religions (persons without a religious affiliation are the reference group). In contrast, people with high scores on the religiosity index were more likely to support Bush. The effects of national economic evaluations are statistically insignificant, and personal economic evaluations are perversely signed in terms of prevailing economic voting theories. The composite model estimates suggest that people making positive judgments about their personal economic condition were more likely to vote for Bush, rather than for Gore who had been vice president in the outgoing Clinton administration. This result again suggests that Gore failed to capitalize on the economic "good times" that the electorate had enjoyed during the Clinton years.

Since logit estimates defy easy interpretation, we calculate changes in the probability of voting for Bush as various predictors are varied across their range and others are held at their means or other plausible values.[15] The results, displayed in Figure 5.7, are consonant with our previous discussion. Although several predictors can invoke substantial changes in the probability of voting for Bush or Gore, those with the biggest effects are associated with party identification, Clinton administration performance evaluations, position issues, and candidate images. Party identification has a substantial impact, with a shift from Democratic to Republican partisanship enhancing the likelihood of a Bush vote by 64 points (from -.36 to .28, see Figure 5.7). As for performance evaluations, both the economy-crime and moral climate-national security dimensions were very influential. *Ceteris paribus*, the former could

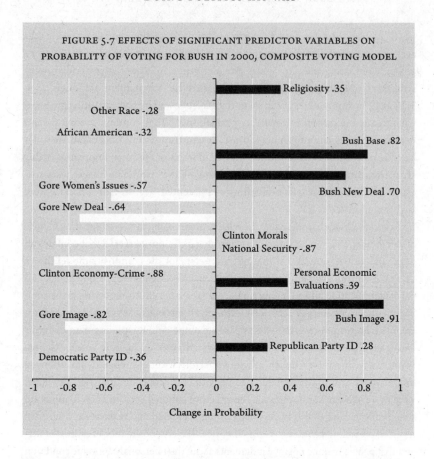

FIGURE 5.7 EFFECTS OF SIGNIFICANT PREDICTOR VARIABLES ON
PROBABILITY OF VOTING FOR BUSH IN 2000, COMPOSITE VOTING MODEL

change the probability of a Bush vote by fully 88 points, and the latter could change it by 87 points. All four issue-proximity (position issue) dimensions were powerful too, showing that they could alter the likelihood of voting for Bush by 57 to 82 points. As for candidate images, other things equal, favorable impressions of Al Gore could lower the probability of supporting Bush by 82 points, whereas favorable impressions of Bush could raise the probability of voting for him by fully 91 points.

Viewed globally, our multivariate analyses indicate presidential voting in 2000 was strongly influenced by several factors. The analysis of the composite model summarized in Table 5.6 shows that no single model is able to encompass its competitors (Charemza and Deadman, 1997). Rather, several models testify that they can contribute to the larger story about what influenced the choices voters made when they opted for Bush or Gore. Moreover, the Akaike model selection criterion value for the composite model is better (smaller) than for any of the individual models: this despite the fact that the former is much more richly parameterized than any of the latter.

We believe these results make sense. Before casting their ballots in presidential elections, American voters are bombarded with vast quantities of information/propaganda and interpretation/spin by the competing candidates' campaigns, media commentators, political pundits, and the motley miscellany of professional "talking heads" that populate the nation's TV screens and daily newspapers. The inevitable result is that multiple considerations come into play when voters make up their minds (Zaller, 1992). However, it is equally true that not all considerations are equally important. Valence politics factors—candidate images, government performance evaluations, and partisanship—supplemented by perceptions of candidates' positions in policy spaces that they work to define to their advantage, are key. In 2000 Vice President Gore relied heavily on using the campaign to exploit what he believed would be a decisive image advantage over his rival. In the conclusion, we reconsider this strategy and how it and other factors contributed to the election outcome.

CONCLUSION: DOING AN ELECTION HIS WAY

We began this book by noting that every election is a "risky business." However, the 2000 American presidential election appeared to be one in which both Venus and Mars were favorably aligned for a Democratic victory and the beginning of an Al Gore administration. It was not to be, and the question we posed here is, why? Why did eight years of peace and prosperity and economic good times, a discernible lead in party identification, and an initially positive image not result in Gore rather than Bush taking the oath of office as president on January 20, 2001?

One reason may have been that in Gore's mind, winning may have not looked all that easy. Rather, he needed to square a political circle by claiming credit for the eight good years and imploring voters to keep the good times rolling by electing him president. However, to do so he had to embrace the incumbent president, William Jefferson Clinton, closely; an embrace which for political, and perhaps personal, reasons Gore was hesitant to make. After all, Clinton had only recently been impeached by the House of Representatives and tried by the Senate. Like Andrew Johnson, Abraham Lincoln's vice president, the Senate acquitted Clinton. Nonetheless, Gore may have concluded that millions of Americans, not all of whom were staunch Republicans, found Clinton's personal behavior, in particular his bizarre affair with a 23-year-old White House intern, reprehensible. Indeed, Gore's running mate, Joe Lieberman, had risen in the Senate to sharply denounce Clinton, his president and party leader, for precisely that behavior. By selecting Lieberman as his running mate, Gore seemed to be sending a strong signal to the electorate that he shared Lieberman's revulsion with the president's conduct.

There were, of course, other reasons that could have accounted for Senator Lieberman's selection. It was a "political first"—Lieberman was the first Jewish

American to be on a presidential ticket. A foreign policy "hawk," he was a strong supporter of Israel. His presence on the ticket thereby might help the Democrats win Florida, a battleground state where the Clinton administration had alienated a large number of Cuban Americans. Lieberman might offset this by appealing strongly to south Florida's sizable Jewish population. His reputation for being able to "work across the aisle" on legislative matters, because he had many friends among his Republican colleagues, could also have been a consideration if, as was distinctly possible, the Republicans retained control over Congress. Irrespective of whether choosing Lieberman as a running mate fulfilled some of the expectations Gore may have had for him, the choice was a strong symbolic rejection of Clinton. It also angered the Congressional Black Caucus leaders in Congress because of Lieberman's stand on social issues such as school vouchers and welfare reform. Gore's strategy of distancing himself from Clinton thus had both pluses and minuses.

What if he had done it differently? Embracing Clinton definitely would have had upside potential on some issues. Most important, a large majority of voters were enthusiastic about the state of the economy, and many of them credited President Clinton for the prosperity that they had enjoyed while he was in the Oval Office. As we have seen, Gore gained almost no traction from these highly favorable economic evaluations, something that would have been very likely had he identified himself with a president who had presided over the economic boom.

On other issues, the outcome would have been less certain. When questioned about which party was best able to deal with problems facing the nation, voters gave the Democrats a lead, albeit a modest one, over the Republicans. However, and perhaps significant in light of eight years of peace and prosperity presided over by a Democratic administration, a majority said there was no difference in party preference or they did not know which party would do better. Being close to Clinton likely would not have helped with these voters. In addition, voters judged Clinton harshly for the moral tone he had set for the nation and, as Gore undoubtedly feared, these judgments could influence electoral choices. The vice president also did not have a decided advantage on position issues. On some such issues he was closer to voters, but on others Bush was closer and, generally, the differences were small. Again, there is no reason to believe allying himself closely with Clinton would have enabled Gore to reshape the policy space to his advantage.

In sum, although Gore may have made a strategic error in overestimating the costs of tying himself more closely to the Clinton record—particularly the president's successes with the economy, and a tactical one in not employing Clinton's still formidable skills as a campaigner—it is unlikely that Gore would have had a "lock" on the election if he had been willing to take greater advantage of the president's record. As just noted, many voters were undecided which party was best on important valence issues, and differences between voters and the candidates on position issues did not give a clear advantage to either Gore or Bush. Nevertheless, it is clearly the case that Gore's decision to distance himself from Clinton minimized an often-documented incumbent advantage on a powerful electoral fundamental: a buoyant economy. In addition, by severing himself from the Clinton record, Gore made his behavior on the campaign trail a determinative consideration in his quest for the White House. Rather than running as an incumbent, he ran as a challenger.

As is the norm in presidential elections, candidate images had highly significant effects in 2000. We have argued that a key component of valence politics to which national election campaigns are heavily freighted is the importance of leader image as a heuristic device for voters concerned about what the future might bring. In fact, many voters had positive images of Al Gore. However, and contrary to a basic assumption of strategists in the Gore camp, many voters also had positive images of George W. Bush. And, on the key trait of strong leadership, the canonical ANES data say Bush bested Gore.

Gore's strategy placed a premium on his ability to use the campaign to convince the electorate that he indeed had the "right stuff" to be president. In particular, the presidential debates presented a major opportunity to demonstrate his superiority over a man the Gore team dismissed as an unworthy rival. Gore blew it. The debates and their subsequent interpretation by the media did nothing to enhance and much to dull the lustre of the vice president's image as a leader into whose hands the nation should be trusted for the next four years. Although it must remain in the ever hazy realm of historical counterfactuals, if the debates had affected public perceptions of the candidates in the way that Gore and his advisors had anticipated, there is good reason to believe his electoral fate would have been a comfortable victory rather than a bitter defeat.

Notes

1   In 2000 respondents were randomly chosen to receive the prospective and retrospective questions about their own economic situation in either the pre- or post-wave of the survey. Respondents were also chosen at random to either receive the batteries of questions asking about improvements and declines in key policy areas over the 1992–2000 period and Clinton's responsibility for the state of affairs across policy domains in either the pre- or post-election study. For all "split" batteries, we present results from the full sample using the combined pre-post summary variables provided in the ANES dataset and codebook.

2   Respondents were asked how they thought the state of the economy, budget deficit, national security, crime rate, and moral climate in 2000 were "compared to 1992," the year Clinton was elected to office. Each question had five response categories and high responses (coded five) indicated that the respondent thought that the moral climate, crime rate, and economy had gotten "much better," the

nation had gotten "much more secure," and the budget deficit had gotten "much smaller." Responses coded four thought that national trends in each of the areas had improved "somewhat," and respondents refusing to answer the question or who did not know how to answer the question, or those believing that there was no change during the Clinton era were coded at the mid-point value of three. Respondents judging that progress in the policy domain had taken a turn for the worse (or that the budget deficit was larger and the nation less secure) were coded two, if the respondent indicated that there was "somewhat" of a decline, and coded one if they reported things as getting "much" worse.

3   Respondents were also asked about "Clinton's effect" on each policy domain mentioned in endnote two. Response categories and coding are the same as described above.

4   A random half-sample of respondents to the 2000 ANES were asked the open-ended question: "What do you think are the most important problems facing this country?" Those providing multiple answers to the question were subsequently asked to pick the most important of the issues and to evaluate how good a job the government in Washington was "doing dealing with this problem." Respondents could answer that the incumbent government was doing a "good" (coded three), "fair" (coded two), or "poor" (coded one) job. Respondents also were asked which party was best on the issue they deemed most important. Since only a half-sample was asked to designate a "best party," we include the "party best" variable only in an auxiliary multivariate analysis (see Appendix 5.A after the endnotes).

5   "Other social issues" included responses often disproportionately provided by conservatives, such as abortion and problems with the values of the youth. Those giving such responses were likely to disapprove of the administration's overall approval of handling social issues (see Table 5.1).

6   According to Gore's vice presidential biography produced by the Senate Historical Office and available online, even President Clinton chimed in and described Gore as a "most powerful" vice president.

7   As was the case in 2004, respondents could respond that a trait described Gore or Bush "extremely well," "quite well," "not too well," or "not well at all." Trait variables had a range of one to five. Maximum scores signified that the respondent thought the positive trait described the candidate extremely well or that a negative trait described the candidate not well at all. Respondents that did not evaluate a candidate on a trait were given a score of three. Separate principal components analyses (PCAs) of both Gore and Bush's seven traits indicated that the traits could be seen as a consequence of a single latent dimension (the latent factors for both Bush and Gore each had a single eigenvalue (λ) slightly above 3.40). For each candidate, all of the positive traits had loadings greater than .70. Negatively worded traits had slightly more modest loadings (range = .48–.57), with question wording a possible culprit for the additional unexplained variance for this group of traits.

8   Each of the spatial issue questions in the 2000 ANES was subject to branching experiments with some respondents receiving the standard seven-point range between extreme policy positions to place

themselves and the candidates. A randomly selected experimental group received a "branched format" of the policy question where they were asked their position on the issue before receiving a follow-up question probing the intensity of their position. The experimental group was also asked to estimate Gore's and Bush's positions on the issues using this format. For comparability across subject pools, the liberal-conservative question was recoded to a five-point scale: "strong" liberals were coded one; "not strong" liberals were coded two; "not strong" conservatives coded four; and "strong" conservatives coded five. Moderates, including those that reported an ideological direction "if they had to choose" were coded three. Other questions were also reduced to five-point scales, but abortion retained its standard four-point scale described in endnote eight in Chapter Four. Before modelling the issue space, we multiplied the absolute distance between the candidates and the candidates on the abortion question by 5/4 to match the five-point scale used for the other policy questions for 2000.

9   The eigenvalues (λ) for the position issue dimensions are as follows: Bush New Deal = 2.5; Bush Base = 1.0; Gore New Deal = 2.6; and Gore Women's Issues = 1.1. All factors are scored after verimax rotation.

10 The final religiosity variable was the respondents' factor scores extracted after a PCA of three variables: frequency of prayer, church attendance, and belief in the authenticity of the Bible. Responses to these questions were assigned the same values given to responses in 2004 (see endnote 13 in Chapter Four). The PCA yielded a single factor ($\lambda = 1.9$), and each of the three indicator variables had loadings greater than .74.

11 Respondents' answers to the four questions covering their assessments of their own and the nation's prospective and retrospective economic situations were given the same values assigned to the questions in Chapter Four (see endnote nine). The eigenvalue (λ) for the personal economic evaluations factor was 1.6, and the eigenvalue (λ) for the national economic evaluations factor was 1.0. The questions have rotated loadings on their respective factors that ranged from 0.63 to 0.66.

12 As was the case for our analyses of the 2004 models of the vote, we follow Miller (1991) and only consider the respondents to be Democratic and Republican identifiers if they said so when asked the first branch of the standard ANES party identification question.

13 The PCA of the four Clinton performance questions yielded eigenvalues (λ) of 2.1 for the factor containing Clinton's performance on the economy and crime questions and .8 for the factor containing the moral climate-national security questions. The rotated factor loadings of the questions on their respective dimensions ranged from .72 to .89.

14 The "party best on most important issue" data are available for only a random half-sample of 2000 ANES respondents. Since "party best" variables are typically major players in valence politics models of electoral choice, we replicated the multivariate analyses for this half-sample and included

Republican and Democratic "party best" dummy variables. The results show that both of these variables have significant effects on voting behavior net of all other considerations, including Clinton performance evaluations. The half-sample composite model is presented in Appendix 5.A.

15 As was the case with the analyses of the 2004 data, for scenarios where the impact of a specific dichotomous variable was not being considered, we assumed that the respondent was white, female, Independent, secular, and from the Northeast.

APPENDIX 5.A COMPOSITE MODEL OF FACTORS AFFECTING VOTING FOR GEORGE W. BUSH IN THE 2000 PRESIDENTIAL ELECTION INCLUDING PARTY BEST ON MOST IMPORTANT ISSUE

	B	S.E.
Predictor Variables		
Valence Politics:		
Clinton Performance:		
General	-0.95***	.24
Moral Climate	-0.46*	.23
Party Best Most Important Issue:		
Democrats	-1.85***	.60
Republicans	1.50*	.67
Leader Image:		
Gore Traits	-0.73**	.30
Bush Traits	1.04***	.30
Policy Spaces:		
Bush Base	1.10***	.31
Bush New Deal	1.33***	.35
Gore New Deal	-1.28***	.36
Gore Women	-0.82***	.25
Party Identification:		
Democrat	-1.58***	.52
Republican	2.11***	.63
Economic Evaluations:		
Personal–Retrospective & Prospective	0.15	.27
National–Retrospective & Prospective	0.03	.27
Demographics:		
Age	-0.01	.01
Gender	0.06	.50
Income	0.03	.06
Race: African American	-3.48***	1.01
Hispanic	-1.99*	1.12
Other	-2.14*	1.03
Region: North Central	-0.84	.61
South	-0.26	.63
West	-1.64*	.70
Religion: Catholic	-0.32	.85
Protestant	-0.53	.83
Other	-0.13	1.51
Religiosity	0.19	.41
Religiosity x Protestant	-0.92	.56
Constant	0.44	.74

McFadden R^2 = .76   McKelvey R^2 = .93

Per Cent Correctly Classified = 93.2, λ = .86   AIC = 236.81

N = 547 (random half-sample of ANES respondents)

*** p < .001; ** p < .01; * p < .05; one-tailed test.
†—Akaike Information Criterion (AIC)—smaller values indicate better model performance.

CHAPTER SIX

A Big Blue Wave

The 2006 American Congressional Election

Despite the often-quoted conventional wisdom, perhaps best articulated by former Democratic Speaker of the House of Representatives Tip O'Neil that "all politics are local," in fact some are not. This was cogently argued by David Brady (1978) in a study of how congressional election outcomes affect public policy. The former speaker's wisdom to the contrary notwithstanding, Brady observed that some congressional elections become "nationalized," usually over one or more highly salient "hot button" issues that have failed to be resolved over the years. Illustrative of such issues are the extension of slavery to the territories, which climaxed in 1860 with the election of Lincoln and the Civil War; the changes brought by industrialization that sparked controversies such as those over tariffs and bimetallism, which came to a head in 1896 with the election of McKinley; and the protracted economic hardships of the Great Depression that led to the election of Franklin D. Roosevelt in 1932 and the New Deal. In this chapter, we will argue that the congressional election of 2006 was such a nationalized contest. In 2006 the focus was on President George Bush and the major issues were the Iraq War and several sordid scandals involving Republican members of Congress and other prominent political figures allied with the GOP.[1]

As the war in Iraq dragged on into its third year, Americans increasingly began to compare it with the ill-fated war in Vietnam some four decades earlier.[2] Just as President Johnson's public support diminished as the Vietnamese conflict escalated, so did President Bush's. Bush's approval rating in monthly Gallup polls had reached almost 90 per cent shortly after 9/11 in the autumn of 2001 and stood at 70 per cent in April 2003, immediately after the invasion of Iraq. However, it then declined to 49 per cent just before the November 2004 presidential election. The slide continued, with Bush's approval rating falling to 37 per cent when voters went to the polls in November 2006 (see Figure 6.1).

Although analogies between Iraq and Vietnam were frequently made by the press and public alike, perhaps a more appropriate comparison of the erosion of Bush's popularity because of Iraq would be with the decline of former President Harry Truman's support during the Korean War. Iraq and Korea were major military conflicts and, in both cases, American involvement was largely a result of decisions made by the president. Although the Korean War began disastrously, American forces soon drove the North Koreans out of South Korea. US troops then continued into

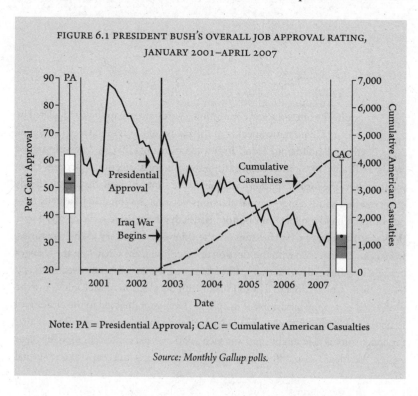

FIGURE 6.1 PRESIDENT BUSH'S OVERALL JOB APPROVAL RATING, JANUARY 2001–APRIL 2007

Note: PA = Presidential Approval; CAC = Cumulative American Casualties

Source: Monthly Gallup polls.

the North until they approached the Chinese border. This prompted China to enter the war. After "human wave" attacks by hundreds of thousands of Chinese troops forced a humiliating American retreat, the military situation eventually stabilized at the North-South border (the 38th parallel) where the conflict began. President Truman's political position during the conflict was seriously weakened after he fired highly popular General Douglas MacArthur, the commander of American forces in the Pacific during World War II. Truman had appointed MacArthur as supreme commander of the largely American United Nations forces under whose auspices the Korean War was ostensibly fought (Manchester, 1978).

Unlike Harry Truman and George W. Bush who in a real sense initiated US involvement in what became unpopular wars, Lyndon B. Johnson inherited a deteriorating military situation in which his country was already involved. Although Johnson is still regarded as the most powerful and effective Senate majority leader in American history, he was not widely known outside the Washington Beltway during his tenure on Capitol Hill (Caro, 2002). To the extent that he was, he was regarded as a Southern conservative oil and gas senator from a Southern oil and gas state, Texas. That perception quickly changed when he succeeded to the presidency in 1963 after the assassination of President Kennedy. Actions such as the passage of the Civil Rights Bill of 1964, the agreement with the Soviets to stop atmospheric testing of nuclear weapons, and the beginning of the War on Poverty showed that Johnson was an activist president with an ambitious and wide-ranging political agenda (Dallek, 1999).

In November 1964, Johnson won one of the most lopsided election victories in American history, besting the conservative Republican, Senator Barry Goldwater. Although it seemed at the time that Johnson could do "no political wrong," events soon conspired against him. Making a decision that eventually helped drive him from office, Johnson followed the advice of his defense secretary, Robert McNamara, and ordered a dramatic increase in US military support for the embattled South Vietnamese government. Thereafter, his approval ratings trended downward, just a Truman's had at the time of Korea, and Bush's would some 40 years later.

Figure 6.2 illustrates the erosion both Truman's and Johnson's approval suffered from the time they took office after their respective elections in 1948 and 1964, to their key decisions on Korea and Vietnam, to their exits from office after 1952 and 1968 presidential elections. As Figures 6.2A and 6.2B indicate, Truman and Johnson received similar approval ratings after their respective victories in 1948 and 1964. For a variety of reasons that need not be elaborated here, Truman's numbers had already "gone south" when he decided to repel the North Korean invasion, whereas Johnson continued to enjoy widespread public support in the summer of 1965 when the American escalation in Vietnam began. However, only one year later, Johnson's popularity had fallen by more than 20 points (to 48 per cent). And, as Figure 6.2A

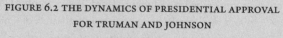

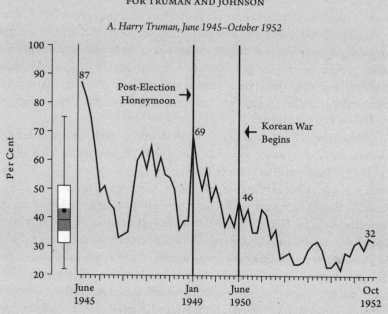

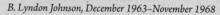

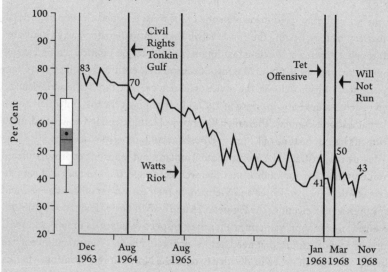

shows, Truman's approval had sunk even lower by the summer of 1951 (to 25 per cent). Although Truman's poll numbers were truly dismal when he left office in January 1953, subsequently he has become a venerated political icon, claimed by Democrat and Republican presidents alike as their model and spiritual guide. In contrast, Johnson remains unclaimed and, to a great extent, unloved. Whether presidential scholars and presidents alike will someday extol the current president, George W. Bush, as an exemplary role model, one can only speculate.

A MID-TERM REFERENDUM ON AN EMBATTLED PRESIDENT

We argue that the 2006 election was, in great part, a referendum on President Bush. We do this recognizing that many observers claim that the most important variables in congressional elections, particularly off-year ones, are incumbency, the balance of Democratic and Republican party identifiers in the congressional districts, and the resources, especially financial, available to the local candidates (e.g., Cover, 1977; Green and Krasno, 1988; Tufte, 1975). These resources enable incumbent members of Congress to perform a variety of electorally beneficial advertising, credit-claiming, and position-taking activities (Mayhew, 1974). In turn, these activities contribute to shaping public opinion such that voters "love their (local) congressmen" even if, as is often the case, they simultaneously hold a low opinion of Congress as a whole (e.g., Fenno, 1978).

In earlier chapters we have investigated the explanatory power of three alternative models of electoral choice—the valence model, the position issue/issue proximity model, and the sociological model. The latter emphasizes the importance of factors such as gender, race, region, religion, and social class. As elaborated by social psychologists at the University of Michigan, social characteristics acquire political relevance via voters' acquisition of highly durable attachments to political parties (Campbell et al., 1960; Miller and Shanks, 1996). These attachments are correlated with sociological characteristics such that, for example, overwhelming percentages of African Americans identify with the Democratic Party, and large numbers of middle-class white men identify with the Republican Party.

Unlike variants of the sociological model, the issue-proximity model is premised on the assumption that voters are rational, utility-maximizing actors who determine which party or candidate is closest to them on specific "pro-con" issues and more general ideological orientations (e.g., Downs, 1957; Adams, Merrill, and Grofman, 2005). Calculations of distances between voters' "ideal points" and party locations in issue/ideological space are what drive electoral choice. According to the valence model, the issues that matter are of a different sort. As discussed in earlier chapters, election agendas tend to be dominated by issues for which there is almost universal public agreement about what is desirable. Political debate concerns "means" not "ends," i.e., which candidate, leader, and party is best able to achieve consensually agreed-upon goals (Clarke et al., 1996; Stokes, 1963, 1992). Partisan attachments are also important in the valence model, but party identifications are not "fixed in stone" as social psychologists in Ann Arbor would have one believe. Rather, many voters have flexible party ties, and they update their partisanship in light of ongoing party and leader performance evaluations (e.g., Clarke et al., 2004).

JOB PERFORMANCE EVALUATIONS

Pace observers who tout the strength of local factors in congressional elections, we contend that the 2006 election was largely a referendum on President Bush's performance. Although widespread unhappiness with the president's handling of the Iraq War was especially important, we will also demonstrate that he received low grades for his performance on other salient issues, including terrorism, immigration, and the economy. Adverse judgments about the economy must have been especially perplexing to Bush and his advisors since objective indicators pointed to only modest levels of unemployment and inflation. Moreover, the stock market was putting money in investors' pocketbooks by moving upward to levels not seen since

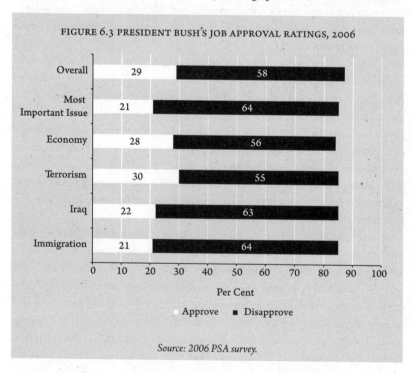

FIGURE 6.3 PRESIDENT BUSH'S JOB APPROVAL RATINGS, 2006

Source: 2006 PSA survey.

before the post-9/11 meltdown. Although significant, widespread negativism about the performance of the Bush administration was not the only factor working against the Republicans in 2006. Another feature of the election, one that had its parallel in the 2006 Canadian federal election discussed in Chapter Two, was a series of widely publicized scandals involving Republican candidates and other public figures with close ties to the GOP. Before discussing public reactions to these events, we consider Bush's approval ratings, and how his party fared on key issues.

Figure 6.3 illustrates how respondents in the 2006 Political Support in America (PSA) survey rated the president's performance.[3] Less than three in 10 (29 per cent) approved of Bush's overall performance in office, whereas nearly six in 10 (58 per cent) disapproved.[4] Bush's dismal overall rating rested on a number of specifics—the economy on which 56 per cent disapproved; on terrorism, which was so important in his re-election two years earlier, on which 55 per cent disapproved; on Iraq on which 63 per cent disapproved; and on his position on immigration on which 64 per cent of the public disapproved. On the issue respondents deemed most important, 64 per cent again disapproved. Failing job performance grades were clearly the norm for the president in 2006.

As observed, the president's failure to receive credit for his management of the economy must have mystified his advisors given that objective economic conditions

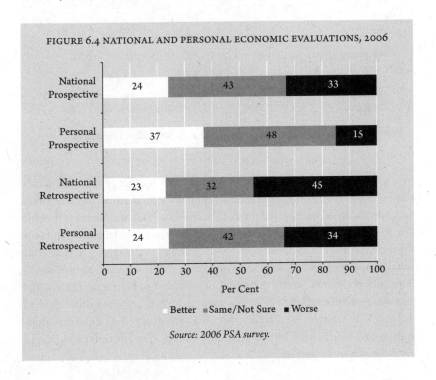

FIGURE 6.4 NATIONAL AND PERSONAL ECONOMIC EVALUATIONS, 2006

Source: 2006 PSA survey.

TABLE 6.1 PRESIDENT BUSH'S JOB EVALUATIONS BY PARTY IDENTIFICATION, 2006 CONGRESSIONAL ELECTION STUDY

| | PARTY IDENTIFICATION | | | |
	REPUBLICAN	DEMOCRAT	OTHER	INDEPENDENT
Job Evaluation				
Overall:				
Approve	72%	7%	22%	19%
Neither	14	8	14	19
Disapprove	14	85	65	62
Most Important Issue:				
Approve	54%	5%	16%	13%
Neither	20	8	17	18
Disapprove	25	87	67	69
Economy:				
Approve	70%	8%	28%	19%
Neither	18	8	11	20
Disapprove	13	84	61	62
Immigration:				
Approve	35%	7%	9%	11%
Neither	33	25	22	30
Disapprove	33	68	69	59
Iraq:				
Approve	59%	5%	19%	14%
Neither	19	7	13	18
Disapprove	23	88	68	67
Terrorism:				
Approve	72%	9%	25%	21%
Neither	14	12	15	20
Disapprove	15	79	61	60

Note: *Vertical percentages; percentages may not sum to 100 because of rounding.*

were quite positive. Still, the survey data clearly indicate that people were decidedly less than enthusiastic about the economy and their personal financial situation. Specifically, 45 per cent judged that the economy had worsened over the past year. An additional 32 per cent believed the economy had stayed the same, and only 23 per cent judged that it had improved (see Figure 6.4).[5] As usual (e.g., Clarke et al., 2004; Krause, 1997), people were somewhat more sanguine about their own conditions. Still, one-third reported that their pocketbooks had been squeezed over the past year, two-fifths said their situations were unchanged, and one-quarter claimed that they were better off. Similar patterns characterized judgments about the future, with positive judgments about national and personal economic conditions being a distinctly minority viewpoint.

As demonstrated in earlier chapters, judgments about the candidates are strongly correlated with voters' partisan attachments. As anticipated, in the 2000 and 2004 presidential elections Republican identifiers generally gave the Republican candidate, Bush, higher grades. Democrats gave him much lower ones, and self-identified Independents, arguably the most objective reviewers, fell in between. However, what must have been particularly troubling to the administration in 2006 was that judgments offered by Independents were much harsher than they had been only two years earlier. With respect to overall presidential approval ratings, Table 6.1 shows that 72 per cent of Republican identifiers gave Bush a favorable rating, as opposed to only 7 per cent of Democratic identifiers and 19 per cent of Independents. Similarly, although 54 per cent of the Republican identifiers approved of his performance on what they regarded as their most important issue in the election, only very small minorities of Democrats (5 per cent) and Independents (13 per cent) did so. Even on the "War on Terror," an issue that worked strongly in the president's favor in the 2004 election among Independents and even among some Democratic partisans, only 9 per cent of Democratic identifiers and only 21 per cent of Independents gave him a favorable evaluation in 2006. In contrast, fully 72 per cent of Republican identifiers approved of how the president was dealing with the issue. Similarly, large differences between Republicans and the rest of the country characterized evaluations of how the president had handled immigration, the Iraq War, and the economy.

Given strong partisan differences in evaluations of presidential job performance on the economy, it is not surprising that partisanship was strongly correlated with people's judgments about the health of the economy and their personal financial circumstances. Whereas 51 per cent of Republican identifiers said the economy had improved over the past year and 39 per cent said the same of their own financial condition, comparable percentages for Democrats were 9 per cent and 18 per cent, and for Independents 16 per cent and 19 per cent (see Table 6.2). As for the future, 48 per cent of Republicans said the economy would get better in the next year or so, and 50 per cent made the same judgment about their own economic position. In contrast, less than one in five Democrats or Independents were optimistic about the economy's future, and only three in 10 were sanguine that their own position would evolve.

IMPORTANT (VALENCE) ISSUES

A key piece of evidence supporting the valence politics model concerns the kinds of issues voters emphasize. When given the opportunity to select which election issues are most important, they regularly cite valence rather than position issues. As Table 6.3 shows, this tendency was readily apparent in 2006. Overall, only one PSA survey respondent in 20 mentioned a position issue other than Iraq.[6] Yet even

TABLE 6.2 ECONOMIC EVALUATIONS BY PARTY IDENTIFICATION,
2006 CONGRESSIONAL ELECTION STUDY

| | PARTY IDENTIFICATION | | | |
Economic Evaluation	REPUBLICAN	DEMOCRAT	OTHER	INDEPENDENT
Personal Retrospective:				
Better	39%	18%	28%	19%
Same	40	42	39	45
Worse	22	40	33	37
National Retrospective:				
Better	51%	9%	27%	16%
Same	31	30	28	35
Worse	18	61	46	49
Personal Prospective:				
Better	50%	31%	47%	31%
Same	42	52	40	50
Worse	8	17	13	19
National Prospective:				
Better	48%	14%	16%	16%
Same	39	44	50	44
Worse	13	43	34	39

Note: Vertical percentages; percentages may not sum to 100 because of rounding.

Iraq was acquiring valence characteristics; over three-fifths of those surveyed in Gallup polls conducted in 2006 stated that they opposed the war. In the 2006 PSA pre-election survey, Iraq dominated the issue agenda, with 35 per cent citing it as a key concern. As indicated in Table 6.3, virtually all of the other issues were valence ones, but all were cited by relatively small numbers of respondents. Specifically, the economy, crime, terrorism, health care, and the environment were cited by 2 per cent to 15 per cent of those surveyed.

On several of these issues, the Democratic Party was judged superior to its Republican rival.[7] For example, the Democrats were favored by large margins on Iraq, the economy, health care, the environment, and various social issues which collectively accounted for over three-fifths of all issues mentioned. The Republicans led on immigration, terrorism, crime, national security, and miscellaneous position issues, but collectively these issues were cited by only three out of 10 survey respondents. Altogether, the Democratic issue edge over the Republicans was sizable (34 per cent to 24 per cent), with another 36 per cent stating that no party was best on the most important issue or they did not know which one was best. With less than one person

TABLE 6.3 MOST IMPORTANT ISSUE FACING THE COUNTRY
AND PARTY BEST ABLE TO HANDLE IT, 2006

| | PARTY | | | | |
| | | | | NONE | |
Issue	DEMOCRAT	REPUBLICAN	OTHER	DK	TOTAL
Economy	37	17	7	39	15
Health	42	10	7	42	7
Other Social	34	14	13	40	4
Iraq	45	16	3	36	35
Immigration	7	50	10	34	5
Terrorism	13	62	2	23	12
Crime	8	13	0	78	1
National Security	20	36	7	37	7
Scandals, Leadership	54	6	11	29	9
Environment	29	0	12	58	2
All Position Issues	17	43	9	31	5
Miscellaneous	42	15	10	33	9
Total Party Best	34	24	6	36	

Source: 2006 PSA pre-election survey.

in four preferring their party on important issues, and large majorities giving their party's leader, President Bush, failing grades, Republican congressional candidates were in a distinctly disadvantageous position as they traversed the campaign trail in 2006.

POSITION ISSUES

Although the salience of valence issues was readily apparent in 2006, the power of position issues cannot be summarily dismissed. Indeed, some observers (e.g., Hunter, 1991, 1994; Frank, 2004) have described the contemporary United States as two ideological nations—one conservative, one liberal—warring within the bosom of a single state. PSA survey data indicate that the liberal, or at least left-of-center, group was somewhat larger than the conservative right-of-center one in 2006. When presented with a 10-point scale anchored by the options of spending much more or much less on defense, 46 per cent put themselves on the "spend less" (liberal) side of the scale, and 32 per cent put themselves on the "spend more" (conservative) side. The remainder (22 per cent) located themselves at the middle of the scale. The division on a 10-point, "tax less-spend less on services" versus "tax more-spend more on services" scale was more evenly balanced, with 39 per cent on the liberal "tax and spend" side,

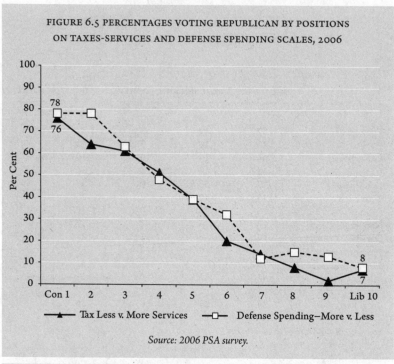

FIGURE 6.5 PERCENTAGES VOTING REPUBLICAN BY POSITIONS ON TAXES-SERVICES AND DEFENSE SPENDING SCALES, 2006

Source: 2006 PSA survey.

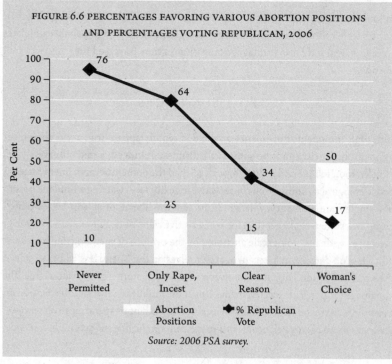

FIGURE 6.6 PERCENTAGES FAVORING VARIOUS ABORTION POSITIONS AND PERCENTAGES VOTING REPUBLICAN, 2006

Source: 2006 PSA survey.

and 36 per cent on the conservative "cut and cut" side. The remainder (26 per cent) were at the mid-point of the scale.[8] As illustrated by Figure 6.5, positions on these two scales were strongly correlated with voting for the House of Representatives in 2006. Over three-quarters of those placing themselves at the conservative end of the two scales voted Republican as compared to less than one in 10 of those placing themselves at the liberal end of the scales.

These patterns are repeated for the abortion issue, a continuing matter of bitter contention in American politics since 1973, when the Supreme Court concluded in its *Roe v. Wade* decision that laws against abortion violated a woman's right to privacy under the due process clause of the Fourteenth Amendment to the Constitution. In the 2006 PSA survey, 50 per cent said that women should be able to make their own decisions about whether to terminate a pregnancy, and a further 15 per cent said that abortions should be permitted if a "clear reason" could be established (see Figure 6.6). One person in four wanted to restrict abortion to situations where rape or incest had occurred, and only one in 10 wanted to outlaw abortions completely.[9] Positions on abortion were strongly related to voting, with the percentage opting for a Republican House candidate declining from 76 per cent among those wishing to outlaw abortions entirely to 17 per cent among those wishing to make the termination of pregnancy a woman's choice. Later in this chapter, we will see if these strong statistical relationships between voters' locations on position issues and their electoral choices are sustained in multivariate models that control for other potentially influential factors.

SCANDALOUS BEHAVIOR

Scandals often have a relatively short shelf life in American politics. However, in 2006 there was reason to believe that lurid tales involving Republican members of Congress and their financial and ideological supporters may have had a substantial impact on the vote. Although several scandals made national headlines, the two most widely publicized cases involved prominent lobbyist Jack Abramoff and Congressman Mark Foley. In the early months of 2006, Abramoff, an influential "fixer" and long-time Republican activist with contacts at the highest levels of government, was tried and convicted on five criminal charges involving fraud and corruption of public officials. Foley, Republican congressman for Florida's 16th District, resigned in late September 2006 after it was revealed that he had sent sexually suggestive e-mails and text messages to teenage boys whom he had met when they were congressional pages. The political fallout from the case multiplied when it became known that Republican leaders in Congress had been advised about Foley's possible misconduct long before the scandal broke. The clear implication was that they were aware of the situation and had done nothing.

FIGURE 6.7 REACTIONS TO REPUBLICAN SCANDALS

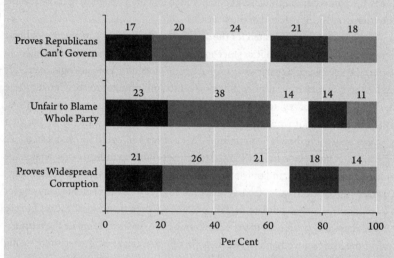

A. *Evaluating the Scandals*

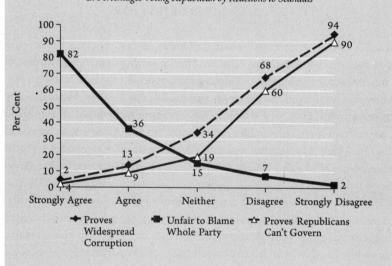

B. *Percentages Voting Republican by Reactions to Scandals*

Source: 2006 PSA survey.

In the 2006 PSA survey, we posed three questions to gauge public reactions to the scandals.[10] The responses summarized in Figure 6.7A indicate that 37 per cent of the PSA respondents strongly agreed or agreed with the statement that the scandals prove that Republicans cannot govern. Perhaps more damning was that fully 47 per cent agreed that the scandals were proof of "widespread corruption in the Republican party." These negative attitudes towards Republicans were mitigated somewhat by the 61 per cent who said it was unfair to blame the entire party for the scandals, as opposed to the 25 per cent who judged that blame was warranted. In sum, although the willingness to attribute blame was not pervasive, there was a sizable group of voters who were ready to castigate the Republicans for the illegal and unethical behavior of their friends and colleagues.

As might be expected, reactions of Democratic and Republican identifiers to the scandals were virtually mirror images of one another. For example, on the question of whether there was widespread corruption within the Republican Party, 70 per cent of Democrats agreed as opposed to only 10 per cent of Republicans. On the issue of whether the scandals indicated that the Republicans were unable to govern, 60 per cent of the Democrats agreed as opposed to only 6 per cent of Republicans. Finally, on the issue of whether it was unfair to blame the entire Republican Party for the actions of relatively few, whereas 90 per cent of the Republicans agreed with that statement and only 4 per cent disagreed, fully 44 per cent of Democrats agreed that it was fair as opposed to the 39 per cent who disagreed. As was the case with other issues, Independents were much closer to the views of the Democrats than they were to the Republicans.

Analyses suggest that voters' reactions to the scandals may well have mattered. Figure 6.7B shows that the percentage of people voting Republican diminished substantially as judgments about the affairs became increasingly negative. For example, among those strongly agreeing that the scandals prove the existence of widespread corruption in the Republican Party, less than one person in 20 voted Republican. However, among those disagreeing strongly with this proposition, more than nine in 10 cast a GOP ballot. The pattern for those agreeing or disagreeing with the statement that the scandals prove the Republicans cannot govern effectively is identical. Also, as one would expect, the pattern is exactly opposite when voters are divided according to their responses to the question about whether it is fair to blame the whole Republican Party. Among those who say blame was warranted, only one in 50 voted Republican, whereas among those who say it was unfair to blame the entire party, over eight in 10 opted for the GOP. Below, we will determine if these strong bivariate relationships hold up when other influential factors are brought into play.

FIGURE 6.8 TRENDS IN PARTY IDENTIFICATION, JANUARY 2001–APRIL 2007

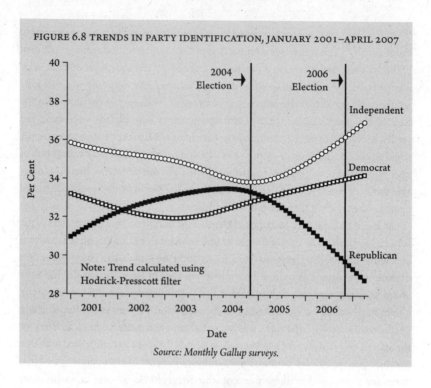

Source: Monthly Gallup surveys.

PARTY IDENTIFICATION: DONKEY RISING, ELEPHANT FALLING

Another problem for Republican candidates in 2006 was that they were facing an electorate that was considerably more "Democratic" than had been the case in 2004. Figure 6.8 illustrates underlying trends in the Gallup measure of party identification since 2000.[11] As shown, the Democrats' edge over their GOP rivals was initially quite substantial. However, the GOP then closed the gap, and by 2004 had actually overtaken the Democrats. At that time both parties enjoyed the support of about one-third of the electorate. Thereafter, the Republican share quickly eroded, with the GOP decline being accompanied by modest increases in the numbers of Democratic identifiers and Independents. As observed in earlier chapters, sizable partisan dynamics such as those occurring over the relatively brief time interval between the 2004 and 2006 elections accord well with the idea that party identification has flexible qualities, changing in response to an ongoing stream of information about the performance of political parties and their leaders.

Some analysts (e.g., Bishop et al., 1994) discount evidence on the dynamics of party identification provided by Gallup polls because Gallup asks a party identification question that is slightly different than the one asked in the American National

TABLE 6.4 INDIVIDUAL-LEVEL DYNAMICS OF PARTY IDENTIFICATION, 2004–2006

		2004			
		DEMOCRAT	INDEPENDENT	REPUBLICAN	TOTAL
2006	Democrat	91.3%	30.4%	11.8%	43.6%
	Independent	6.8	53.8	13.3	26.0
	Republican	1.9	15.8	74.9	30.4
	Total	31.5	36.5	32.1	100.0
		(207)	(240)	(211)	(658)

Source: 2004–2006 ANES pilot survey.

Election Study (ANES) surveys.[12] However, data from the 2004–06 ANES panel survey that poses the traditional party identification question also indicates substantial partisan instability, with nearly three people in 10 (28 per cent) moving between parties or shifting between partisanship and independence. The pattern of movement in the ANES data is somewhat different from that revealed by the Gallup surveys, but the result for the balance of partisan forces is basically the same. The ANES data show the Democrats as big winners, with the number of Democratic identifiers growing by fully 12 per cent between 2004 and 2006. As Table 6.4 documents, the Democrats held onto 91 per cent of their 2004 identifiers, and gained 12 per cent of the 2004 Republicans and fully 30 per cent of the 2004 Independents. In contrast, one-quarter of the 2004 Republicans changed their partisanship by 2006, and nearly half of 2004 Independents also did so. Many in the latter group migrated to the Democrats. This pattern of big net Democratic gains in party identification is exactly what one would expect in a context of widespread unhappiness with the performance of an incumbent GOP administration, a liberal tilt in the balance of opinion on major position issues, and massive negative publicity about scandals involving prominent Republicans.

LOVE AND LOATHING ON THE CAMPAIGN TRAIL?

One very interesting feature of American public opinion, according to congressional scholar Richard Fenno (1978) is that Americans traditionally have held their local members of Congress in high regard, but have had a low opinion of Congress as an institution. The PSA survey data indicate that Fenno's widely cited observation was an exaggeration in 2006. As shown in Figure 6.9A, 41 per cent of the PSA respondents reported that their local representative was doing a "very good job" or a "good job," but nearly as many, 36 per cent, said "bad job" or "very bad job." The comparable figures for Congress as a whole are 22 per cent and 65 per cent (see Figure 6.10).[13] Thus, while it appears that Fenno's characterization of public opinion about Congress continued to be basically accurate, affection for local members of Congress was not especially widespread. Consonant with the generally sour mood that suffused the electorate in the run-up to the 2006 election, a sizable minority of the electorate was dissatisfied with the performance of both Congress and its members.

Since the majority of members of Congress before the 2006 election were Republicans, judgments about both the institution and individual incumbents were correlated to the Republican vote. Figure 6.9B indicates that in districts where incumbents were Republicans and were judged to be doing a very good job, they received 90 per cent of the vote. However, as evaluations of them became more negative the percentage of people voting Republican diminished sharply. Also, when incumbent Democrats were judged to be doing a very good job, the Republican opponents gained a meagre 11 per cent of the vote. As also expected, the proportion of people voting Republican increased as judgments about incumbent Democrats became more negative. However, this relationship was weaker, although nontrivial, in races where there was a Democratic incumbent. In these contests, the percentage voting Republican varied from a low of 11 per cent when a Democratic incumbent's performance was deemed very good, to 41 per cent when it was judged very bad. In open races, i.e., contests in which there was no incumbent, and thus there was no basis on which to judge, the correlation between job performance and the vote was weaker still. Thus, 30 per cent of those judging that their (former) representative had done a very good job voted Republican, but so did 25 per cent of those who judged that the representative had done a very bad job.

Finally, as Figure 6.10 illustrates, judgments about the performance of Congress also correlated with Republican voting in a predictable way. Among those evaluating the institution's performance positively, a substantial majority opted for the GOP, but among those evaluating the institution's performance negatively, less than four in 10 did so. Below, we will see if these patterns persist in a multivariate voting model.

BALANCING ACT?

The framers of the American Constitution were preoccupied with the dangers of concentrated political power, and were at pains to thwart what they called "the mischief of faction." Accordingly, they designed a set of governmental institutions that would curtail the exercise of power in the service of organized interests. Inspired by the ideas of James Madison, the framers established a federal system; divided political authority among the executive, legislative, and judicial branches of the national government; and created an intricate system of "checks and balances" to ensure that one branch would not dominate the others. With these institutional barriers in place,

FIGURE 6.9 EVALUATIONS OF PERFORMANCE OF INCUMBENT
REPRESENTATIVE AND PER CENT VOTING REPUBLICAN BY EVALUATIONS OF
PERFORMANCE OF MEMBER OF CONGRESS, 2006

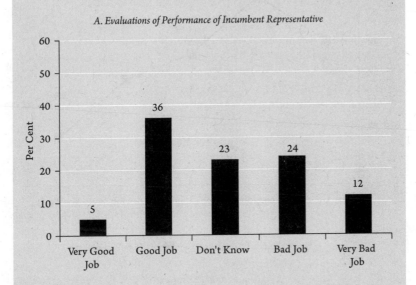

A. Evaluations of Performance of Incumbent Representative

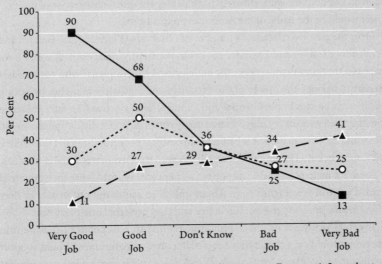

B. Per Cent Voting Republican by Evaluations of Performance of Member of Congress
Controlling for Party of Incumbent Member

Source: 2006 PSA survey.

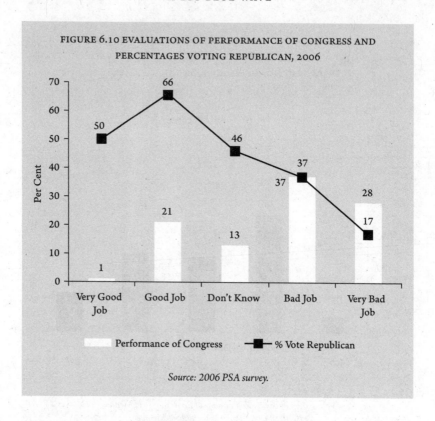

FIGURE 6.10 EVALUATIONS OF PERFORMANCE OF CONGRESS AND
PERCENTAGES VOTING REPUBLICAN, 2006

Source: 2006 PSA survey.

Madison and his colleagues ensured that blocking the unilateral exercise of political power would be the name of the American political game.

Over the past two decades, a number of observers (Fiorina, 1992; Garand and Lichtl, 2000; Carsey and Layman, 2004; but see Burden and Kimball, 2002) have proposed that American voters may be "electoral Madisonians" who consciously attempt to balance the power of the executive and legislative branches by voting for different parties in presidential and congressional elections. In fact, evidence from the 2006 PSA survey suggests that many voters do prefer divided government. When asked, "Do you think it is better when one party controls both the Presidency and Congress, better when control is split between the Democrats and Republicans, or doesn't it matter?" a sizable minority (45 per cent) reported that they preferred divided control (see Figure 6.11). About one-third said it did not matter or they "didn't know," and only one person in five said they preferred one-party rule.

If voters really act on these opinions, then with a Republican president in office one would expect that those preferring divided government would support Democratic candidates for Congress, and those preferring unified government would support Republican candidates. Figure 6.11 shows exactly this pattern, with the

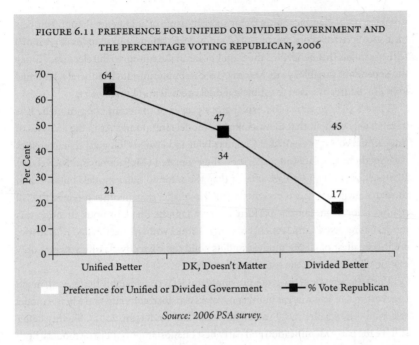

FIGURE 6.11 PREFERENCE FOR UNIFIED OR DIVIDED GOVERNMENT AND THE PERCENTAGE VOTING REPUBLICAN, 2006

Preference for Unified or Divided Government ■ ■ % Vote Republican

Source: 2006 PSA survey.

percentage voting Republican falling from 64 per cent among those favoring unified government to 17 per cent among those preferring divided government. Although statistically impressive, perhaps this pattern simply reflects voters using an abstract principle of American government—perhaps one that they dimly recall from their Political Science 101 courses—to rationalize choices made for other reasons. In the next section of this chapter, we will see if this is the case.

MODELLING THE VOTE

The 2006 PSA survey data enable us to assess the explanatory power of sociological, issue-proximity, and valence models of voting behavior in the 2006 congressional election. Given the heavy emphasis in studies of congressional elections on local effects in these contests, we also consider a model which specifies that the vote is a function of evaluations of the job performance of the local Member of Congress, whether one of the candidates is an incumbent, and campaign expenditures by rival Republican and Democratic candidates. The sociological model includes several demographic characteristics (age, education, ethnicity/race, gender, income, military status, religion, and religiosity).[14] In contrast, the issue-proximity model has only one predictor variable. This is a factor score generated by an exploratory factor analysis of the tax reduction-social services spending, defense spending, and abortion variables discussed above. We specify the valence model using the following variables: party identification, a factor-score measure of judgments about Bush's performance, a factor-score measure of economic evaluations, and an index of reactions to the scandals that bedevilled the Republicans in the run-up to the election.[15] Since the dependent variable is a dichotomy (vote Republican, vote Democrat), binomial logit procedures are used to estimate model coefficients (Long, 1997).

Table 6.5 summarizes the explanatory power of the competing models. It is immediately evident that the sociological model fares poorly. As in the analyses of presidential voting presented in Chapters Four and Five, sociological characteristics have mediocre explanatory capacity—the estimated (McFadden and McKelvey) R^2 statistics (Long, 1997) are smaller than those for all other models but one, and the percentage of voters correctly classified is smaller than in other models. The "all politics is local" model also performs poorly. Despite the enormous attention this model has received from students of congressional voting, its estimated R^2 statistics are the smallest of all the models, and its ability to correctly classify voters is only marginally better than the sociological model.

The performance of the issue-proximity model is considerably better, with much larger estimated R^2s, a larger number of voters classified correctly, and a better model selection (i.e., smaller AIC) value (Burnham and Anderson, 2002). Slightly better still are the party identification and party best on most important issue models. Both of these models are components of the larger valence politics model, which also

TABLE 6.5 RIVAL MODELS OF VOTING IN THE 2006 HOUSE OF REPRESENTATIVES ELECTIONS

MODEL	MCFADDEN R^2	MCKELVEY R^2	PER CENT CORRECTLY CLASSIFIED	AIC
Demographics	.13	.24	68.6	2097.73
Local (Incumbency, Congessman Evaluation Congressional District Campaign Spending)	.09	.16	70.4	2175.36
Issue Proximity (Liberal-Conservative)	.36	.55	81.3	1452.83
Party Identification	.40	.55	83.5	1429.41
Party Best on Most Important Issue	.46	.62	84.5	1292.93
Bush Performance, Economic Evaluations	.52	.64	87.7	1146.14
Bush Performance, Economic Evaluations, Scandals	.57	.71	89.3	1039.24
Composite Model, All Significant Predictors	.66	.80	91.0	832.77

†—Akaike Information Criterion (AIC)—smaller values indicate better model performance.

Note: Binomial logit analyses; Republican voting versus Democrat and other party/candidate voting.

includes judgments about the president's job performance, economic evaluations, and reactions to the Republican scandals. As Table 6.5 documents, these latter variables (i.e., job performance judgments, economic evaluations, reactions to scandals) collectively perform very well. Their model has the largest estimated R^2s, the best voter classification performance (over 89 per cent), and the smallest AIC value of any of the models considered thus far.

Although these results testify that key variables in the valence politics model have powerful effects, they do not have the playing field to themselves. Similar to presidential voting, a composite congressional voting model that includes all of the predictor variables provides the strongest explanation. As the bottom row of Table 6.5 shows, the composite model has the largest R^2s and is slightly better at correctly classifying how the voters behaved. Although the composite model is more elaborately parameterized (has more predictor variables), it performs best in terms of the AIC model selection criterion, which penalizes models according to the number of parameters estimated. Thus, the valence politics model of congressional voting does very well, but other models also contribute to the explanation.

The idea that models based on competing theoretical perspectives can contribute to explaining the vote gains force when one considers the detailed results of estimating the composite model. These results, displayed in Table 6.6, reveal that all of the core variables in the valence politics model, i.e., party identification, party best on important issues, and presidential performance evaluations, have statistically significant and properly signed coefficients. These variables are joined by economic evaluations and Republican scandals to form a congressional voting version of the valence politics model. However, as the table also shows, several other variables have significant effects. Issue-proximity effects work as advertised, i.e., people with more liberal positions on issues such as abortion, defense spending, and tax-social services trade-offs were less likely to vote Republican. The district-level variables favored by congressional scholars weigh in, too. Although campaign spending by the local candidates is not significant once other factors are controlled, having a Republican incumbent running as a candidate increases the likelihood of casting a Republican ballot. And positive evaluations of the performance of a local member of the House bolster the probability of supporting that candidate.

There are several other significant effects. A preference for unified rather than divided government enhances the chances of voting for a Republican candidate, a sensible result given the presence of a Republican president. Some demographic characteristics are significant as well. Older voters and better educated ones are less likely to support Republican candidates and Protestants and people in the "other" ethnicity/race category are more likely to do so.

How large are the effects of various predictor variables? Which ones are substantively, as well as statistically, significant? As in earlier chapters, we answer this

TABLE 6.6 COMPOSITE MODEL OF REPUBLICAN VOTING
IN THE 2006 HOUSE OF REPRESENTATIVES ELECTIONS

PREDICTOR	B	S.E.
Bush Performance Evaluations	0.87***	.16
Economic Evaluations	0.27***	.12
Republican Scandals	-0.20***	.05
Issue Proximity (Liberal-Conservative)	-0.46***	.15
Party Best Most Important Issue:		
Democrat	-0.95***	.32
Republican	0.57*	.28
Other Party	0.14	.43
Party Identification:		
Democrat	-1.39***	.31
Republican	0.62**	.25
Other Party	-0.16	.46
Evaluations:		
Representative	0.32***	.09
Congress	-0.06	.10
Electoral District Incumbency:		
Republican Incumbent	0.90***	.28
No Incumbent	0.65	.42
Electoral District Campaign Spending:		
Republican Candidate	-0.00	.00
Democratic Candidate	0.00	.00
Prefer Unified-Divided Government	0.44***	.13
Demographics:		
Age	-0.01*	.007
Education	-0.19*	.08
Ethnicity/Race:		
African American	-1.06	1.06
Asian	0.67	0.64
Hispanic	-0.44	0.64
Other	1.39***	0.44
Gender	-0.05	0.21
Income	-0.01	0.03
Military Status	-0.13	0.29
Religion: Protestant	0.56*	0.33
Catholic	0.47	0.37
Other	0.28	0.34
Religiosity	0.03	0.11
Constant	0.70	0.77

McFadden R^2 = .66, McKelvey R^2 = .80
Per Cent Correctly Classified = 91.0
Lambda = .76, AIC = 832.79

*** $p < .001$; ** $p < .01$; * $p < .05$; one-tailed test.
†—Akaike Information Criterion (AIC)—smaller values indicate better
model performance.

question with illustrative scenarios in which a predictor variable of interest is set at its lowest value while other predictors are held constant at their means or other plausible values.[16] The probability of voting Republican is calculated. Then that probability is recalculated when the predictor variable of interest is set at its highest value. The resulting changes in probability of voting for the GOP are displayed in Figure 6.12. These numbers emphasize the importance of President Bush's job performance evaluations for understanding why voters behaved as they did in 2006. *Ceteris paribus*, changing these evaluations from their lowest to their highest value increases the probability of voting Republican by fully 69 points. Other variables in the valence politics model have lesser, but still sizable, effects. Thus, changing economic evaluations can alter the probability of a Republican ballot by 28 points, selecting the Republicans rather than the Democrats as best on an important issue can alter the probability by 25 (13 + 12) points, and being a Republican rather than a Democratic Party identifier can do so by 32 (19 + 13) points. The scandals mattered

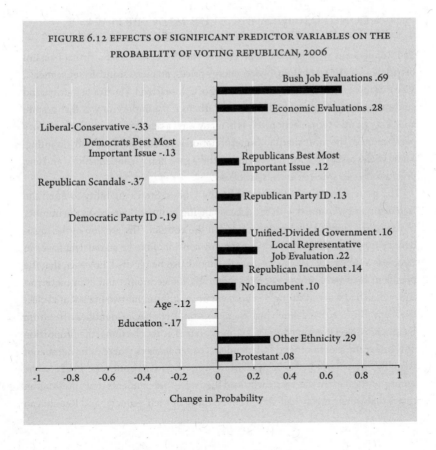

FIGURE 6.12 EFFECTS OF SIGNIFICANT PREDICTOR VARIABLES ON THE PROBABILITY OF VOTING REPUBLICAN, 2006

too. As opinions about what the scandals said about the Republican Party varied from positive to negative, the likelihood of a GOP vote decreased by fully 37 points.

Of the remaining significant predictors, position issues have the strongest impact. Changing one's location from liberal to conservative on the issue-proximity factor boosts the probability of a Republican vote by 33 points. Other variables have weaker effects. Other things equal, having a Republican incumbent and having a favorable evaluation of a local representative enhances the likelihood of choosing the GOP by 14 points and 22 points, respectively. A preference for unified rather than divided government increases that likelihood by 16 points. Demographic effects also tend to be relatively weak—their probability change scores average 17 points. Taken together, the numbers in Figure 6.12 underscore the point that the "big action" in congressional voting in 2006 had to do with the valence judgments voters were making about the president and his party. Unfortunately for Republican congressional candidates, these judgments tended to be very negative. *Pace*, Tip O'Neil, the politics that mattered most in 2006 were national, not local.

CONCLUSION: A BIG BLUE MID-TERM WAVE

The Republicans went into the 2006 congressional election after a virtual tsunami of bad news—the war in Iraq, higher energy prices, financial scandals, sex scandals, Vice President Chaney's accidental shooting of a close friend, Hurricane Katrina, and continuing budgetary and trade deficits. Perhaps most important was that despite 2006 being a mid-term election, it was in many ways a referendum on the president's performance. The most charitable interpretation is that the public found it wanting. Many voters assigned him a failing grade, others gave him a "gentleman's C," and few, precious few, awarded an enthusiastic pass.

The issue agenda was dominated by the United States' inability to quell the Iraq insurgency, coupled with the accompanying monthly increase in the number of American troops killed and wounded in the conflict. The erosion of the president's support, largely because of what many considered to be an outright fiasco in Iraq, was a key factor driving the vote. It should also be recalled, however, that the president received low grades on immigration, the economy, and even on terrorism, which had worked strongly in his favor in 2004. As in his two presidential election runs, Bush received much higher grades from Republican identifiers than from Democrats. However, in contrast to the 2000 and 2004 elections, the proportion of Democratic identifiers and Independents had increased, whereas the number of Republican partisans had decreased. Moreover, whereas in both 2000 and 2004 the same one-third of the electorate who said they were Independents took positions on issues that were roughly half-way between those of the Democrat and Republican identifiers; Independent positions on the issue agenda in 2006 were much closer to those of Democrats than they were to the Republicans.

A series of scandals—some financial, some sexual, all tawdry—also took a toll on the image of the president, his party, and its congressional candidates. As demonstrated above, although Republican identifiers were more forgiving than Democrats and Independents, even Republican supporters were affected by the scandals. Together, these several factors proved to be an archetypical scenario for valence politics to produce substantial large individual- and aggregate-level effects. As the title to this chapter indicates, the resulting "big blue wave" was one that the Democrats surfed to power, electing majorities in both houses of Congress.

The impressive dynamics of party identification over the brief interval separating the 2004 and 2006 elections underscores that partisan attachments are not the "unmoved mover" as claimed by proponents of the venerable Michigan model of electoral behavior. Between the 2004 and 2006 elections, only a minority of the electorate were perfectly stable identifiers in terms of direction and intensity, with one in four changing identification, typically to and from independence and identification. Additionally, although campaign spending and evaluations of an incumbent's job performance were of considerable significance on voting, they paled in comparison to the several "Bush effects," especially the negative assessments of him because of his leadership of the war in Iraq. Historically, the erosion of Bush's support paralleled the experiences of Presidents Truman and Johnson, who led American involvement in the Korean and Vietnam wars, respectively. Like Iraq, the Korean and Vietnam conflicts were unpopular among broad segments of the electorate, many of whom reacted by withdrawing support from the president and his party.

Americans have little tolerance for protracted military conflicts in which their country is not a clear and decisive victor, whether it is because casualties are mounting or the public comes to believe that the chances of a military victory are remote. That said, in all cases other factors also fuelled the decline in the three presidents' public approval ratings. For Truman, it was charges of corruption, charges of Communists infiltrating the State Department, and his leadership style. For Johnson, it was the supposed failure of the War on Poverty; scandals associated with some of his key staffers; the defection of the Deep South because of Johnson's advocacy of civil rights legislation; and the enmity of former President Kennedy's brother, Robert Kennedy, who had many supporters in the Democratic Party. For Bush, it can be argued that his personal style, the purported loss of American prestige in the international community, rising energy prices, an unending parade of scandals, and his administration's inept response to the Hurricane Katrina crisis all were contributing factors.

Finally, all three presidents lost public support for the wars they led in part because of problems created for them by key appointments they had made. Truman seemed to lose the affection of more Americans with every tickertape parade given to General MacArthur after his firing by the president as commander in Korea and his return to the United States. The popularity of Presidents Johnson and Bush suffered because of the actions of their defense secretaries, Robert McNamara and Donald Rumsfeld, respectively. Both McNamara and Rumsfeld seemed to become albatrosses who, the longer they presided over the defense department, the less popular their presidents became. Certainly, it would be hard to argue that Secretary McNamara's continued expressions of optimism in the face of a deteriorating military situation ("I can see the light at the end of the tunnel") and casualty figures not seen since the Korean War helped to generate public confidence in and support for President Johnson. The same might be said of Secretary Rumsfeld, whose contemptuous dismissal of all criticisms of his tenure, despite the rising number of casualties and the continued inability to terminate the insurgency in Iraq, tarnished the image of President Bush as a competent commander-in-chief.

Republican politicos did not enjoy waking up on November 8, 2006, to glaring headlines declaring a national and global repudiation of their party's sitting president and the so-called do-nothing Congress that was in their control. A further indignity was that the 2006 election marked the first time in history that the Republicans had failed to capture a single House or Senate seat held by a Democrat. Thirty-one House and six Senate seats changed hands, and all of them went to the Democrats.

Although national-level forces clearly drove the 2006 result, it would be erroneous to assert that local factors were irrelevant. Voters' evaluations of the performance of their local members of Congress influenced the vote net of all other considerations. Also, as emphasized in the literature on congressional voting, incumbency played a predictable role—net of other factors, the presence of a Republican incumbent boosted GOP support in a congressional district. There is additional evidence that incumbents continued to have sizable advantages in their districts; most obviously, fewer than 10 per cent of challengers defeated sitting members of Congress in 2006. In addition, in a political world where money matters (a lot), sitting House members typically amassed large campaign war chests that they used to their advantage, outspending their opponents by an average of almost one million dollars.

Other possible local-level effects involve counterfactuals which, by their nature, are more difficult to calibrate. For example, one can only speculate as to the number of Independents and ideological moderates who would have supported Democratic congressional candidates if the Democrats had failed to pursue National Party Chairman Howard Dean's "50 State Strategy." Dean had argued that the party should not concede conservative and moderate voters to the Republicans. He recommended that the Democrats recruit candidates that fit the mold of many conservative and moderate districts in the nation's heartland. One anecdotal example of the success of Dean's strategy was that the Democrats were able to recapture Indiana's

9th District by persuading a conservative "blue dog Democrat," Baron Hill, to again contest the seat for them.

As Converse (1966) argued long ago, in a sense, every mid-term congressional election constitutes a kind of referendum on the sitting president and his administration. Historically, the pattern has been that the high regard in which presidents are held by the public immediately after their election tends to decline before picking up slightly at the end of their term in office. In most instances, the extent of this decline is reflected in the magnitude of the loss of congressional seats the president's party suffers in a mid-term election. The loss was particularly heavy in 2006 because of adverse reactions to an increasingly unpopular war, highly negative evaluations of the president's performance, and several odious scandals. These events and conditions combined to create a tidal wave of public disaffection. On November 7, 2006, that wave surged ashore, sweeping a large number of Republicans out of the House and Senate and ending, at least temporarily, their party's control of Congress.

Notes

1   GOP (Grand Old Party) is a synonym for the Republican Party.

2   Among others, Milstein (1974), Mueller (1971; 1973), and Gartner and Segura (1998) note the downward trend in support for the Vietnam and Korean conflicts as casualties began to mount. A competing school argues that declining public support for conflicts is more directly linked to citizens coming to the realization that success in attaining the goals that necessitated using the military are unattainable (cf. Feaver and Gelpi, 2004; Eichenberg, 2005; Gelpi, Feaver, and Reifler, 2005). For tests of these hypotheses that highlight the conflict in Iraq, see Voten and Brewer (2006), Eichenberg, Stoll, and Lebo (2006), and the exchange between Klarevas and Gelpi and Reifler (2006).

3   As is the case with the 2006 Political Support in Canada (PSC) survey, the 2006 PSA study was a nation-wide "pre-post" Internet study (N = 3660) conducted by the British firm YouGov shortly before and after the 2006 mid-term election. More information on the survey, including the full questionnaire, is available at http://www.utdallas.edu/~hclarke.

4   The question read: "Overall, do you approve or disapprove of the way George W. Bush is handling his job as president?" This question and questions asking about President Bush's performance in specific areas were coded as follows: 5 = strongly agree; 4 = agree; 3 = neither agree nor disagree/don't know; 2 = disagree; and 1 = strongly disagree.

5   The four economic evaluation questions were worded as follows: a) national prospective: "Thinking ahead, would you say that over the *next year*, the *nation's economy* will ... ?"; b) Personal Prospective: "Thinking ahead, how do you think the financial situation of *your household* will change over the *next*

12 months? Will it ... ?"; c) national retrospective: "Would you say that over the *past year*, the *nation's economy* has ... ?"; and d) personal retrospective: "Thinking about economic conditions, how does the financial situation of *your household* now compare with what it was *12 months ago*? Has it ... ?" Responses to these questions were coded: 5 = much better; 4 = better; 3 = stay about the same/not sure; 2 = worse; and 1 = much worse.

6   The most important issue variable was constructed from responses obtained from the following open-ended question: "As far as you are concerned, what is the single most important issue facing the country at the present time?"

7   Following the open-ended most important issue question, respondents were asked the following two questions: a) "Do you approve or disapprove of the way President Bush is handling this particular issue?"; and b) "Which political party is best able to handle this particular issue?" Evaluations of the president's job performance were coded 5 = approve strongly; 4 = approve; 3 = neither approve nor disapprove/don't know; 2 = disapprove; and 1 = disapprove strongly. Respondents could choose the Democrats, the Republicans, or another party as the party best able to handle the issue or state that they could not choose between the two or lacked the confidence in both of the parties to handle the issue.

8   The taxes and services question was phrased as follows: "Some people think the government should provide fewer services even in areas such as health and education in order to reduce taxes. Other people feel it is important for the government to provide many more services even if it means an increase in taxes. On a scale from 0 to 10, where 10 means 'government should raise taxes in order to provide many more services' and 0 means 'government should reduce services in order to cut taxes,' where would you place yourself on this scale?" The defense spending question was worded: "Some people believe that we should spend much less money for defense. Others feel that defense spending should be greatly increased. On a scale from 0 to 10, where 0 means 'government should spend much more on defense' and 10 means 'government should spend much less on defense,' where would you place yourself on this scale?" For both questions, those who said that they did not know where to place themselves were coded at the mean, 4.9 for the taxes and services question and 5.6 for the defense spending question.

9   The abortion question on the PSA survey was worded as follows: "There has been a lot of discussion about abortion in recent years. Which one of the following statements comes closest to your own view?" The statements were: a) "By law, abortion should never be permitted"; b) "The law should permit abortion only in case of rape, incest, or when the woman's life is in danger"; c) "Don't Know"; d) "The law should permit abortion for reasons other than rape, incest, or danger to the woman's life, but only after the need for the abortion has been clearly established"; and e) By law, a woman should always be able to obtain an abortion as a matter of personal choice."

10 The three-question scandal battery was prefaced with the following statement: "Here are some state-ments people are making about recent scandals involving some Republican Members of Congress. Please indicate if you *agree* or *disagree*." The statements were: a) "The scandals prove that there is widespread corruption in the Republican Party"; b) "It is unfair to blame the entire Republican Party for the scandals"; and c) "The scandals show that the Republican Party cannot govern the country effectively." The question coding and available options are similar to those presented for responses to Bush's job approval (see endnote four above).

11 The wording for the Gallup party identification question is: "In politics, as of today, do you consider yourself a Republican, a Democrat, or an Independent?".

12 As noted in endnote four of Chapter Four, we draw the boundary between identifiers and noni-dentifiers by considering partisans to be only those who identified themselves as Republicans or Democrats when asked the first question in the ANES party identification battery. The question is: "Generally speaking, do you think of yourself as a Republican, a Democrat, an Independent, or what?" In the vote models, we use three dummy (0–1) variables, one for Republican identifiers, one for Democratic identifiers, and one for other party identifiers. Independents and nonidentifiers are the reference category.

13 The two questions were: a) "Overall, how good or bad a job do you think the Member of Congress from your US House District has been doing in recent years?"; and b) "Overall, how good or bad a job do you think the Congress in Washington has been doing in recent years?" Responses were coded: 5 = very good job; 4 = good job; 3 = don't know; 2 = bad job; and 1 = very bad job.

14 Age is a continuous variable with missing values recoded to the mean. Education is a six-category variable: 1 = less than secondary school; 2 = some secondary school or graduated secondary school; 3 = some community or technical college, including those with associate's degrees; 4 = some college or university; 5 = college or university graduate (BA/BSc); and 6 = graduate/professional school attended or completed. Using Caucasian respondents as a reference category, separate dichotomous variables were created for African American, Hispanic, and Asian respondents, as well as those who said they belong to (an)other racial/ethnic group. A dichotomous variable was also created for gender, with men coded one, and women, zero. Income was a 12-category ordinal variable ranging from 1 = under $20,000, to 12 = $200,000 or more. Those that did not report an income were recoded to the mean value of 4.9. Military status was a variable coded one if the respondent or an immediate member of their family (brother, sister, spouse, father, mother, son, daughter) was serving in the military, two if the respondent and immediate family members were both serving in the military, and zero otherwise. Separate dichotomous variables were created for those of Catholic, Protestant, and other faiths (with the nonreligious respondents serving as the reference category). Religiosity was an ordinal variable with church attendance coded as follows: 1 = never attends church or did not know; 2 = attends once

or a few times a year; 3 = attends once a month but not more than once a week; and 4 = attends at least once a week.

15 Two principal components analyses (PCA) were conducted to obtain factor scores. A PCA with the abortion, defense, and tax spending variables as indicators yielded a one-factor solution. A second PCA of the Bush performance and economic evaluations variables described in endnotes four and five yielded a two-factor solution. Variables tapping evaluations of Bush loaded on the first factor, and the four economic evaluations variables loaded on a second factor. The scandal index sums responses to three statements soliciting opinions about the scandals (see endnote ten above).

16 Changes in vote probabilities are computed by allowing a variable of interest to move across its full range, with other predictor variables held at their mean values (in the case of continuous variables) or at zero (in the case of dummy variables). Probabilities were computed using the CLARIFY package implemented in STATA 9 (Tomz, Wittenberg , and King, 1999).

CHAPTER SEVEN

Mulroney, Reagan, and Three Big Elections

This chapter focuses on the 1988 and 1993 Canadian federal elections and the 1980 American presidential election. Our interest in these elections stems from the fact that all three are considered issue-based contests that should provide strong tests of the rival models of electoral choice investigated in earlier chapters. In the 1980 American presidential election campaign, Republican candidate Ronald Reagan advocated controversial policy proposals for reducing the role of government. As Reagan liked to quip, "Government isn't the solution to our problem, Government *is* the problem." In the campaign he also called for a more aggressive foreign policy, with massive increases in defense spending as the corner-stone. Reagan and his advisors cast his campaign as involving real policy choices—on spending priorities and the scope of governmental involvement in economy and society. However, contentious positional issues were not the whole story. Reagan also invited voters to judge the leadership abilities of his Democratic rival, incumbent President Jimmy Carter, as manager of the national economy and defender of US interests around the world. Both position and valence issues had been much discussed when American voters went to the polls in November 1980.[1]

The 1988 Canadian federal election also had a strong position issue emphasis. In fact, the campaign was dominated by one such issue, the desirability of a free trade agreement (the FTA) with the United States. Members of the opposition Liberals previously had used their Senate majority to thwart the efforts of Prime Minister Brian Mulroney and his governing Progressive Conservatives (PCs) to pass the FTA. The Liberal Party was led by John Turner. First elected to Parliament in 1962, Turner went on to head two powerful ministries during the Trudeau governments of the late 1960s and early 1970s. He then resigned to return to private business, becoming one of Canada's leading corporate attorneys. For several years afterward, hundreds of Liberal admirers considered the handsome, well-connected, and wealthy Turner a kind of "emperor in exile," waiting to assume his rightful place as Canada's next great prime minister.[2] When long-time Prime Minister Pierre Trudeau announced his intention to retire, Turner's many fans pleaded with him to enter the Liberal leadership contest, which he did, and easily won. Despite his previous successes in politics and business, he proved to be stunningly inept as a leader and campaigner in the 1984 federal election (Kornberg and Clarke, 1988).

Many Liberal insiders subsequently blamed Turner personally for his party's defeat and the Mulroney-led Conservative landslide victory that gave the PCs 75 per cent (211 of 282) of the seats in Parliament. Although public support for the Conservatives declined substantially after their 1984 victory, internecine grumbling about and hostility towards Turner's leadership continued and, in fact, intensified. In a panic, the desperate Turner seized upon opposition to the FTA as the issue that would turn the tide, one that would galvanize public opinion for him and his party. Opposition to the FTA had the added merit of simultaneously eroding support for the increasingly popular New Democratic Party (NDP) who appeared "wishy-washy" on the issue. In Turner's view, free trade could be represented as an issue that would make Canada a social-cultural and political, as well as an economic, satellite of the United States. Mulroney and the Conservatives could be cast as serving the colossus to the south, and Turner as "Captain Canada," who would rally voters to save their country from the rapacious Yankees and their Tory running dogs.

Students of Canadian history could be forgiven if they were dumfounded by Turner's ploy. In effect, Canada's two major federal parties would be switching their historic positions on economic policy towards the United States. After all, it was C.D. Howe, the most powerful minister in a series of Liberal governments in the 1940s and 1950s who was the architect of the economic policy that came to be labelled "continentalism." Howe was convinced that the key to post-war prosperity was a significant expansion of the country's industrial and economic base. To this end, Canada needed to aggressively pursue American capital investment. In the event, it appeared that Howe's plan worked. Canada's economy did grow significantly in the decade after World War II, bringing unprecedented affluence to millions of average people. The additional resources made it possible for the federal and provincial governments to implement a variety of highly popular social programs. Unimpressed by the new wealth and the public services it made possible, Canadian left-nationalists would subsequently stigmatize this policy as the "Great Liberal Sell-Out" (e.g., Watkins, 1968; Lumsden, 1970; Laxer and Laxer, 1977).

Notwithstanding disbelief by students of Canadian history, however, there was John Turner, using a nationally televised debate among the party leaders to accuse Mulroney of selling out his country for a "mess of potage" by pursuing free trade. Although Turner was successful in making free trade *the issue* of the 1988 election, the Liberals still lost. Polls showed that the free trade fireworks Turner generated during the leadership debate helped to ignite public support for his party, but the effect proved temporary (Johnston et al., 1992). Reacting to their slippage in the polls, the PCs counterattacked by mounting a series of television advertisements that savaged Turner's leadership abilities and extolled the virtues of free trade. As election day approached, the Conservatives regained their lead in the polls and, when the ballots were counted, they won a comfortable majority of seats in Parliament.

The 1993 Canadian federal election was very different. As noted elsewhere (e.g., Clarke and Kornberg, 1996), the 1993 election was a dramatic contest that resulted in the virtual annihilation of the governing Conservative Party, the decimation of the NDP, and the dramatic emergence of two new parties, Reform and Bloc Québécois. Specifically, the Liberals won a majority (177) of parliamentary seats, and the PCs lost fully 167 of their 169 seats and their vote share plunged from 43 to 16 per cent. The NDP seat and vote totals fell from 43 to 7 and from 20 per cent to 7 per cent, respectively. The two new parties collectively captured fully 33 per cent of the vote and 106 parliamentary seats. Reform took 19 per cent of the vote and elected 52 MPs; the Bloc Québécois (BQ) gained a 14 per cent vote share and elected 54 MPs. Ironically, the separatist BQ became the official opposition in Parliament, with Reform assuming the roles of spokesperson for the interests of the Western provinces and populist champion of the virtues of direct democracy.

It could be argued that Mulroney brought many of his problems on himself. After returning to office in 1988, the Tories quickly implemented the controversial free trade pact with the USA. They also introduced a hugely unpopular Goods and Services Tax (GST) to generate revenues needed to halt spiralling budget deficits. The result was that Conservative popularity fell precipitously. To build political support in Quebec, Mulroney negotiated a constitutional agreement (the Meech Lake Accord) in 1987 which he hoped would satisfy Quebeckers' aspirations for a new federalism and keep them in the Conservative fold. However, the agreement failed to secure the necessary ratification by all 10 provinces. Many Quebeckers reacted to Meech's failure with frustration and anger at what they considered to be rejection by the rest of Canada. Support for Quebec independence escalated rapidly, and Cabinet Minister Lucien Bouchard resigned from the Mulroney government to form a new separatist party, the Bloc Québécois.

The failed attempt at constitutional renewal produced very significant collateral damage. By emphasizing Quebec's interests, Mulroney alienated a substantial segment of public opinion in Western Canada. This provided a mass base for the new Reform Party. Many of Reform's supporters were erstwhile PCs. Recognizing the threat posed by the reinvigorated independence movement in Quebec and mounting hostility towards him in the West, Mulroney tried the constitutional gambit again. "Rolling the dice," as he put it, Mulroney attempted to strike a deal that would appeal simultaneously to Quebec, the West, and other parts of Canada. The agreement came to be called the Charlottetown Accord.

Although the accord was supported by virtually the entire Canadian political establishment, including the old-line parties and the mainstream media, it was opposed by both new parties. According to Reform and the Bloc, the accord was just another "insider deal" formulated by ruling elites who had blocked the aspirations of Quebec and the West for over a century. Making a politically pointed pun and playing on Western suspicions about the motives of Mulroney and other architects of the Charlottetown deal, Reform leader Preston Manning urged people to "know more" and vote "no." After Mulroney campaigned vigorously on behalf of the accord, it was decisively defeated in an October 1992 national referendum. Already suffering from the adverse political effects of a serious recession and widespread antipathy to the new GST, rejection of the accord was "strike three" for the prime minister and his party.

Recognizing the situation for what it was, Mulroney soon resigned. Conservative strategists hoped that he would take public disaffection with him, and thereby enable the PCs to make a fresh start in a forthcoming federal election under the leadership of Kim Campbell. It was not to be. The 1993 federal election was an unmitigated disaster for the Conservatives who lost all but two of their seats in Parliament. The almost total destruction of the party's parliamentary base shocked many political scientists who had easily accepted the argument that mature democracies with large numbers of party identifiers tend to have very stable party systems (e.g., Campbell et al., 1966). Indeed, some observers have contended that national party systems are basically "immortal" (e.g., Bartolini and Mair, 1990). If this contention is a rule, Canada showed itself to be a decided exception. The 1993 result dramatically illustrated that a single election could profoundly alter the contours of a long-lived national party system.

THE 1980 US PRESIDENTIAL ELECTION

"A recession is when your neighbor loses his job.
A depression is when you lose your job, and
recovery is when Jimmy Carter loses his."
—Ronald Reagan during the 1980 presidential campaign
(cited in Patterson, 2005: 148).

Unlike Canada, the United States seemingly provides the archetypical example of party-system longevity. Since the mid-nineteenth century, two-party competition between Democrats and Republicans has been the focal point of successive elections. However, sometimes the game changes, at least to a limited extent. The 1980 presidential election is a case in point. In that year the customary Democratic-Republican duopoly was challenged by a third candidate, Republican Congressman John Anderson. Despite becoming the favorite of many academics and media pundits, Anderson failed to attract the support of a substantial section of the electorate, getting less than 7 per cent of the national vote and failing to win a seat in the electoral college. However, Anderson's failure to "break the mold" of American party politics was not the really big story of 1980. That story was the successful candidacy of an avowed conservative, Ronald Reagan. Reagan mounted a clear ideological challenge to the centrist "Downsian-style" politics that had been a mainstay of national party competition. Candidates who chose to violate centrist platforms went down to decisive defeats. Such was the case with the candidacy of conservative Republican, Arizona Senator Barry Goldwater, in the 1964 presidential election and the liberal Democrat from South Dakota, George McGovern, in the 1972 contest.

To be sure, the 1980 American campaign was not totally devoid of valence forces that typically dominate the issue agenda. As noted above, candidate images were among the most prominent of these forces. Reagan faced an incumbent, Jimmy Carter, who, because of a variety of domestic and foreign policy problems (some of his own making), had become widely unpopular and eminently beatable. We begin with an overview and analysis of the 1980 presidential election.

History, we are told, is written by and about winners. Ronald Reagan won the 1980 presidential election, and became the 40th president of the United States. Although he was easily re-elected in 1984, we confine our attention to the 1980 election and his victory over the Democratic incumbent James Earl (Jimmy) Carter and John Anderson, who ran as an Independent. Winston Churchill might well have dismissed Reagan, as he allegedly did Labor Party leader Clement Atlee, as "a modest man with much to be modest about." Reagan would probably have agreed with the first part of Churchill's characterization.

Reagan's biographer, Lou Cannon (2000), who covered him from the time he was still an actor and pitchman for corporations such as General Electric, through his years as governor of California, to two terms in the White House, and throughout his life after his presidency, contended that not even President Abraham Lincoln was as self-deprecating as Reagan. Reagan's great gift was to use that self-effacement to communicate with ordinary people and explain very large matters in very simple ways. His principal means of communicating was humor. He used jokes and funny stories to break the ice with strangers, to amuse and ingratiate himself with an audience, to deflate political adversaries, and to fill awkward silences at meetings when the topic either bored him or was beyond his comprehension.

Reagan knew people liked to laugh about good-humored jokes about their jobs. So he told anti-lawyer jokes to lawyers, anti-clerical jokes to ministers, and anti-Soviet jokes to then Soviet leader, Mikhail Gorbachev. However, Cannon (2000: ch. 8) asserts Reagan's most frequent target was himself. No president was ever as effective at self-ridicule about his work habits, his memory lapses, his age, his vanities, his ideology, the widely held view that he was unintelligent, and even his long career as an actor in "B" movies. For example, pointing to an old studio picture showing himself with a chimpanzee in the movie *Bedtime for Bonzo*, Reagan told a reporter, "I'm the one with the watch!" About his less than stellar work habits, Reagan quipped, "It's true hard work never killed anybody, but why take the chance?" About his falling asleep at afternoon cabinet meetings, he said, "I'm concerned about what is happening in government and it has caused me many a sleepless afternoon." And in response to a reporter's query that his lack of diplomacy coupled with an ignorance of foreign policy could lead him to blow up the world, he retorted, "Only between the hours of 9 and 5." Responding to another reporter's concern that his ignorance of economic policy could lead to enormous budget deficits, he said, "I'm not worried about the deficit; it's big enough to take care of itself."[3]

However, while he was modest, Reagan would never agree with the idea that he had much to be modest about. Just the opposite—Cannon (2000) argues that Reagan could poke fun at his ignorance because he considered himself abundantly blessed with common sense, and he could laugh at himself because he knew he had a serious purpose and worked diligently at things that mattered most to him (see also Kiewe and Houck, 1991 and FitzGerald, 2000). Cannon rejected the assessments of many "Washington insiders" and liberal power-brokers that Reagan was "an amiable dunce." His amiability did not deter him from firing his first campaign chairman, John Sears, nor did it prevent him from declining to reward his second campaign chairman, William Casey, with the secretary of state's position that he coveted, nor from refusing to make ultra-loyal Ed Meese his chief of staff. Later, he fired Donald Regan, his first treasury secretary and chief of staff, as well as a number of other cabinet secretaries and several national security advisors.[4] Also, early in his first term, despite being warned that it would raise havoc with the transportation system, he fired most of the country's air traffic controllers when their union defied his order not to strike (cf. Nordlund, 1998).

Nor was Reagan a dunce. Rather, he was capable of shrewdly assessing what people wanted and what they were most troubled and worried about. He was also an incurable optimist whom Patterson (2005) argued truly believed his message during both his 1980 and 1984 campaigns that America was not in decline but, rather, that its best days were still ahead. In the 1980 campaign in particular, his message that Americans had and would continue to perform great deeds and could resolve any problem facing them, simply because they were Americans, resonated strongly with the electorate (cf. Troy, 2005). After years of economic stagflation and political turmoil, Reagan's message of "hope, growth, and opportunity" found a welcome audience.[5]

In addition, Reagan was a powerful orator capable of moving large television audiences to tears, as his did with his address following the explosion of the Space Shuttle *Challenger*. He was also capable of evoking great national pride and patriotism in his audiences. An example was his 1984 televised D-Day address on a Normandy beach overlooking steep cliffs that a group of young Rangers had climbed 40 years earlier to clear the German guns firing on American troops below. Despite his age, he was an athletic-looking physically fit individual who in the 1980 campaign belied his 69 years. Patterson (2005: 147) notes that he had a "marvellously soothing voice and an easy platform manner, and was a captivating public presence and speaker." These attributes contrasted sharply with those of his 1980 rival, Jimmy Carter. The latter's speaking voice, delivery, and cadence when giving a major television address to the nation frequently puzzled, and at other times, amused his audience. A sharp contrast to Carter, Reagan truly was "the Great Communicator."

This is not to say Reagan was a political genius. As columnist and conservative icon William F. Buckley noted (cited by Cannon, 2000: 110), "People say he is a simpleton which isn't right, and when they realize he isn't, they're apt to go to the other end of the spectrum and compare him with Socrates which doesn't work either." As Cannon (2000: 115, 118) states: "The presidency proved both the best and worst of offices for Ronald Reagan. His amiable temperament inoculated him against the maladies provoked by the exercise of unaccustomed power. His perspective was unaltered by the presidency, perhaps because he did not need high office to impart a sense of self-esteem.... Since Reagan was not in need of self-esteem, he had no interest in changing. Indeed, Reagan was so self-confident and set in his ways that he refused to allow the presidency to challenge him. It was at once his most appealing quality and his greatest defect as president."

Reagan's 1980 opponent, incumbent Jimmy Carter, was one of the most intelligent and unlucky presidents in the history of the republic. A small town, Georgian,

he won an appointment to the United States Naval Academy from which he graduated with a degree in nuclear engineering. He served on a nuclear submarine and
his intellectual ability brought him to the attention of Admiral Hyman Rickover, the
"father of the nuclear submarine." When Carter's own father fell ill, he resigned from
the navy and returned to Georgia to head the family business. Carter won election
to the Georgia state legislature and in 1970 to the governor's office. He was a pioneer
of the strategy, now commonplace in presidential campaigns, of starting early—in
Carter's case some two years early. He also employed the tried and true practice
of running for national office by pledging to eliminate the pernicious influence of
"Beltway bandits," "Washington insiders," and miscellaneous other miscreants, real
and imagined (cf. Jones, 1998). The problem with that approach is that if elected, you
need the assistance and support of those same insiders to get things done (Jones,
1998; Greenstein, 2000).

Patterson notes that many influential liberals in the Democratic Party, as well as
moderate Republicans, considered Carter a "hick" who was in over his head. Carter
also erred seriously in spurning the advice of Democratic Speaker of the House of
Representatives Tip O'Neill, who wanted to help him develop good relations with
Congress: "O'Neill and others found it especially hard to warm to Carter's aloof,
largely humorless manner" (cited in Patterson, 2005: 111). Kaufman (1993: 210) noted
that Carter struck many congressmen as a "morally self-righteous prig." Liberal jour-
nalist James Fallows (1979: 33–48), who initially liked Carter, later described him as
"complacent, arrogant, and lacking in sophistication." To Fallows, Carter was bliss-
fully ignorant about how to get things done and was a passionless paper-pusher.
Exacerbating his problems, he was a "control freak" who, even with his own staff,
monopolized decision-making on small and seemingly irrelevant details, such as
who would be permitted to use the White House tennis courts.

As for misfortunes, domestically there was the environmental disaster of the Love
Canal neighborhood in 1978 in upstate New York. Much scarier were the partial meltdown of the radioactive core and the release of radioactive steam from the nuclear
facility at Three Mile Island in Middletown, Pennsylvania. Thousands of nearby residents in upstate New York evacuated their homes and plans for new nuclear power
plants across the nation ground to a halt.

Carter soon lost the support of substantial numbers of an important component of the Democratic Party base—organized labor. Labor was concerned that
the president had failed to back legislation designed to protect workers from recessions by providing public employment to those who had been laid off. Many of
these blue-collar workers subsequently became so-called Reagan Democrats. The
root of Carter's problems with maintaining the support of working people was
"stagflation"—a stagnant economy that led to high unemployment, coupled with
seemingly endless increases in inflation that led to double-digit interest rates. These

problems, in turn, had their genesis in the enormous increases in energy prices generated by the Arab Organization of Petroleum Exporting Countries (AOPEC) oil embargo imposed after the 1973 Arab-Israeli War. A second energy crisis occurred after the Iranian revolution in 1979. The resulting gasoline shortages led to long lines of frustrated angry motorists at service stations throughout the country.

In foreign policy, Carter's secretary of state, Cyrus Vance, and his national security advisor, Zbigniew Brzezinski, waged bureaucratic war with one another over American policy towards the Soviet Union. The foreign policy flashpoint during Carter's presidency happened in Iran, where the ruling shah of Iran, Mohammed Reza Pahlavi, had been put in power by a 1953 CIA-backed coup. He subsequently received billions in military aid from the United States, and he was sometimes referred to as America's policeman in the Persian Gulf region. However, his harsh rule over his people eventually led to his overthrow by the Ayatollah Khomeini in 1979. In October of that year, a Tehran mob seized the US embassy, taking 66 American embassy workers hostage. Thereafter, the media networks dwelled on the "hostage crisis," running nightly broadcasts featuring the number of days the Americans had been held captive. An ill-fated rescue attempt by helicopter-borne American Special Forces in April 1980 proved a political and public relations disaster, and further eroded Carter's prospects for re-election. The combination of foreign policy disasters and serious economic problems contributed to a widespread perception that Carter was a weak and ineffective leader who could not control events.

John Anderson, the third newsworthy presidential aspirant in 1980, was a fiscally conservative congressman from Illinois with a reputation for being a social liberal. Anderson was concerned that Ronald Reagan seemed to have bought into the supply-side economic theory, which promised significant benefits if taxes were sharply reduced. The problem was that Reagan announced that he would accompany these tax cuts with sharp increases in defense expenditures. To Anderson, this was "smoke and mirror" economics rather than sound economic policy.[6] Unable to make any headway in the 1980 Republican presidential primaries, Anderson was sufficiently motivated to begin what he knew would be the impossible task of becoming president by running as an Independent. His principal attractiveness was to younger, better educated Americans and to fiscal conservatives in both parties. However, even among such persons his appeal was limited, in part at least by his often-reiterated promise to increase gasoline taxes by 50 cents. His persistence in a futile vastly underfunded campaign was in some respects a tribute to a dedicated public servant (Lacy and Monson, 2002). However, it also reflected his need to obtain 5 per cent of the popular vote in order to get federal funds to pay off his campaign debts. On Election Day Anderson met this goal, obtaining 7 per cent of the ballots cast.

CANDIDATE IMAGES AND PERFORMANCE

The 1980 American National Election Study (ANES) data show how voters saw the candidates. Both incumbent President Jimmy Carter and his principal challenger, Ronald Reagan, were viewed by substantial majorities of Americans as moral, knowledgeable, and honest, with Carter holding an edge in the first two attributes. They differed substantially with respect to perceptions of their personal and leadership

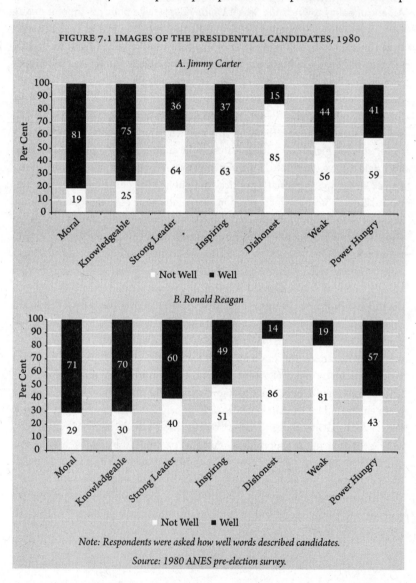

FIGURE 7.1 IMAGES OF THE PRESIDENTIAL CANDIDATES, 1980

A. Jimmy Carter

B. Ronald Reagan

Note: Respondents were asked how well words described candidates.

Source: 1980 ANES pre-election survey.

strengths. Reagan was regarded as personally strong and a strong leader by 81 per cent and 60 per cent of the ANES respondents, respectively. Similar perceptions of Carter were held by only 56 per cent and 36 per cent (see Figure 7.1). As shown in our analyses of voting in the 2000 and 2004 presidential elections (see Chapters Four and Five), "strength" is an extremely important component of presidential leadership in the eyes of the public. Carter's chances of re-election were thus negatively affected by the judgment that his principal rival, Ronald Reagan, was a stronger candidate.[7]

As also observed in earlier chapters, candidates tend to be seen by the public through the lens of partisanship. In the 2000 and 2004 presidential elections, Democratic and Republican identifiers viewed their party's candidate much more positively and the opposition party's candidate more negatively, with the Independent identifiers' views falling in between. Similarly, in 1980, neither Democrats nor Independents were as favorably impressed with Reagan as were Republicans. On each of the seven leader-image traits, Democratic and Independent perceptions were statistically and substantively different from those of Republicans (data not shown in tabular form). Independents' views of Carter with regard to his leadership, personal weakness, and the extent to which he was inspiring and hungry for power were significantly different from those of Republican identifiers. In sum, Independents' images of Reagan and, to a lesser extent, of Carter were closer to those of Democratic identifiers than to those of Republican identifiers. This was a plus for Carter.

However, public views of Carter's performance in office were decidedly unhelpful to him.[8] A charitable interpretation was that the public gave him a "D" for diligence. Realistically, an "F" for failure is more accurate. Specifically, 77 per cent judged his

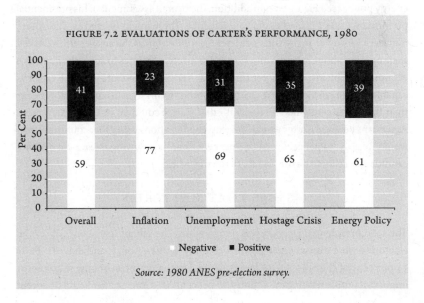

FIGURE 7.2 EVALUATIONS OF CARTER'S PERFORMANCE, 1980

Source: 1980 ANES pre-election survey.

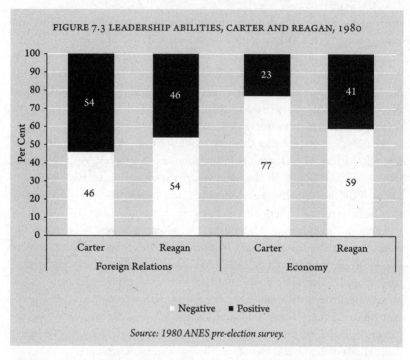

FIGURE 7.3 LEADERSHIP ABILITIES, CARTER AND REAGAN, 1980

Source: 1980 ANES pre-election survey.

ability to handle inflation negatively; 69 per cent made a similar judgment on battling unemployment; 65 per cent were negative about his handling of the hostage crisis; and 61 per cent, probably remembering the long gas lines, negatively assessed his energy policy (see Figure 7.2). In addition, the overall assessment of his presidential performance was a dismal 59 per cent negative. These might be read as "sure loser" numbers. However, many voters did not regard Reagan as the answer either. Asked their opinion about Reagan's and Carter's respective abilities to solve the country's economic problems, only 41 per cent of the ANES respondents judged Reagan as capable of doing the job (see Figure 7.3). To be sure, this was still considerably better than the 23 per cent who still had faith that Carter could do it. Conversely, more Americans believed Carter would "develop good relations with other countries" than would Reagan (54 per cent versus 46 per cent), hardly a glowing assessment of either candidate's ability to be the "leader of the free world."

ISSUES THAT MATTERED

The 1980 presidential election was one in which the salient issue concerns of the electorate were overwhelmingly the economy, foreign policy, and defense. Fully 54 per cent of the 1980 ANES respondents designated the economy as the most important problem facing the country, 27 per cent cited foreign affairs, and 8 per cent

TABLE 7.1 MOST IMPORTANT PROBLEM FACING THE COUNTRY AND
GOVERNMENT PERFORMANCE, THE UNITED STATES, 1980

	PER CENT MENTIONING	GOVERNMENT PERFORMANCE		
		GOOD	FAIR	POOR
Most Important Issue				
Health/Social Welfare	2	0	41	59
Education	0.9	0	42	58
Elder Care	2	9	48	44
Economy	54	2	32	66
Defense	8	5	31	65
Foreign Affairs	27	9	40	51
Terrorism	0.1	0	0	100
Race	0.2	0	0	100
Abortion	0	–	–	–
Crime	0.8	10	30	60
Government Functioning	2	7	32	61
Immigration	0.7	11	11	78
Environment	2	5	50	46
Miscellaneous Other	0.5	0	33	67
DK, None	0.2	–	–	–
Total		4	35	61

Party Best Most Important Issue
All Issue Mentions:
Republican = 40%
Democrat = 10%
No Difference, DK = 50%

N = 1355
Source: 1980 ANES post-election survey.

mentioned defense (see Table 7.1). All other issues lacked immediate salience for most voters. For example, only 2 per cent cited health and social welfare, and equal numbers mentioned care of the elderly and the environment. All other issues, including education, terrorism, race, abortion, crime, and immigration, were referenced by less than 1 per cent of the survey respondents.

Also, as observed above, on big issues such as the economy, foreign affairs, and defense, public perceptions of the Carter administration's success in handling them was that it had failed. As Table 7.1 shows, fully two-thirds of the ANES respondents judged that the government had done a poor job with respect to the economy and defense, and slightly over half felt this way about its handling of foreign affairs. Nor was the administration considered more successful in other areas. Indeed, on only two issues—elder care and the environment—did a majority give the administration

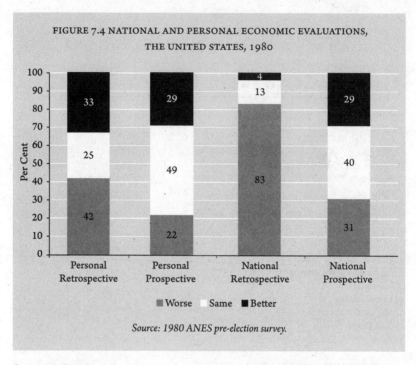

FIGURE 7.4 NATIONAL AND PERSONAL ECONOMIC EVALUATIONS, THE UNITED STATES, 1980

Source: 1980 ANES pre-election survey.

fair or good marks. As to which party was best on the most important problem facing the country, 40 per cent chose the Republicans and only 10 per cent, the Democrats. The remaining 50 per cent said either there was no difference between the parties or that they did not know which one was better.

Unlike leader images, there were virtually no differences between Democrats and Republicans regarding the most important problems facing the country. Not surprisingly, the sluggish economy affected people's perceptions of national economic conditions.[9] As Figure 7.4 illustrates, fully 83 per cent judged that the national economy had worsened in the past year or so. In addition, as is typical, people were considerably more optimistic about their own circumstances. Thus one-third (33 per cent) judged their own position had improved over the past two years, as opposed to the minuscule number (4 per cent) who said the same about the national economy. Although 42 per cent acknowledged their own economic positions had eroded, that was still only half the number who made a similar judgment about national conditions. Smaller differences between national and personal economic situations were observed when respondents were asked about what the future would bring. The same proportions (29 per cent) judged that both the national economy and their own financial condition would shortly improve. There was also only a 9 per cent difference between the proportions estimating that the national and their own condition would worsen during that period.

ISSUES—PRIORITIES AND PROXIMITIES

The 1980 campaign featured several issues. Discussions as to how to deal with the Soviet Union after that nation's incursion into Afghanistan, the need for a defense buildup, and how to combat rising inflation and unemployment all figured prominently in the candidate debates, campaign commercials, and media coverage. As noted above, over half of the ANES respondents listed the economy as their principal concern, followed by the 35 per cent who listed either defense or foreign affairs. Historically, the Republican Party traditionally had been seen as stronger on these issues, whereas the Democrats were viewed as the "caring" party, more concerned with and better able to handle social issues, education, health care, and other public services. As the 1980 election approached, the fact that issues customarily "owned" by the Republican Party were being designated as most important not only by Republicans but also by huge numbers of Democrats and Independents did not bode well for Carter.

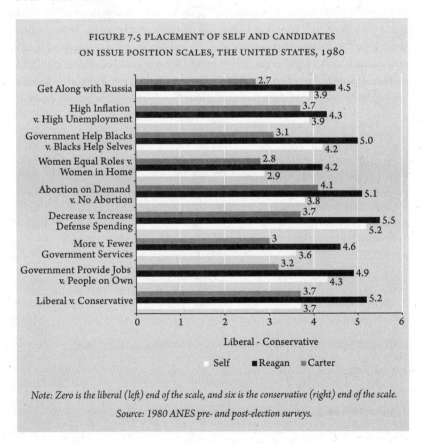

FIGURE 7.5 PLACEMENT OF SELF AND CANDIDATES
ON ISSUE POSITION SCALES, THE UNITED STATES, 1980

Liberal - Conservative

■ Self ■ Reagan ■ Carter

Note: Zero is the liberal (left) end of the scale, and six is the conservative (right) end of the scale.

Source: 1980 ANES pre- and post-election surveys.

However, there is another side to the story. Adopting a ploy that the Canadian Liberals would use a quarter of a century later in their attacks on Stephen Harper, Carter and his allies claimed Reagan was dangerously far to the right of the ideological spectrum on a host of positional issues. The ANES data enable us to determine if voters agreed that Reagan was a "right-wing nut." Figure 7.5 illustrates how the survey respondents placed themselves and the two presidential candidates on these issues with lower values indicating more "left" or "liberal" positions. Considering the average scores, Carter did not look too bad. For example, respondents perceived themselves as much closer to him on abortion and women's rights—social issues that had received heavy media coverage throughout the 1970s. Perhaps people *did* view Reagan as "too far out there" when it came to such issues. However, Reagan was closer to the public's average position on US-Soviet relations, the need for more defense spending, minority rights, and the responsibility of individuals to find a job.

Calculating mean absolute differences between voters and the candidates shows that Carter maintained an advantage on the social issues of abortion and women's rights (see Table 7.2). However, Carter did poorly on other issues. That is, when mean absolute distances between candidates and voters on various issues are calculated, Reagan was significantly closer. Indeed, Reagan could be said to "own" and dominate issues in the international affairs domain. In sum, although Carter had the advantage on selected social issues that scholars such as Inglehart (1971) came to

TABLE 7.2 MEAN INDIVIDUAL-LEVEL ABSOLUTE DIFFERENCES
IN PROXIMITY TO JIMMY CARTER AND RONALD REAGAN
ON POSITION ISSUES, 1980

	CARTER	REAGAN	T	P
More v. Fewer Government Services	1.96	1.87	-1.85	.064
Decrease v. Increase Defense Spending	2.18	**1.40**	-16.36	.000
Government Provide Jobs v. People on Own	1.93	**1.53**	-8.80	.000
Government Help Blacks v. Blacks Help Selves	2.02	**1.53**	-11.92	.000
Inflation v. Unemployment	1.64	**1.45**	-5.84	.000
Women Equal Roles v. Women in Home	**1.43**	2.19	15.76	.000
Abortion on Demand v. No Abortion	**1.05**	1.26	8.84	.000
Get Along with Russia	1.82	**1.42**	-8.92	.000
Magnitude of a Proposed Tax Cut	1.53	**1.34**	-6.77	.000
Overall Liberal v. Conservative Scale	**1.79**	2.51	25.67	.000

Note: Boldface numbers indicate statistically significant difference in proximity between candidates and voters (p < .05, two-tailed test).

Source: 1980 ANES pre- and post-election surveys.

view as high on the emergent "post-materialist" issue agenda of the 1970s, the state of the economy and perilous situations across the globe had the average American worried more about the standard "materialist" issues of "peace and prosperity" in 1980. On economic and national security issues, Reagan came out ahead. To map the dimensions underlying voters' positions vis-à-vis the two candidates, we employed separate principal components analyses of the distances between where the ANES respondents placed themselves and the two candidates. Reagan's analysis yielded a single factor that encompassed "liberal" and "conservative" or "left-right" positions on seven issues. Voters saw their positions vis-à-vis Reagan's along a single continuum that we label Reagan's "New Deal" dimension.[10] The structure of Carter's issue space is only slightly more complex. For him, the issue-proximity space has two dimensions, with all of the issue variables but one loading on a single factor. The sole exception concerns voters' perceptions of the distance between themselves and Carter on women's issues. Given this pattern, we label the first dimension of the Carter issue-proximity space as Carter's "New Deal" dimension and the second, Carter's "Women's Issues" dimension.[11]

In sum, Carter was viewed by voters as having obvious and often large shortcomings on the valence items of competency and candidate image. Voters also perceived significant differences in the locations of the two candidates on positional issues. Again, Reagan tended to be favored on several of these issues. Thus, the balance

TABLE 7.3 SUMMARY OF PERFORMANCE OF RIVAL MODELS OF VOTING
IN THE 1980 PRESIDENTIAL ELECTION

	MCFADDEN R^2	PER CENT CORRECTLY CLASSIFIED	AIC†
Rival Models			
Demographics	.13	60.6	1588.83
Performance of Economy	.03	51.6	1720.97
Federal Party Identification	.23	72.5	1373.21
Party Best Important Issues	.21	71.4	1400.17
Party Best Important Issues + Carter Performance	.34	77.4	1181.47
Position Issues	.33	76.8	1186.73
Party Leader Images	.45	79.1	996.01
Valence Politics	.55	84.4	837.53
Composite Model	.62	80.1	791.84

†—Akaike Information Criterion (AIC)—smaller values indicate better model performance.

Note: Multinomial logit models with Carter vote as the reference category.

of issue positions and concerns, whether valence or positional, appeared to favor Reagan, a circumstance that gave him a decided advantage in his run for the presidency. However, the relative importance of valence and position issues for determining electoral choice in 1980 remains to be investigated. This is our next topic.

RIVAL MODELS OF ELECTORAL CHOICE

How do various models of voting behavior discussed in earlier chapters perform in the 1980 US presidential election? Table 7.3 helps us to answer this question. The table reports the results of estimating these models in a series of analyses of factors affecting voting for Carter, Reagan, and Anderson. Generally speaking, the results are very similar to those for more recent elections in the US and Canada. For example, demographic variables and economic evaluations have very modest effects; party identification, position issues, and valence issues have stronger effects; and party leader images have still stronger effects. However, none of these models perform as well as the larger valence politics model that includes party identification, leader images, and party best on important issues. Despite having more variables than the simpler, more specific models, the valence politics model has a considerably smaller (i.e., better) Akaike Information Criterion (AIC) value.[12] However, similar to all other voting analyses we have considered, a composite model that includes all of the predictor variables from various specific models performs best, having the largest estimated R^2 value (.62), and the smallest AIC value (791.84). As in our analyses of voting in other elections, no single model can tell the whole story of why voters did what they did in the 1980 US presidential election.

Table 7.4 presents the composite model analyses.[13] As expected, components of the valence politics model have a variety of significant effects. Positive evaluations of the performance of the incumbent president, Jimmy Carter, increased the probability of voting for him and decreased the probability of supporting either Reagan or Anderson. Anticipated Republican performance on important issues mattered as well, with positive expectations enhancing the probability of a Reagan vote and lessening the probability of choosing Carter or Anderson. Party identification also works as expected, with Republican identifications increasing the likelihood of voting for Reagan or Anderson (a former Republican congressman) and decreasing the probability of voting for Carter. Democratic identification had the opposite kinds of effects, boosting the probability of a Carter vote and lessening the likelihood of choosing Anderson. Candidate images were important as well, with the leadership and integrity components of these images exerting a variety of significant and predictable effects.

Controlling for these several valence politics effects, position issues also mattered—proximity to Carter on the New Deal dimension increased the likelihood of

TABLE 7.4 COMPOSITE MODEL OF FACTORS AFFECTING VOTING
IN THE 1980 PRESIDENTIAL ELECTION

| | PANEL A | PANEL B | |
	CARTER	REAGAN	ANDERSON
Predictor Variables			
Carter Performance	.76***	-.73***	-.78**
Leader Images:			
Carter Leadership	.62***	-.57***	-.90***
Carter Integrity	.41**	-.26	-.63***
Reagan Leadership	-.43***	.72***	-.35*
Reagan Integrity	-.62***	.74***	.25
Anderson Leadership	-.26*	-.02	.70***
Anderson Integrity	-.08	-.23	.93***
Party Best Important Issue:			
Republican	-1.02***	1.00***	.77*
Democrat	.13	-.53	-.14
Position Issues:			
Carter New Deal	.68***	-.85***	-.22
Carter Women	.13	-.17	-.30*
Reagan New Deal	-.43***	.72***	.15
Party Identification:			
Republican	-1.67***	1.69***	1.64**
Democrat	.88***	-.53	-1.16**
Economic Evaluations	.10	-.14	.11
Demographics:			
Age	.02***	-.02*	-.05***
Gender	.22	-.12	-.46
Income	.04	-.05	-.01
Race/Ethnicity:			
African American	2.30***	-2.00***	-1.76
Hispanic	1.02	-1.32	-.49
Other	-.18	.40	.73
Region: North Central	-.48	.47	.61
South	-.46	.44	.30
West	-.66*	.76*	.26
Religion: Catholic	.65	-.46	-1.00*
Protestant	.83*	-.68	-.88*
Other	.84	-.39	-.96
Religiosity x Protestant	-.14	.25	-.07
Constant	-2.82***	1.89*	.85
McFadden R^2 =	.63	.62	
McKelvey R^2 =	.83	x	
Per Cent Correctly Classified =	88.7	80.1	
AIC =	536.67	.84	

*** p < .001; ** p < .01; * p < .05; one-tailed test.
N = 958
x—undefined for multinomial logit analysis.
†—Akaike Information Criterion (AIC)—smaller values indicate better model performance.

Note: Panel A is a binomial logit analysis—vote Carter versus vote Reagan or Anderson. Panel B is a multinomial logit analysis—vote Reagan or vote Anderson, with vote Carter as the reference category.

voting for him rather than Reagan. Predictably, proximity to Reagan had the opposite effects. Proximity to Carter on the women's issue dimension did not matter for choosing between him and Reagan, although it did lessen the likelihood of voting for Anderson. In addition, some of the demographic variables were influential. Younger voters were more likely to choose Reagan or Anderson rather than Carter, and African Americans were more likely to favor Carter over Reagan. Westerners preferred Reagan, and both Protestants and Catholics were less likely than those with no religious affiliation to favor Anderson.

To illustrate the strength of various predictor variables, we calculate the probability of voting for Reagan as a particular predictor is varied over its entire range, while other predictors are held at their means or other reference values.[14] As Figure 7.6 shows, the results indicate that several valence politics variables had strong effects. Similar to voting in other elections, leader images mattered a great deal in 1980. Changing views of Reagan's leadership and integrity could alter the probability of

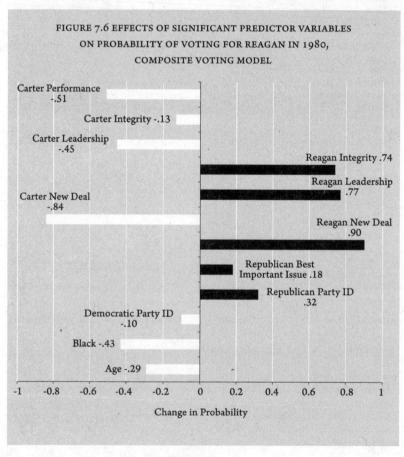

FIGURE 7.6 EFFECTS OF SIGNIFICANT PREDICTOR VARIABLES ON PROBABILITY OF VOTING FOR REAGAN IN 1980, COMPOSITE VOTING MODEL

voting for him by 77 and 74 points, respectively. Similarly, varying views of Carter's leadership could change the likelihood of a Reagan vote by 45 points. Judgments about Carter's performance mattered as well, with highly positive evaluations lessening the likelihood of a Reagan vote by 51 points. Partisanship had nontrivial effects too, with a shift from being a Democratic to being a Republican identifier increasing the probability of voting for Reagan by 42 points.

Figure 7.6 indicates that other factors were at work in 1980. Issue proximities exerted strong effects. As proximity to Reagan is varied across his New Deal issue dimension, the probability of voting for him increased by fully 90 points. Similarly, as proximity to Carter is varied across his equivalent dimension, the probability of a Reagan vote decreased by an impressive 84 points. Race mattered, too. Net of all other considerations, the probability of supporting Reagan dropped by 43 points if a voter was African American.

In sum, it is clear that a combination of factors were at work in the 1980 presidential election. As described above, many voters had concluded that Carter's performance as president left much to be desired. Simply stated, he was a weak leader who could not do the job, either at home or abroad. These are precisely the kinds of judgments that fuel valence politics effects on electoral choice. However, there was more. Carter's principal rival, Ronald Reagan, had a strong positive image in the minds of many voters, thus magnifying the importance of leadership considerations. Yet Reagan was also a self-styled ideological conservative. This latter aspect of his image helped the Carter camp to portray Reagan as out of step with mainstream thinking, while raising the salience of position issues in people's minds. The overall result was that a combination of valence and position issues joined leadership images as key factors driving the choices voters made in the 1980 presidential election.

THE 1988 AND 1993 CANADIAN FEDERAL ELECTIONS

Party Leader Images

Sadly for a man who had enjoyed great success for almost his entire adult life as an athlete, a cabinet minister, and a lawyer/businessman, in 1988 John Turner was regarded as a considerably less able party leader than either Brian Mulroney or NDP chieftain Ed Broadbent. As Figure 7.7 illustrates, Broadbent was regarded more highly than either of the two major party leaders in terms of honesty. Five years later, in 1993, the new Conservative leader and prime minister, Kim Campbell, was clearly viewed as less able than her predecessor, Brian Mulroney, but also less able than any of her opponents, Liberal leader Jean Chrétien, Bloc Québécois leader Lucien Bouchard, Reform leader Preston Manning, and NDP leader Audrey McLaughlin. Chrétien's image is particularly noteworthy, because before the election he had been

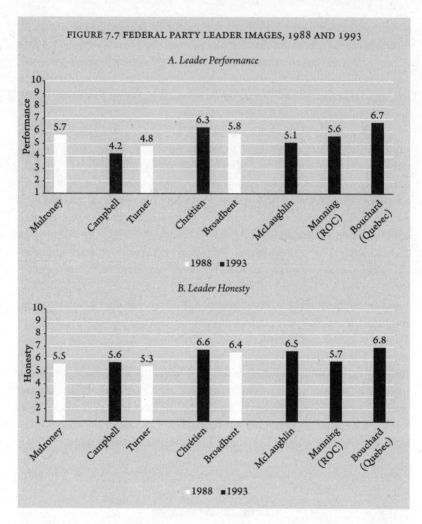

FIGURE 7.7 FEDERAL PARTY LEADER IMAGES, 1988 AND 1993

A. Leader Performance

B. Leader Honesty

widely derided as "yesterday's man"—an irrelevant relic of an earlier era. Campbell did much better on the honesty dimension but, again, less well than McLaughlin, Bouchard, or Chrétien (see Figure 7.7). To the extent that leader images were important, Campbell clearly was at a disadvantage in 1993.[15]

This conclusion is reinforced by the leaders' scores on 100-point "feeling thermometers." In 1988 Mulroney had an average score of 50, exactly the mid-point of the scale. Five years later, his successor Kim Campbell had an average score of only 39—decidedly in the negative range but still better than Mulroney's truly dismal 1993 average of 24. There were big changes in feelings about the leaders of the other parties, too. Whereas John Turner had averaged only 44 points in 1988, Jean Chrétien's average of 56 points is one of the highest ever recorded. NDP leader scores went in the opposite direction; although Broadbent was clearly in the positive range with a 54-point average in 1988, the party's new leader, Audrey McLaughlin, averaged only 43 points in 1993. Reform leader Preston Manning had an even lower overall average score (41 points), but in Saskatchewan, Alberta, and British Columbia he averaged 47, 57, and 48 points, respectively. The other new party leader, the BQ's Lucien Bouchard, was even more popular in his home province of Quebec, where he averaged 56 points. These large differences in how people reacted to the party leaders were important for the choices voters made in 1993.

Most Important Problems, 1988 and 1993

Table 7.5 indicates that 1988 was virtually a one-issue election—free trade. It was cited as most important by an overwhelming 90 per cent of people participating in the 1988 PSC national survey. Clearly, the Liberals had succeeded in making free trade *the issue*. As noted above, the Conservatives represented free trade as simply a good

TABLE 7.5 MOST IMPORTANT PROBLEM FACING THE COUNTRY AND GOVERNMENT PERFORMANCE, CANADA, 1988

	PER CENT MENTIONING	GOVERNMENT PERFORMANCE		
		GOOD	FAIR	POOR
Most Important Issue				
Abortion	0.7	0	10	90
Deficit	1.6	25	46	29
Environment	0.7	10	20	70
Free Trade	90.1	14	42	44
Meech Lake	0.8	0	27	73
Taxes	0.2	0	0	100
Unemployment	0.1	0	50	50
Other	3.0	18	39	44
DK, None	2.7	—	—	—
Total		4	35	61

Party Best Most Important Issue
All Issue Mentions:
Liberal = 26%
Progressive Conservative = 45%
NDP = 16%
Other Party = 2%
No Difference, DK = 12%
N = 1473

Source: 1988 PSC post-election survey.

economic policy, one that would help ensure the future of Canada and Canadians. In contrast, the Liberals invested it with far greater significance as a policy that would make Canada a subservient client-state of the all-powerful United States.

Unfortunately for the Liberals, they were unable to translate their success in raising the salience of free trade into success at the polls. One reason was that they were unable to persuade a majority of voters that the Tories were making a hash of their handling of the issue—56 per cent of respondents in the 1988 PSC survey thought the Mulroney government was doing either a fair or good job on free trade. Similarly, fully 45 per cent of the electorate concluded that the PCs were best able to handle the most important election issue, and, for most people, that issue was free trade. The comparable figures for the Liberals and NDP were 26 per cent and 16 per cent, respectively. Perhaps more surprising was that the Meech Lake Accord, Mulroney's then ongoing attempt to broker a deal that would be embraced by Quebec and accepted by the rest of Canada (Monahan, 1991; Russell, 1992) was cited by less than 1 per cent of the PSC respondents. This, despite the fact that the failure to get the accord ratified

TABLE 7.6 MOST IMPORTANT PROBLEM FACING
THE COUNTRY, CANADA, 1993

MOST IMPORTANT ISSUE	PER CENT MENTIONING
Social Issues	1.5
Economy	73.8
Environment	0.4
Free Trade	1.4
Health Care	1.9
Government Functioning	7.8
Education	0.5
Law and Order	0.5
Immigration	0.3
Regionalism	3.1
Other	2.0
DK, None	6.8

Party Best Most Important Issue
All Issue Mentions:
Liberal = 40%
Progressive Conservative = 12%
NDP = 7%
Reform = 17%
Bloc Québécois = 7%
Other Party = 2%
No Difference, DK = 16%
N = 1394

Source: 1993 PSC post-election survey.

by all 10 provinces would subsequently precipitate a constitutional crisis and sharp increases in support for the separatist Parti Québécois and its new federal counterpart, the Bloc Québécois.[16] Other supposedly "hot button" issues, such as abortion, the escalating deficit, the environment, taxes, and even the perennial problem of unemployment, all paled into insignificance in the public mind. In 1988, free trade dominated the issue agenda.

Five years later, everything had changed. In 1993 free trade was no longer *the issue*. Indeed, it was barely mentioned. It was the economy that held pride of place in the public mind. The 1993 PSC survey indicates that nearly three out of four Canadians judged the economy to be the most important issue facing the country (see Table 7.6). Once again, the electorate's fascination with one issue meant that other issues that would normally be invested with importance, such as health care, education, immigration, social issues, and law and order, were rarely cited. In fact, these several issues *together* were cited by only 7 per cent of the PSC respondents. Public judgments about the economy turned decidedly negative after 1988 and this in part is reflected in the widespread view in 1993 that the PCs were not the party that could best handle this issue.[17] Only 13 per cent of the PSC respondents judged that the PCs were best on the economy—not much more than the 5 per cent who referenced the New Democrats or the Bloc, and 12 per cent *less* than the number who thought that the new Reform Party could do the best job.[18] In contrast, although the Liberals had been out of office for almost a decade, 43 per cent of the public pinned their faith on the Grits, while 17 per cent judged that there really was no difference in the ability of various parties to manage the country's most important problem, the economy.

Why would a party that had been out of office for a decade be viewed as able to do a better job of managing the economy than an incumbent party that had been in office for nine years? First, managing a country's economy well, and more important for electoral reasons, getting credit from the public for doing a good job, is no easy thing in a mature democracy with a market-oriented economy. In an age of increasing globalization, many of the factors that affect an individual country's economy are beyond the control of its government. Moreover, the economies of mature democracies are incredibly complex, and the instruments available to affect them by either a government or some central banking authority are relatively limited. The principal ones, other than taxing and spending and trade policy, are managing the money supply and interest rates. Of course, these can and do have important consequences for the economy, but manifestations of their effects may not be immediately apparent, especially to ordinary people not versed in the principles of economics.

Moreover, economic policy instruments do not always work. In Canada and the United States, attempts to control inflation by steadily increasing interest rates in the 1970s and early 1980s seemingly had no impact other than to further erode economic performance and increase the financial problems of the nation's citizens.

Nevertheless, sizable majorities of people believe that government bears responsibility for the state of the economy. For example, when the economy improved between 1984 and 1987, a substantial number of Canadians judged that the government was doing a good job (see Figure 7.8). When it began to decline after the 1988 election, there was a sharp increase in the number of people who judged that the government was doing a bad job.

Unfortunately for governments of mature democracies such as Canada and the United States, responsibility attribution is likely to be asymmetric and a kind of "one-edged sword" (e.g., Bloom and Price, 1975). Thus, the more positively people judge the nation's economy and the more they feel good about their own material circumstances, the less likely they are to credit the government. Conversely, when people are unhappy about the national economy, or their own personal financial situation, they are more likely to hold the government at fault. Data from the PSC surveys indicate that this kind of one-sided attribution process is at work in Canada (cf. Kornberg and Clarke, 1992; Clarke, Kornberg, and Wearing, 2000). This finding is consequential because, as Figure 7.9 shows, between 1988 and 1993 there was a five-fold increase in the number of people who believed that the national economy had become worse over the past few years. Evaluations of changes in personal finances were more muted, but a pattern of increasing pessimism is apparent.

The Mulroney-Campbell PC government thus faced the prospect of going to the people in a context of very widespread unhappiness with economic conditions. Adding to the government's woes was a corresponding decline in evaluations of government performance across several policy areas.[19] Some of these evaluations were

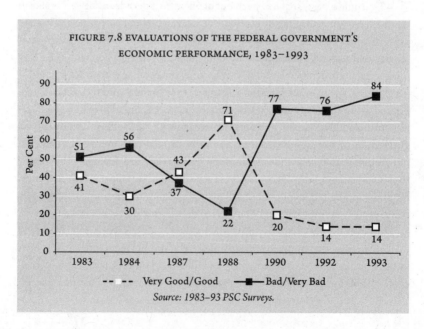

FIGURE 7.8 EVALUATIONS OF THE FEDERAL GOVERNMENT'S ECONOMIC PERFORMANCE, 1983–1993

Source: 1983–93 PSC Surveys.

closely related to the poor economic conditions facing the country. Table 7.7 shows that the portion of the 1993 sample reporting that the government was doing "not very well" in providing opportunities for work was 38 per cent higher than it had been in 1988. A smaller, but still significant, decline in confidence regarding the government's handling of inflation is also apparent. Further, for a Progressive Conservative government that had campaigned in 1984 on a platform that social programs were a "sacred trust," citizen evaluations of that government's performance in the areas of health care and education had also declined. The only improvements were in the areas of environmental protection and the provision of welfare services. Overall, this was hardly a report card that the incumbent PC party could point to with pride when trying to make a case to the voters when it went to the polls in the 1993 election.

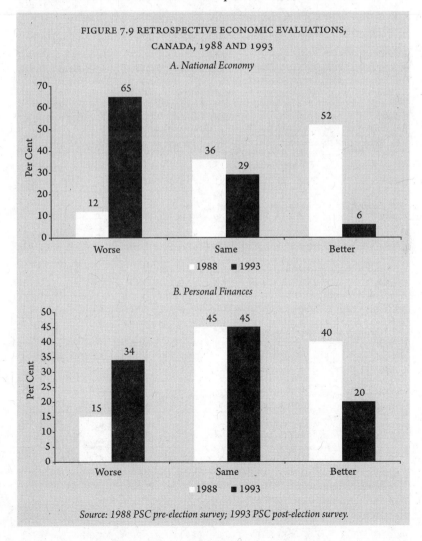

FIGURE 7.9 RETROSPECTIVE ECONOMIC EVALUATIONS, CANADA, 1988 AND 1993

A. National Economy

B. Personal Finances

Source: 1988 PSC pre-election survey; 1993 PSC post-election survey.

TABLE 7.7 EVALUATIONS OF GOVERNMENT PERFORMANCE,
CANADA, 1988–1993

Question: "For each of the following statements, please tell me if you think the federal government is doing very well, fairly well, or not very well."

	NOT VERY WELL	FAIRLY WELL	VERY WELL	χ^2
A. Provide welfare services for anyone that needs them?				
1988	18.4	56.2	25.3	
1993	14.6	52.8	32.7	25.52
B. Make sure that everyone who wants to work has the opportunity to do so?				
1988	35.8	52.1	12.1	
1993	74.0	22.8	3.2	508.57
C. Protect people's lives and property?				
1988	16.4	66.4	17.2	
1993	22.3	63.8	13.9	22.47
D. Ensure that the personal liberties and rights of people are never endangered?				
1988	19.9	61.3	18.7	
1993	24.2	60.4	15.4	12.42
E. Ensure that inflation is kept under control?				
1988	28.9	60.1	11.0	
1993	43.8	42.4	13.8	110.19
F. Ensure that everyone has their health needs looked after?				
1988	13.2	49.3	37.0	
1993	13.8	57.5	28.7	29.41
G. Clean up and protect the environment?				
1988	61.6	32.5	5.9	
1993	45.3	48.1	6.7	96.45
H. Ensure that people get all the education they are capable of?				
1988	26.5	53.7	19.8	
1993	38.0	50.1	12.0	70.34

Note: Questions from the 1988 pre-election and 1993 post-election PSC studies. All $\chi^2(df=2)$ tests (i.e., whether answers were significantly different across years) were significant ($p < .05$). Answers are in percentages.

VOTING IN 1988

Table 7.8 presents the results of estimating composite models of voting in the 1988 federal election. The table tells a now familiar story, with leader images, judgments regarding which party is best able to handle important issues, and party identification all exerting significant effects in expected directions. Thus, for example, positive feelings about Brian Mulroney, perceptions that the PCs are best on the most important issues, and PC partisanship are all positively associated with Conservative voting and negatively associated with voting for the Liberals or the NDP. In all of the other elections we have considered, these variables formed the core of the valence politics model of electoral choice. However, in 1988, since 90 per cent chose free trade as the most important election issue, party best on most important issue overwhelmingly refers to free trade. Of course, free trade is a position not a valence issue, with large numbers of voters favoring the FTA and large numbers opposing it. The importance of this issue is underscored by the finding that, aside from its role in the voting models as the dominant most important issue, opinions on the desirability of the FTA also have significant and properly signed effects. Controlling for all other factors, pro-FTA attitudes were positively associated with PC voting and negatively associated with Liberal and NDP voting.[20]

Other significant predictors in Table 7.8 include tactical voting and various demographics. As in the analyses of more recent Canadian elections discussed in Chapters Two and Three, the latter effects are quite weak. Overall, the estimated (McFadden) R^2 in the models of PC, Liberal, and NDP voting with just the demographic variables is only .05 (analysis not shown). In contrast, the effects of tactical voting considerations are consistently statistically significant ($p < .001$) in these models, with these effects working to help the PCs and hurt both the Liberals and the NDP. Finally, the effects of both economic evaluations and attitudes towards the Meech Lake Accord are very weak, with the former having a marginal positive impact on NDP voting ($p \leq .10$), and the latter, a marginal positive impact on Liberal voting ($p \leq .10$).[21]

Overall, the composite model fares well. The estimated R^2s are quite large—.79 in the PC versus other parties analysis (Table 7.8, Model A), and .73 in the Liberal and NDP versus PC analysis (Table 7.8, Model B)—and the percentages of voters correctly classified are impressive, 94.8 per cent for the former analysis and 90.5 per cent for the latter one. Also, key predictor variables are similar to those in voting models for other elections. As Table 7.9 shows, the strongest predictors in the PC versus other party voting models are feelings about Mulroney and Turner, and perceptions that the PCs are best able to handle the most important issue. Changing feelings about Mulroney and Turner can alter the probability of a PC vote by 83 and 53 points, respectively, whereas changing perceptions of the party best on the most important issue can change that probability by 55 points. In addition, net of these and other

TABLE 7.8 COMPOSITE MODEL OF FACTORS AFFECTING VOTING
IN THE 1988 CANADIAN FEDERAL ELECTION

| | MODEL A | MODEL B | |
	PC	LIBERAL	NDP
Predictor Variables			
Leaders:			
Turner	-.03***	.05***	.01
Mulroney	.05***	-.06***	-.05***
Broadbent	-.01	-.01	.04***
Party Closest Most Important Issue:			
Liberal	-1.23**	1.26**	.61
PC	2.53***	-2.38***	-2.70***
NDP	-1.35*	.40	2.19***
Other	1.60	-1.94	-1.02
Party Identification:			
Liberal	-.69*	1.20**	-.23
PC	1.28***	-1.16**	-1.38***
NDP	-2.72***	1.99**	2.75***
Other	.28	-.07	-1.02
Economic Evaluations:			
Prospective	-.08	.00	.20
Retrospective	-.18	.11	.29a
Tactical Voting	2.33***	-2.28***	-2.80***
Position Issues:			
Free Trade	1.24***	-1.44***	-1.08***
Meech Lake	-.20	.35a	.04a
Demographics:			
Age	.01	-.00	-.00
Gender	-.40a	.29	.46a
Income	.12a	-.07	-.21*
Atlantic	.52	-.67	-.40
Quebec-French	-.04	-.74*	.85*
Quebec-Non-French	-.64	.54	-.30
Prairies	.92*	-1.07*	-.77*
British Columbia	.53	-1.05*	.39
Constant	-3.20***	2.91***	1.38a
McFadden R^2	.79	.73	
McKelvey R^2	.88	–	
Per Cent Correctly Classified	94.8	90.5	
AIC	417.82	818.50	

*** p < .001; ** p < .01; * p < .05; a p < .10; one-tailed test.
– not defined for multinomial logit analysis.
†—Akaike Information Criterion (AIC)—smaller values indicate better model performance.
Note: Model A is a binomial logit contrasting PC voting with voting for the Liberal and NDP parties. Model B is a multinomial logit of Liberal and NDP voting with PC voting as the reference category.

TABLE 7.9 VOTING PROBABILITIES IN THE 1988 CANADIAN FEDERAL
ELECTION, STRONGEST PREDICTORS

PARTY VOTED FOR	CHANGE IN VOTING PROBABILITY
A. *Progressive Conservative*	
Feelings about PC Leader Brian Mulroney	+.83
PCs Best on Most Important Issue	+.55
Feelings about Liberal Leader John Turner	-.53
Free Trade	+.50
B. *Liberal*	
Feelings about Liberal Leader John Turner	+.73
Feelings about PC Leader Brian Mulroney	-.66
Free Trade	-.39
C. *NDP*	
Feelings about NDP Leader Ed Broadbent	+.57
NDP Best on Most Important Issue	+.52
NDP Party Identification	+.36
Free Trade	-.14

Note: *PC vote probabilities are calculated using Model A in Table 7.8. Liberal and NDP vote probabilities are calculated using Model B in Table 7.8.*

effects, changing opinions about the desirability of free trade can alter the probability of voting PC by 50 points.

As Table 7.9 also shows, changing feelings about party leaders have strong effects on the likelihood of voting Liberal or NDP. In addition, attitudes towards free trade, expressed either directly or indirectly via party best on most important issue, have large effects on the probability of casting a Liberal ballot, and party best on most important issue and being an NDP identifier have large effects on support for the New Democrats. Although the direct effect of attitudes towards free trade on the probability of voting NDP are not especially large (-.14), the sizable impact of select-ing the New Democrats as best on the most important issue (+.52) again testifies to the importance of free trade in 1988. Regardless of which party's vote one considers, opinions about the FTA are important. These opinions, together with party leader images, did much to drive the vote.

VOTING IN 1993

Similar to more recent Canadian federal elections, analyses of voting behavior in 1993 are complicated by the presence of different party systems in Quebec and the rest of the country. We accommodate this difference by performing separate analyses

TABLE 7.10 COMPOSITE MODEL OF FACTORS AFFECTING VOTING
IN THE 1993 CANADIAN FEDERAL ELECTION IN QUEBEC
AND REST OF CANADA (ROC)

	MODEL A PC	MODEL B LIBERAL	MODEL B NDP	MODEL B REFORM	MODEL C BQ
Predictor Variables					
Leaders:					
Campbell	.03***	-.03***	-.01	-.03***	-.01
Chrétien	-.03**	.06***	-.01	.01	-.02*
McLaughlin	-.00	.01	.04***	-.01	.01
Manning	-.00	-.01	-.02a	.05***	X
Bouchard	X	X	X	X	.01
Party Closest Most Important Issue:					
Liberal	-.71*	1.43***	-.08	.07	-.84a
PC	2.69***	-2.76***	-1.73*	-2.21***	.50
NDP	-1.18a	-1.03	1.99*	.72	.91
Reform	-2.50***	-.50a	.09	2.56***	X
BQ	X	X	X	X	1.58*
Party Identification:					
Liberal	-.69	.95***	-.15	.20	-.89a
PC	2.31***	-2.63***	-2.12***	-.85a	.09
NDP	.24	-1.05a	1.17a	-.17	-.63
Reform	-.61	-3.17*	.25	1.98*	X
BQ	X	X	X	X	1.84**
Economic Evaluations:					
Prospective	.10	.04	.14	-.25	-.71**
Personal Retrospective	.10	-.02	-.33a	-.07	.31
Strategic Voting	-1.02*	2.66***	-.16	.39	.20
Free Trade	.20*	-.16	-.12	-.10	.07
Quebec Sovereignty	X	X	X	X	.76*
Demographics:					
Age	.02*	-.03*	-.03*	-.00	-.02a
Gender	.22	-.39	-.13	-.03	.46
Income	-.19	.33***	-.00	.09	-.12
Atlantic	.85*	-.69	.11	-1.45*	X
Quebec-French	X	X	X	X	.09
Prairies	.25	-.69a	-.11	.08	X
British Columbia	-1.18*	.36	2.07***	.97*	X
Constant	-2.91**	-.29	1.58	-1.02	.25
McFadden R²	.64	.71			.63
McKelvey R²	.72	–			.79
Per Cent Correctly Classified	94.2	88.6			90.2
AIC	334.43	795.44			198.61

*** p < .001; ** p < .01; * p < .05; a p < .10; one-tailed test.

X—variable not included in model.

†—Akaike Information Criterion (AIC)—smaller values indicate better model performance.

Note: Model A is a binomial logit contrasting PC voting with voting for any of the opposition parties, ROC voters only. Model B is a multinomial logit of Liberal, NDP, and Reform voting with PC voting as the reference category, ROC voters only. Model C is a binomial logit contrasting BQ and Liberal voting, Quebec only. ROC N = 934; ROC, Quebec N = 308.

of voting in Quebec and the ROC.[22] Results, displayed in Table 7.10, provide strong support for the valence model of electoral choice. All of the "usual suspects" exert statistically significant, properly signed effects. For example, in the analysis of PC voting (see Table 7.10, Model A), attitudes towards Kim Campbell have a significant positive effect, and attitudes towards Jean Chrétien have a significant negative effect. Selection of the PCs as best on the most important issue has a significant positive impact on Conservative support, and selection of the Liberals, NDP, or Reform has a significant negative impact. Also, controlling for these and other effects, PC party identification has a significant positive influence on Conservative support. In varying

TABLE 7.11 VOTING PROBABILITIES IN THE
1993 CANADIAN FEDERAL ELECTION, STRONGEST PREDICTORS

PARTY VOTED FOR	CHANGE IN VOTING PROBABILITY
A. Progressive Conservative	
PCs Best on Most Important Issue	+.43
Feelings about PC Leader Kim Campbell	+.20
PC Party Identification	+.19
Free Trade	+.02
B. Liberal	
Feelings about Liberal Leader Jean Chrétien	+.84
Reform Party Identification	-.64
Income	+.50
C. NDP	
Feelings about NDP Leader Audrey McLaughlin	+.40
NDP Best on Most Important Issue	+.35
NDP Party Identification	+.26
D. Reform Party	
Feelings about Reform Leader Preston Manning	+.82
Reform Party Identification	+.63
Reform Best on Most Important Issue	+.59
E. Bloc Québécois	
Prospective Economic Evaluations	-.52
Feelings about Liberal Leader Jean Chrétien	-.34
BQ Party Identification	+.26
Age	-.26
Attitudes towards Quebec Independence	.23

Note: PC vote probabilities are calculated using Model A in Table 7.10; Liberal, NDP, and Reform vote probabilities are calculated using Model B in Table 7.10; and BQ vote probabilities are calculated using Model C in Table 7.10.

combinations, party leader images, party best on important issue perceptions, and partisanship also significantly affect voting for the Liberals, NDP, and Reform parties (see Table 7.10, Model B).

Finally, it is noteworthy that the effect of free trade, which was *the* issue in 1988, has largely disappeared. As discussed above, the mix of issues cited as most important in 1993 is dominated by heavily valenced economic concerns, and the direct effect of attitudes towards free trade is significant only in the PC voting analysis. And, as Table 7.11 indicates, this effect is very weak. Setting other variables at their means (for continuous variables) or their reference values (for dummy variables), and varying attitudes towards free trade alters the probability of voting PC by only two points. As is typical in Canadian federal elections, the "big action" is with party leader images, valence issues, and party identification. This is true not only for the old line parties but also for the then new Reform Party. In Reform's case, increasingly positive feelings about its party leader, Preston Manning, added to the probability of a Reform vote by fully 82 points. The effects of adopting a Reform identification and selecting the party as best on the most important issues were also very sizable, enhancing the likelihood of casting a Reform ballot by 63 and 59 points, respectively.

Factors driving support for the other new federal party, the Bloc Québécois, are similar. As Table 7.10 indicates, although feelings about Bloc leader, Lucien Bouchard, are not significant, selection of the party as best on the most important issue, being a BQ identifier, and feelings about Liberal leader Jean Chrétien have significant predictable effects on BQ voting. Prospective economic evaluations are also significant and, as one would anticipate, voters with negative views about what the future holds for the Canadian economy and their own financial situation are more likely to endorse the separatist BQ.

A major position issue was also at work in Quebec in 1993. Controlling for all other predictors, believing that sovereignty is a desirable option for Quebec has a significant influence on BQ voting. There are other marginally significant ($p < .10$) effects too. These include a belief that the Liberals are best on the most important issue, Liberal party identification, and age. Those favoring the Liberals on important issues, Liberal identifiers, and older people are all less likely to support the BQ.

Of these several predictors, economic evaluations, feelings about Jean Chrétien, BQ identification, and age have the strongest ability to shift the probability of voting for the Bloc. Changing economic evaluations can vary the probability of casting a BQ ballot by 52 points, while changes in feelings about Chrétien, BQ identification, and age can change that probability by 26 to 34 points (see Table 7.11, Panel E). Attitudes towards Quebec sovereignty also have a sizable effect, being able to shift the likelihood of voting BQ by 23 points. Taken together, these findings paint a portrait of a typical Bloc supporter as a young person who combines economic pessimism with a dislike of the leader of the major opposition party, the Liberals. These

characteristics, together with (a newly adopted) BQ identification rooted in a positive view of Quebec sovereignty drove support for the Bloc and enabled it to make a
dramatic breakthrough in the 1993 federal election (see also Clarke, Kornberg, and
Wearing, 2000). As in 1988, a major position issue was at work in 1993.

CONCLUSION: VALENCE POLITICS
CONFRONTS POSITION ISSUES

The 1980 US presidential election and the 1988 and 1993 Canadian federal elections were emotionally charged, highly consequential events. In 1980 an incumbent Democratic president was thrown out of office and replaced by an avowedly
neo-conservative Republican intent on taking US economic and foreign policy in
radically new directions. In 1988 a single issue in Canada, a hotly disputed free trade
agreement between Canada and the United States, dominated an exciting election
campaign. Victory by the incumbent Progressive Conservatives paved the way
for PC leader Prime Minister Brian Mulroney to implement the free trade agreement, impose a major new tax (the GST), and broker two unsuccessful constitutional accords designed to revamp the Canadian federal system. In 1993 the failure
of these constitutional initiatives, coupled with widespread antipathy to the GST
and a deep persistent recession, paved the way for the ouster of the PCs and the dramatic electoral successes of two regionally based federal parties, Reform and the Bloc
Québécois. A principal motor of BQ support was increasing sympathy for Quebec
sovereignty. Revival of the sovereignty option brought a quintessential deeply divisive position issue into the electoral arena. Its injection into the 1993 federal election
affected the outcome of that contest and thereby helped to change the contours of
Canada's national party system.

   Thus, significant position issues were at work in the American and Canadian
political arenas during these three elections. As well, analyses presented in this chapter document that these issues exerted substantial effects on electoral choice. Voters'
proximities to Reagan and Carter on what we have termed the "New Deal" issue
dimension had a sizable impact on the choices Americans made in 1980. Similarly,
since free trade was virtually the only issue in the 1988 Canadian federal election,
voters' positions on free trade dominated the selection of which party was deemed
best on the most important issue which, as usual, was an important factor affecting
voting behavior. Although the issue agenda in the 1993 Canadian federal election had
changed greatly since 1988, the presence of an avowedly separatist opposition party
in Quebec meant that attitudes towards Quebec sovereignty had direct and indirect
effects on how voters in that province behaved.

   While documenting the reality of position issue effects, analyses of voting in these
three elections also confirm important elements of the valence politics model. Party

leader images, a key component of that model, exerted large, sometimes massive, effects. Party identifications were also influential and, again, their effects were often decidedly nontrivial. In addition, similar to more recent elections in the two countries, analyses indicate that composite models informed by multiple theoretical perspectives outperform models informed by particular perspectives. Combinations of valence politics and position issue considerations did much to shape voting behavior in the 1980 US election and the 1988 and 1993 Canadian federal elections. Party leader images and partisanship, key aspects of the valence politics model, were very much in play in all three cases, but important and controversial position issues gained widespread salience. The presence of these issues reshaped the mix of factors governing electoral choice. Although election issue agendas in Canada and the United States are typically dominated by valence issues, the three cases considered in this chapter emphasize that position issues can occasionally be both salient and influential.

Notes

1   For Carter, the most devastating moment in the 1980 presidential candidate's debates came when Reagan made the valence appeal by asking the television audience, "Are you better off than you were four years ago?" (cited by Wirthlin and Hall, 2004).

2   For more insight into the leadership battle in the Liberal Party after Trudeau, with highlights of Turner's strengths and weaknesses, see Carty, Cross, and Young, 2000 (77–79).

3   For an excellent overview of Reagan's use of humor see Cannon 2000 (ch. 8).

4   See Greenstein (2000) for a critical review of Reagan's lack of attention to key staff and what they were doing, something that could have contributed to crises such as "Irangate."

5   In contrast, Carter's team depicted the state of the nation in the late 1970s, with its concatenation of economic and foreign policy problems, as creating a "malaise" that had "descended on American society." It is important to note that the specific words were made by Carter's aide but became associated with the incumbent president's views about the American public (Greenstein, 2000: 135–37).

6   Reagan's leading opponent in the Republican primaries, George H.W. Bush who later became Reagan's vice president and was elected president in 1988, also initially dismissed Reagan's plans to spend more and tax far less as "voodoo economics."

7   Questions about candidate traits are now a standard feature of the ANES. These questions were first asked in 1980, and the battery was introduced by the interviewer with the following lead: "I am going to read a list of words and phrases people use to describe political figures. For each, please tell me

whether the word or phrase describes the candidate I name extremely well, quite well, not too well, or not well at all. Think about [candidate]. The first word on our list is [trait]. In your opinion does the word [trait] describe [candidate] extremely well, quite well, not too well, or not well at all?" Subsequent trait evaluations were obtained by the interviewer asking, "Does [trait] describe [candidate]?" Traits were coded on a scale of one to five, such that high scores reflected the most positive views of the candidate. Nonresponses were coded at the mid-point of three.

In 1980, the traits asked and the distribution of evaluations are displayed in Figure 7.1 for Reagan and Carter. Separate principal components analyses (PCA) of the traits for all three presidential candidates each yielded two-factor solutions. For Reagan and Carter, the first factor with their respective eigenvalues of 3.30 and 3.04 contained the traits falling under the theme of leadership. For Reagan, these were the moral, knowledgeable, inspiring, and strong leadership traits. For Carter, these traits were knowledgeable, inspiring, strong leader, and weak. Reagan's and Carter's second dimension for leadership traits contained those centered on evaluations of the candidates' integrity and the respective candidates' eigenvalues on this second dimension were 0.93 and 1.12. For Reagan, the traits loading on this second "integrity" dimension were dishonest, weak, and power hungry, and for Carter, the traits on the second dimension were moral, dishonest, and power hungry. The two-factor solution explained 60.3 per cent of the indicators' total variance for Reagan and 59.4 per cent of the variance of the indicators for Carter. Citizen evaluations of Anderson's traits took on a slightly different structure. The first factor, with an eigenvalue 2.69, contained many of the integrity traits (e.g. moral, dishonest, weak, power hungry, and knowledgeable), and the second factor, with an eigenvalue of 1.33 contained the leadership traits of inspiring and strong leadership. The knowledgeable trait also had a moderate loading on the second factor. The two-factor solution explained 57.3 per cent of the variance of the respondents' trait evaluations for John Anderson.

8 In the multivariate analyses that follow, we generated a principal components analysis (PCA) of five ANES questions asking whether respondents "strongly approve," "not strongly approve," "not strongly disapprove," or "strongly disapprove" of the job President Carter was doing overall and in the important policy areas of inflation, unemployment, the hostage crisis, and energy policy. The PCA yielded a single factor with an eigenvalue of 2.97 that explained 59.4 per cent of the variance in the respondents' answers to such questions. Each variable was coded from one through five, such that higher scores reflected strongest approval of President Carter's performance in the area, and nonresponses were coded at the mid-point value of three to preserve cases.

9 For the multivariate analyses we ran a PCA of the now familiar (see endnote nine, Chapter Four) respondents' prospective and retrospective economic evaluations of their own fortunes and the national economy. The analysis yielded a single-factor solution with an eigenvalue of 1.62 and 40.4 per cent of the variance explained. All factor loadings were above 0.50.

10 In the multivariate analyses that follow we performed a PCA to obtain the issue space of variables coded to measure the absolute distance between the respondents' positions and those they attributed to Reagan on seven questions or issues: defense spending, government services, aid to Blacks, women's roles, general liberal-conservative position, dealings with Russia, and the government's responsibility to provide jobs. The PCA yielded a one-factor solution with an eigenvalue of 2.78 that explained 39.8 per cent of the variance in responses to the issue variables. All indicators had loadings above 0.50, and we named the variable consisting of the factor scores from the PCA "Reagan New Deal." Variables had a range of zero to six, and respondents who did not place either themselves or the candidate on an issue were coded to the mean absolute differences for the issue.

11 The PCA conducted utilized the same questions used in the above analysis for Reagan and generated a "Carter New Deal" first dimension with an eigenvalue of 2.35 and a "Carter Women" second dimension with an eigenvalue of 0.92. The PCA yields a two-factor solution that explained 49.4 per cent of the variance in the seven variables and, with the exception of the women's roles variable, all had loadings above 0.50 on the first dimension. The variable created to measure the absolute distance between the respondent's views about women and those they ascribed to President Carter was the only variable with a loading above 0.30 on the second dimension.

12 See endnote 12, Chapter Four, for an explanation of the importance of AIC values in judging rival theoretical models of voter choice.

13 The gender variable in the multivariate analysis is coded one for men and zero for women. Income was a 22-category variable. Respondents not reporting their income were given a value of 14. Respondents' religiosity was the factor score obtained after a PCA of two indicators, one measuring the respondents' church attendance and the other measuring their responses to a four-category variable measuring their assessments about the Bible being the true word of God. The single-factor solution generated an eigenvalue of 1.23 and explained 61.2 per cent of the item variance. Respondents not answering these questions (v801176 and v800694 on the 1980 ANES) were assumed to believe that the Bible was the work of humans and not to attend church. The reader may note that we did not include variables that were factor scores generated from a PCA of the mean absolute differences between Anderson and the respondents. This is because, on all issues utilized in the analysis, more than 50 per cent of the sample were not able to locate Anderson in the given space.

14 As in the case elsewhere in the book, probabilities in the multivariate analyses for this chapter were obtained using the CLARIFY software package for STATA.

15 Except where noted, data used for the analyses of Canadian political behavior in 1988 and 1993 come from the Political Support in Canada (PSC) surveys for these years. In 1988 a pre-post wave was conducted, and in 1993 a post-election study was undertaken. Leadership and honesty evaluations of

the party leaders used in the questions depicted in Figure 7.7 had a range of 0–10. In the multivariate analyses, 100-point party leader feeling thermometers are used.

16 If it had been ratified, the Accord would have contained a clause designating Quebec as a "distinct society." This would have given constitutional sanction to the historic claim of Quebec nationalists that Quebec really was not the same kind of province as the others. To most francophone Quebeckers, the distinct society clause was a simple statement of reality. However, it aroused widespread opposition in the rest of Canada.

17 Concern about the economy among Canadians existed well before the 1988 election. Similar to many Western countries, including the United States, the origins of the country's economic problems were grounded in massive increases in energy costs that occurred in the wake of the 1973 Arab oil embargo and the rise of the OPEC cartel. Canada found itself afflicted by stagflation, simultaneous surges in inflation and unemployment, coupled with sagging growth rates. For example, annual rates of inflation that had averaged 2.2 per cent in the 1950s and 1960s rose sharply in the 1970s and peaked at 12.5 per cent in 1981. Unemployment, which stood at 4.4 per cent when the 1970s began, was more than 7 per cent in the latter half of the decade and climbed into double digits in the early 1980s. In Canada, between 1972—the year before the oil embargo and OPEC—and 1982, the well-named "misery index" that combined inflation and unemployment rates rose from 11 per cent to 21.8 per cent (cf. Clarke, Kornberg, and Wearing, 2000: 32–34).

18 Note that these percentages reflect those who chose a party after naming the economy as the most important issue. The party best on most important issue percentages reported in Table 7.6 reflect the party preferences of all the respondents who named an issue as most important.

19 These questions are not used as predictor variables in the multivariate analyses that follow. Instead, they are used to give the reader a sense of the decline in public confidence for the Progressive Conservatives between 1988 and 1993.

20 Support for the Free Trade Agreement in 1988 was coded one and opposition against it was coded -1, as was support for and opposition against the Meech Lake Accord. Unlike the FTA, where almost all of the sample had a position, approximately half of the 1988 sample reported that they either had not heard about or had no position on the Accord and these respondents were given a score of zero.

21 For the multivariate analyses, gender is coded one if the respondent was male. Income is an 8-category variable with the lowest category, 1, indicating that the respondent's household income was under $10,000 and the highest category, 8, indicating that the respondent's income was greater than $70,000 (in 1988). Respondents failing to report their income were given a code of four. Respondents failing to give their age were coded 43.6. The strategic voting question in the 1988 post-election PSC study asked whether, "when the respondent was making up their mind how to vote," they "really

prefer[red] another party." Respondents with an affirmative response were coded one for the tactical voting variable.

A PCA of the economic evaluations questions in 1988 yielded a two-factor solution, the first mostly capturing the respondents' retrospective evaluations and the second capturing their prospective evaluations (eigenvalues for the two dimensions were 1.62 and 0.92, respectively, with 63.4 per cent of the variance explained). In the 1988 PSC pre-election study, the national retrospective question asked about trends in the Canadian economy over the past three to four years. Respondents could answer that it was either "better" (coded three), "worse" (coded one), or "about the same" (coded two) as it had been in the past. For the national prospective evaluation question, respondents were given the same answer choices to a question asking whether they thought the Canadian economy would get better, worse, or stay the same "over the next year or so." For the personal prospective and retrospective questions, respondents were given a three- to four- year time horizon. For all of the questions, nonrespondents and those reporting that the economic situation had or would get better in some areas and worse in other areas were coded a mid-point score of two.

22 In Table 7.10, the gender variable is coded one if the respondent was male. Respondents who did not give their age are given a value of 46.3. Income is a 9-category variable with the lowest category, 1, indicating that the respondent's household income was under $10,000 and with the highest category, 9, indicating that the respondent's income was greater than $80,000 (in 1993). Respondents not reporting their income were given a value of 5.17. The free trade positional variable is an additive index of respondents' answers to questions probing support for both the Free Trade Agreement and the North American Free Trade Agreement. Support was coded three, those not responding or neither opposed or supportive were coded two, and those opposed were coded one. Thus, the index had a minimum value of two and a maximum value of six. Quebeckers answering that they were in favor of sovereignty were coded three, those who did not answer or did not know were coded two, and those opposed were coded one.

The four economic evaluation questions in the 1993 PSC study asked: a) whether the respondent thought their personal finances would be better off in the next three to four years (personal prospective); b) whether the respondent was satisfied with his/her personal material well-being (personal retrospective); c) whether the national economy was better, worse, or the same than in the previous three to four years (national retrospective); and d) whether the Canadian economy would get better, remain the same, or get worse in the next year (national prospective). A PCA of the four economic evaluation questions for 1993 yielded a two-factor solution with 61.5 per cent of the variance explained. The first factor with indicators consisting of all but personal retrospective evaluations had an eigenvalue of 1.44, and the second factor that was mostly generated by personal retrospections had an eigenvalue of 1.02.

CHAPTER EIGHT

At the Polls? Why (Some) People Vote

Democratic politics and voting go hand in hand. In contemporary democracies, new and old alike, voting in periodic elections is the principal—often the only—way by which the vast majority of people express their political preferences. As observed in Chapter One, most research on voting behavior in Canada, the United States, and elsewhere has focused on the choices people make among candidates and parties rather than on the choice of whether to vote. In many mature democracies, including Canada, the historically heavy emphasis on studying party choice seemingly made sense. Turnout levels in national elections were high, with very large majorities of people regularly exercising their right to vote. The idea that democracy and high rates of voting turnout are virtually synonymous was cogently expressed by Butler and Stokes (1969) some four decades ago in their path-breaking study *Political Change in Britain*. They observed that "blurred ideas of popular sovereignty and universal suffrage are so interwoven in prevailing conceptions of British government that the obligation to vote becomes almost an aspect of the citizen's national identity" (Butler and Stokes, 1969: 37).

If they were writing now, Butler and Stokes would not have reached the same conclusion. Turnout rates in Britain and many other mature democracies, including Canada, have fallen substantially (e.g., Dalton and Wattenberg, 2000; Franklin, 2004; Pammett and LeDuc, 2003). In the United States, where relatively low turnout rates were the norm throughout most of the twentieth century, the situation remains substantially unchanged, with concerned observers celebrating if as many as three people in five cast a ballot in a presidential election. Voting turnout has become a problematic aspect of democratic politics. Accordingly, in this chapter we investigate why some people choose to vote and others refrain from doing so. We begin by examining turnout patterns in Canadian federal elections over time. Then, we use survey data gathered in the 2004 Political Support in Canada (PSC) study to analyze individual-level factors that affect the likelihood of casting a ballot. Next, we repeat these analyses for the United States using aggregate data on turnout rates and individual-level survey data from the 2004 American National Election Study (ANES). The conclusion reconsiders major findings.

TURNOUT TRENDS IN CANADA

Figure 8.1 documents trends in turnout in Canadian federal elections since 1945. As shown, for the 15 elections held between 1945 and 1988, turnout fluctuated from a low of 68 per cent in 1953 to an impressive high of 81 per cent in 1958. On average, three in four of those who were eligible to cast a ballot did so, making the 1988 figure of 76 per cent a very typical figure for the entire period. Turnout for all subsequent elections has been lower, with the number of people going to the polls trending steadily downward from 70 per cent in 1993 to 60.5 per cent in 2004. The latter figure is the lowest in history for a Canadian federal election. In 2006 turnout rebounded very modestly to 64.5 per cent. This increase still left the voting rate more than 10 per cent lower than the average figure for the 1945–88 period.

An analyst might entertain four different models for these downward dynamics of turnout in Canadian federal elections. Most simply, it might be hypothesized that turnout has simply decreased as a linear function of time, i.e., there is a tendency in each successive election for turnout to be lower than it was in the previous one. However, it is apparent from the data in Figure 8.1 that a model of progressive decrease in turnout is problematic. Turnout actually increased in the late 1950s and early 1960s before declining in the 1970s and 1980s, and then plummeting after 1988. It thus appears that there is a second possibility that the underlying dynamics of turnout in Canadian federal elections have followed a concave or *quadratic* trend pattern.

A third possibility is that turnout has followed a general quadratic pattern as just described, but that the downward movement was significantly enhanced by lowering

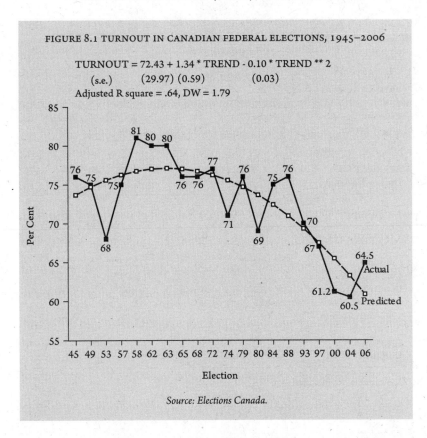

FIGURE 8.1 TURNOUT IN CANADIAN FEDERAL ELECTIONS, 1945–2006

TURNOUT = 72.43 + 1.34 * TREND - 0.10 * TREND ** 2
(s.e.)   (29.97) (0.59)   (0.03)
Adjusted R square = .64, DW = 1.79

Source: Elections Canada.

the voting age to 18 prior to the 1972 federal election. This would be consistent with arguments advanced by analysts such as Franklin (2004), who contend that the decrease in turnout in many mature democracies reflects the presence of successive cohorts of young (18–20-year-old) voters, many of whom never acquire a habit of voting.

A fourth and final possibility is that turnout in federal elections was really characterized by nothing but trendless fluctuation before 1993, i.e., turnout rose in some years and fell in others, but there was no overall pattern. However, since 1993 turnout has simply been lower, with the modest rebound in 2006 signalling that there is no real downward trend in recent elections. This idea of a downward "step shift" in turnout starting in 1993 is, of course, consistent with the major change in Canada's national party system that occurred at that time.

We may investigate these alternative dynamic processes by regressing turnout percentages in the several elections on a time counter and simple 0–1 variables designed to capture downward step shifts in turnout in 1972 and 1993, respectively. As shown in Table 8.1, the linear trend model (Model A) works as hypothesized, with

TABLE 8.1 MODELS OF TURNOUT IN CANADIAN FEDERAL ELECTIONS, 1945–2006

PREDICTOR VARIABLES	MODEL A		MODEL B	
	B	S.E.	B	S.E.
Constant	79.81***	2.14	72.43***	2.69
Linear Trend	-.67***	.18	1.34**	.59
Quadratic Trend			-.10***	.03
Adjusted R^2 =	.41		.64	
Durbin-Watson d	1.03		1.79	

PREDICTOR VARIABLES	MODEL C		MODEL D	
	B	S.E.	B	S.E.
Constant	71.73***	3.02	72.02***	2.52
Linear Trend	1.55*	.71	1.05*	.63
Quadratic Trend	-.10***	.03	-.07*	.04
18-Year-Old Vote	-1.85	3.55	X	X
1993 Party System	X	X	-3.49	3.74
Adjusted R^2 =	.62		.64	
Durbin-Watson d	1.86		1.85	

X—variable not included in model.
*** $p < .001$; ** $p < .01$; * $p < .05$; one-tailed test.

the time trend variable having a statistically significant ($p < .001$) negative coefficient. This linear trend model explains slightly over 40 per cent of the over-time variation in turnout. Model B, which incorporates a curvilinear (quadratic) trend does considerably better. There are two trend terms in this model: a simple time counter that is designed to capture an initial upward movement in turnout, and a squared time counter that is designed to capture the subsequent downward movement. Both trend coefficients are significant and correctly signed, i.e., the first time counter carries a positive sign and the second one, a negative sign. In addition, the percentage of variation in turnout explained increases markedly to 64 per cent, thereby signifying that the quadratic trend model has a much better fit than the simple linear trend model.[1]

Model C is one where we add a post-1968 step-shift variable to the quadratic trend model just described. This enables us to determine if accounting for lowering the voting age to 18 improves our ability to account for the overtime dynamics in turnout. The answer is "no." Model C indicates that "all of the action" is with the quadratic trend. Although the variable measuring the impact of lowering the voting age to 18 is negatively signed, it is not statistically significant $(p > .05)$. In contrast, both trend coefficients remain statistically significant and correctly signed. Results for Model D, which incorporates the post-1988 new party system variable, are similar. As hypothesized, the new party system variable is negatively signed, but it is not statistically significant, whereas the quadratic trend coefficients remain significant $(p < .05)$ and properly signed.

Taken together, these analyses indicate that the unadorned quadratic trend model tells the best story about aggregate dynamics in turnout in Canadian federal elections since World War II. A glance back at Figure 8.1 shows the concave turnout pattern for turnout predicted by this model. What this model suggests is that the downward movement in turnout is the result of a long-term ongoing process rather than an abrupt downward adjustment accompanying changes in the age of majority or the onset of a new party system. In a recent study, Pammett and LeDuc (2003) have argued that the process involves the presence of younger cohorts of people in the Canadian electorate who do not view voting as an important aspect of citizenship. Over time, processes of demographic replacement are making these people a larger and larger proportion of the entire electorate. This, in turn, accounts for the dominant downward curve in turnout depicted in Figure 8.1.

To investigate factors associated with voting turnout in more detail, we turn to individual-level analyses and employ survey data gathered in the 2004 PSC survey. The relationship between age group and turnout is summarized in Figure 8.2. This figure displays percentages of respondents who reported voting in the 2004 federal election, percentages who stated that they were "very interested" in the election, and percentages who said that they have voted in all federal elections for which they have been eligible. The age groups are defined in terms of when members of the group first became eligible to vote in a federal election. The "Harper" group are people who were first eligible to vote in the 2004 election, and the "Chrétien" group are those first eligible to vote in the 1993 election. Other age groups include those entering the electorate in 1984 (Mulroney), 1968 (Trudeau), 1957 (Diefenbaker), and earlier (pre-1957).

The data in Figure 8.2 show striking correlations between age-related cohorts and voting turnout. The percentage reporting that they voted in 2004 increases from slightly over 50 per cent among the 18–21 age group to around 90 per cent or more among the two oldest groups (those 61 or older). Similarly, interest in the 2004 election rises steadily across the age groups, as does the percentage stating that they have voted in every election for which they have been eligible. Again, the age-group differences are impressively large; young people are much less likely to be very interested in the election or to report voting regularly than are older people. These striking patterns are consistent with the idea that age really matters when it comes to involvement in the electoral process.

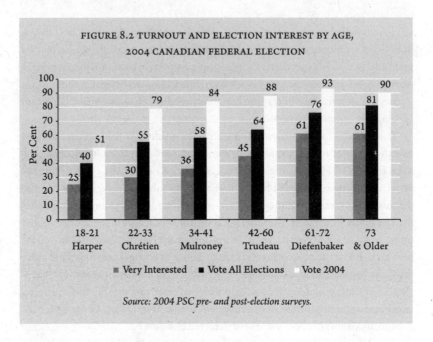

FIGURE 8.2 TURNOUT AND ELECTION INTEREST BY AGE,
2004 CANADIAN FEDERAL ELECTION

Source: 2004 PSC pre- and post-election surveys.

What dynamics underlie these age-related patterns? There are two basic alternatives. One possibility, discussed above, is that recent generations of young people have not been socialized into norms of democratic political participation. Unlike older generations, they fail to see voting as an obligation of citizenship. A second possibility is that the age patterns reflect life-cycle differences. According to this interpretation, young people will gradually become more politically involved as they age. If so, what we call the "Harper" and "Chrétien" groups will eventually participate at rates comparable to their elders, i.e., the "Trudeau" and "Diefenbaker" groups. The two possibilities are not mutually exclusive, i.e., the age patterns seen in the 2004 survey data may reflect a combination of generational and life-cycle effects. In their recent study, Pammett and LeDuc (2003) conclude that this is indeed what is going on in Canada. Currently, young Canadians will vote at higher rates as they age, but they will not participate as much as do people who are currently in older age brackets.

Data limitations make it difficult to distinguish between generational and life-cycle effects with confidence. To ascertain what is actually going on, one would have to re-interview the same people over an extended period of time, repeatedly measuring their levels of electoral participation. If the process were purely generational, then people in currently younger groups would not participate more as they aged. If the process were purely life-cycle, then currently young people would participate more as they became older.

Although the long-run panel data needed to detect these alternatives are unavailable, there is circumstantial evidence of a generational component in the Canadian age-turnout correlation. Particularly intriguing in this regard is Figure 8.3, which shows how the age cohorts in the 2004 survey responded to two questions about their duty to vote. As will be demonstrated below, sense of civic duty is an important predictor of turnout. The patterns in Figure 8.3 are striking—people in the younger age groups are much less likely to express a sense of civic duty than are those in the older groups. Thus, the percentage agreeing with the statement that nonvoting is a "serious neglect" of civic duty rises from 64 per cent among the 18–21 age group, to fully 94 per cent among the 73 and older age group. Similarly, the percentage saying that they would feel "very guilty" if they did not vote rises from 47 per cent in the former group to 90 per cent in the latter one.

Although these patterns clearly indicate that there are large differences in levels of civic duty across age groups, it is not clear whether the observed differences have a generational component. To investigate this possibility, we first regress a measure of sense of civic duty on age, measured in years. Then we repeat the analysis, adding 0–1 dummy variables to designate membership in the Harper, Chrétien, Mulroney, Trudeau, and Diefenbaker age cohorts. If the process is purely a life-cycle one, then we would not expect that the latter variables would contribute to the explanation of variations in civic duty over and above what can be explained by the basic age in years variable. However, if there is a generational component, then the age-cohort variables would significantly increase the goodness-of-fit of the model (Clarke et al.,

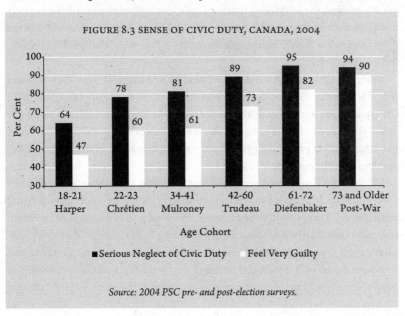

FIGURE 8.3 SENSE OF CIVIC DUTY, CANADA, 2004

Source: 2004 PSC pre- and post-election surveys.

2004; see also Blais, 2000). In fact, this is what happens—the model that includes the age cohort membership variables fits the data significantly better than if only age in years is used (chi-square = 28.77, df = 5, p < .001).[2] This generational component in the relationship between age and feelings of civic duty has implications for what may be expected regarding levels of electoral participation in future federal elections.

MODELLING TURNOUT

Political scientists have advanced a number of different models of voting turnout. Here, we employ the 2004 PSC survey data to investigate how key variables within these models contribute to explaining turnout. The survey data do not contain all of the variables specified in the various expositions of these models, but they do contain several of the most important ones. We will enter these variables in a composite model of turnout to assess their explanatory power.

One of the most influential models of voting turnout is the rational choice model developed by Riker and Ordeshook (1968; 1973). These authors argued that people will vote if the collective benefits of having one party rather than another win an election, discounted by the probability that a person's vote will prove decisive ("pivotal" in their terminology), exceeds the costs of casting a ballot. Voters, being rational, will vote if $P^*B - C > 0$, where P = the probability of casting a pivotal ballot; B = the difference in benefits provided by various parties; and C = the costs of voting. The problem with this simple and elegant formulation lies with the "P" term. As was quickly realized, the probability that any single vote will prove decisive is extremely small (see Gelman, King, and Boscardin, 1998). As a result, the product of P^*B, even if B is large, is less than C, and people do not vote. The model thus predicts nobody will go to the polls!

Riker and Ordeshook amended their model by adding a "D" term. This is where civic duty appears. As modified by the inclusion of the civic duty term, Riker and Ordeshook had a model that worked in the sense that its prediction that some people would vote agreed with the gross fact that many people do go to the polls. However, all of the action in propelling people to the voting booth was in the "D" term. The problem with P remained.

Whitely and Seyd (2002) suggested that what they termed the "general incentives" model could provide a superior explanation of various forms of citizen political participation. As applied to voting turnout, this model adds measures of perceived group and individual benefits associated with voting. It also "softens" the P term from what a strict rational choice theorist would demand. Rather than stipulating that P be perceptions of "pivotality," P becomes a voter's belief that they personally, or people "like them," can influence an election outcome. The result is a "soft" rational choice model of turnout embedded within the larger general incentives model (see Clarke et al., 2004).

Three other models with considerable currency in the literature on turnout are the civic voluntarism model (e.g., Verba, Schlozman, and Brady, 1995; Verba and Nie, 1972), the cognitive mobilization model (e.g., Dalton, 2006; see also Kornberg and Clarke, 1992), and the social capital model. The civic voluntarism model emphasizes the resources that people can access to facilitate participation, as well as their extent of voluntary activity and selected political attitudes (e.g., political interest, strength of party identification). The cognitive mobilization model focuses on voters' awareness of, and engagement with, the political process as indexed by variables such as levels of political knowledge and interest in politics generally and elections in particular. Relevant also are evaluations of specific public policies or the more general functioning of various aspects of the political system. Echoing themes in the civic voluntarism model, the social capital model stresses linkages between society and polity (e.g., Putnam et al., 1993). Feelings of social trust and membership in networks of civic engagement enhance the propensity to participate in politics in various ways, including going to the polls.

In addition to working with one or more of these models, students of voting turnout often have employed two other explanatory variables. Both of these variables are related to the contexts within which particular elections occur. One variable involves perceptions of the extent of competition among competing parties. The idea is that when voters perceive that the race among the parties is close, they will be more likely to vote than when they think that the contest is one-sided. Often, it is claimed that when people perceive a close race, they believe that their vote "matters more," even though, as just discussed, in an electorate comprised of millions of people, the probability that they would actually cast a pivotal vote remains incredibly small. Also, since Canadians do not vote directly to elect a prime minister or a governing party, but rather vote to elect local MPs, it is not clear whether perceptions of national or local inter-party competition are most important. Accordingly, we use measures of perceived competition at both the national and the local level.

A final variable of interest is the extent of party campaign activity. In countries such as Canada, the United States, and Great Britain, local party organizations attempt to "get out the vote" or, more specifically, to get people likely to support their candidate to vote (e.g., Denver and Hands, 1997). However, the effectiveness of parties' activities is controversial, with some analysts arguing that in the modern era all that matters is the national campaign—the "air war" where parties jostle for favorable coverage in both the national media and their media-market-targeted campaign advertisements. However, recent British findings suggest that it would be premature to dismiss the "ground war" of local party campaigning (Clarke et al., 2004). In the analyses that follow, we will investigate whether local party activities influence the likelihood that Canadians and Americans go to the polls.

DISTRIBUTIONS ON KEY VARIABLES

Civic Duty, Costs, and Benefits

Above, we have outlined several competing models of electoral participation. It is informative to see how Canadians stand on some of the key variables in these models. To this end, Table 8.2 presents responses to seven statements posed in the 2004 PSC survey concerning civic duty, the costs of voting, and the group and individual benefits of voting. We have already seen that responses to the civic duty statements vary sharply across age groups. Overall, a very large majority (84 per cent) believe that they would be seriously neglecting their duty if they did not vote. A smaller, but still sizable, majority (68 per cent) say they would feel guilty if they failed to vote.

The idea that most people express beliefs that propel them to vote is sustained when responses to statements about the costs of voting are examined. Thus, fully 83 per cent disagree with the proposition that voting is a waste of time, 73 per cent disagree that people are too busy to vote, and 63 per cent disagree that it takes too much time and effort to vote. Many people also think that there are group and individual benefits to be had from political activity. Group benefits are widely perceived, with nearly three-quarters of the sample agreeing with the idea that political activity is a good way to get benefits for groups they care about. Two-fifths also admit that involvement in politics is a good way to get personal benefits. Overall, an average of nearly 70 per cent of the responses to the several statements is "pro-political involvement."[2]

Inter-Party Competition

To measure how people perceived competition among the parties, we asked the 2004 PSC respondents to rate each party's chances of winning nationally and locally on 0–100 point scales. Smaller differences among the absolute values of the ratings for the parties indicate that a respondent believed the race would be close. Since the Liberals and the Conservatives were the only parties with serious chances of forming a government, we confined our attention to differences in the probability of winning assigned to these two parties as a measure of perceived national competition. However, since riding-level races varied greatly across the country, we employed the average of the pair-wise difference for several parties as the measure of perceived local competition.[3]

TABLE 8.2 PERCEIVED BENEFITS AND COSTS OF POLITICAL ACTIVITY
AND SENSE OF CIVIC DUTY, CANADA, 2004

STATEMENT		AGREE	DISAGREE
A.	I would be seriously neglecting my duty as a citizen if I didn't vote.	84%	16%
B.	Being active in politics is a good way for me to get benefits for me and my family.	42	58
C.	It takes too much time and effort to be active in politics.	37	63
D.	Being active in politics is a good way for people to get benefits for groups that they care about.	75	25
E.	Most of my family and friends think that voting is a waste of time.	17	83
F.	I would feel very guilty if I didn't vote in a general election.	68	32
G.	These days many people are so busy that they don't have time to vote.	27	73

Note: Horizontal percentages.

Source: 2004 PSC pre-election survey.

FIGURE 8.4 ABSOLUTE DIFFERENCES IN PARTIES' CHANCES
OF WINNING THE 2004 FEDERAL ELECTION

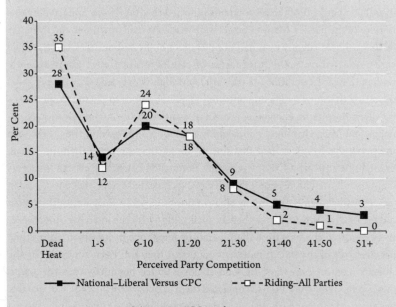

Source: 2004 PSC pre-election survey.

The "perceived inter-party competition" distributions displayed in Figure 8.4 indicate that many Canadians thought the national and local races would be quite close in 2004. Nationally, 28 per cent gave exactly the same probability of winning to the Liberals and the Conservatives, and locally, the "dead heat" number was even greater, 35 per cent. Extending the range of competition somewhat more broadly, we see that over three-fifths of the respondents thought the probability of a Liberal versus a Conservative victory differed by no more than 10 points. At the local riding level, over seven in 10 saw the probability differing by no more than this margin. Quite simply, a lot of voters thought that there was serious national- or local-level competition in 2004. Recall that opinion poll data reported in Chapter Three indicate that this was indeed the case. The Liberals and the Conservatives ran "neck and neck" for much of the campaign, and many voters recognized that they were witnessing a tight race. Below, we will see if these perceptions encouraged them to cast a ballot.

Party Contacting

As noted above, the efficacy of political parties' efforts to persuade people to vote for their candidates and to mobilize supporters who might otherwise stay at home on election day has been a subject of controversy among political scientists. Certainly, the survey data suggest that the parties themselves believe that such efforts have payoffs. The PSC data indicate that a considerable amount of party contacting took place during the 2004 Canadian federal election campaign. Overall, 70 per cent of the respondents reported that they were contacted by one or more of the parties. Many contacts were made via mail brochures and flyers. As Table 8.3 shows, slightly over half (54 per cent) of the respondents said that they were contacted by mail. Other forms of communication were also frequently used, with nearly two-fifths (38 per cent) and slightly over one-fifth (22 per cent) indicating that they had been contacted by telephone or in person, respectively. However, despite its enormous growth as a medium for communication, commerce, and research, e-mail campaigning was not widely used in 2004. Less than one person in 20 mentioned that one of the parties contacted them by e-mail. As might be anticipated, the large parties dominated contacting efforts. In fact, as Table 8.3 indicates, more people reported being contacted by mail, telephone, and in person by the Liberals than by any of the opposition parties. Specifically, 38 per cent said the Liberals had contacted them by mail, and 20 per cent and 11 per cent, respectively, reported contacts from the Liberals by telephone or in person. Altogether, just over half of the PSC respondents said that they had been contacted by the Liberals in one or more ways. The Conservatives trailed, but not by a great deal, with 44 per cent saying the CPC had contacted them in one way or another. Comparable percentages for other parties were 29 per cent for the NDP, 37 per cent for the BQ

TABLE 8.3 PARTY CONTACTS DURING THE
2004 FEDERAL ELECTION CAMPAIGN
(PERCENTAGES OF PSC RESPONDENTS REPORTING CONTACT)

PARTY	TYPE OF CONTACT				TOTAL ALL CONTACTED BY PARTIES
	MAIL	PHONE	IN-PERSON	E-MAIL	
Liberals	38	20	11	1	51
Conservatives	35	15	8	1	44
NDP	24	7	6	1	29
Bloc Québécois†	19	18	7	1	37
Greens	6	X	1	X	8
Total Contacted Various Ways	54	38	22	4	

†—percentages computed for Quebec only.
X—less than .5%.

Source: 2004 PSC post-election survey.

(in Quebec only), and 8 per cent for the Green Party. Clearly, the parties reached out to many voters in 2004. Below, we will see if these efforts helped to bring people to the polls.

Parties' Performance

Cognitive mobilization theories hypothesize that (dis)satisfaction with policies and the functioning of governmental institutions and processes affects political participation. In the context of studying election turnout, we have captured evaluations of the policies on offer by competing parties via a measure of the differential benefits that would accrue should one, rather than another, party win the election. Also, as discussed above, differential benefits are a key variable in the Riker-Ordeshook rational choice theory of election turnout. Thus, cognitive mobilization and rational choice models share this variable.

Regarding evaluations of political institutions, we focus on global judgments about the functioning of the political parties—not a particular party, but parties generally. Table 8.4 displays how the 2004 PSC respondents answered 10 "agree-disagree" statements on various aspects of party performance. What is immediately striking is that many Canadians judge the parties quite harshly. For example, fully 83 per cent agreed that the parties spend too much time bickering, 85 per cent think that there is a big difference between what parties say and what they do, 52 per cent believe that parties are more interested in winning elections than in governing afterwards, and 53 per cent disagree with the idea that parties encourage people to become politically active. Smaller, but still substantial, numbers disparage the parties for failing to look after everyone's interests (42 per cent), for failing to help groups reach agreement (39 per cent), and for spending "too much time catering to minorities" (38 per cent). Widespread negativism about the functioning of political parties was also a feature of PSC surveys conducted in the 1990s (Clarke, Kornberg, and Wearing, 2000), and clearly it has not abated significantly since then.

It is noteworthy that judgments about the parties are not uniformly negative. As Table 8.4 documents, nearly four Canadians in five believe that parties are necessary for democracy, slightly over half think parties give people a say in government, and an equal number reject the proposition that parties divide, rather than unify, the country. In addition, if, as just observed, nearly two-fifths believe parties spend too much time catering to minorities, a slightly larger number rejects this idea. Overall, although the parties' report card has lots of low marks, there are some high and medium grades as well.

Is there a pattern to people's evaluations of the parties? An exploratory factor analysis reveals that three factors organize responses to the 10 statements in Table 8.4. Loading heavily on the first factor are the statements about how well parties govern, such as spending too much time bickering, being more interested in winning than governing, doing other than what they say, and catering to minorities. The second

TABLE 8.4 EVALUATIONS OF CANADIAN POLITICAL PARTIES, 2004
(HORIZONTAL PERCENTAGES)

STATEMENTS ABOUT PARTIES		AGREE	DISAGREE	NOT SURE
A.	Spend too much time bickering.	83	11	6
B.	Needed to make democracy work.	77	13	10
C.	Look after everyone's interests.	37	42	20
D.	Give people say in government.	52	29	19
E.	Difference winning parties say and do.	85	9	6
F.	More interested winning than governing.	52	38	10
G.	Encourage political activism.	24	53	23
H.	Divide don't unify country.	27	53	20
I.	Help groups reach agreement.	27	39	35
J.	Too much time catering to minorities.	38	44	18

Note: Boldface numbers indicate negative evaluation.

Source: 2004 PSC post-election self-completion survey.

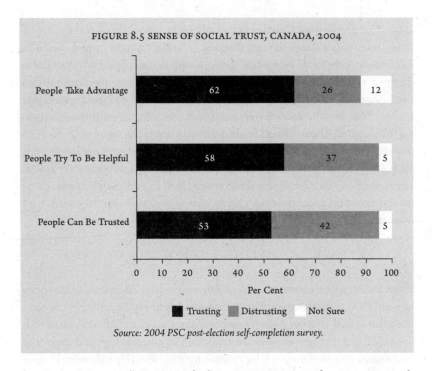

FIGURE 8.5 SENSE OF SOCIAL TRUST, CANADA, 2004

Source: 2004 PSC post-election self-completion survey.

factor concerns parties' activities to facilitate representation and participation, with items such as encouraging political activism, helping groups reach agreement, and representing everyone's interests loading heavily. The third factor, dominated by the statement about parties being needed for democracy, and parties giving people a say in government clearly concerns evaluations of parties as facilitators of democracy.[4] These governing, representation, and democracy factors that structure evaluations of party performance will be included in the turnout analyses presented below. Doing so will enable us to test the relevance of the institutional performance component of cognitive mobilization theories for explaining electoral participation. Since parties are dominant actors in the Canadian electoral process, the expectation is that people who evaluate parties negatively on the governing, representation, and democracy dimensions will be less likely to vote than will those who evaluate them positively.

Social Trust

Feelings of trust in one's fellow citizens are a major component of social capital theories of political participation. The 2004 survey asked respondents if they agreed or disagreed with three statements designed to capture these feelings. The results displayed in Figure 8.5 show that majorities, although not overwhelmingly large ones, provided "trusting" answers. Thus, slightly over three-fifths of the respondents judged that people would "not try to take advantage of you" if they had the opportunity, and nearly as many thought that people "would try to be helpful." Just over half thought "people can be trusted." Constructing an index based on responses to the three statements shows that social trust varies across sociodemographic categories, being greater among older persons, the well-educated, and those with higher incomes.[5] Gender differences are very small, with men being very slightly more trusting than women. There are significant differences across the regions; Quebeckers (especially francophones) and residents of the Atlantic provinces are less trusting than other Canadians. Although these several relationships are statistically significant, collectively they are not especially strong, and can explain only 18 per cent of the variance in the social trust index. In the next section, we will use the social trust index as a predictor variable in our analysis of election turnout.

EXPLAINING VOTING TURNOUT IN CANADA

Earlier in this chapter we outlined several different models designed to explain voting turnout. Here, we assess the ability of these models to explain voting in the 2004 Canadian federal election. Since some of the same variables appear in more than one model (e.g., strength of party identification), we consider a general composite model containing all of the predictor variables from the several specific models. Since election interest is theoretically proximate to actual turnout, we also investigate how well the several predictor variables do in explaining interest in the 2004 election. Since turnout is a "no-yes" dichotomy, binomial logit analysis (Long, 1997) is used to estimate the coefficients in the composite turnout model. Election interest is a four-category ordinal scale, and ordered logit is appropriate for estimating coefficients in the election interest model. The results of the analyses are presented in Table 8.5.[6]

Considering the turnout model first, we see that there are several statistically significant predictors. The modified or "soft" rational choice model performs quite well, with influence-discounted benefits and sense of civic duty having the hypothesized positive effects on turnout. Also, perceived costs have a significant negative effect. Some of the variables from the civic voluntarism and cognitive mobilization models also perform well. Election interest, strength of party identification, and evaluations of parties as facilitators of democracy all have the anticipated positive effects on the likelihood of voting. In addition, social trust has a significant positive coefficient, thereby suggesting that social capital is part of the turnout story. Other variables with significant effects include perceptions of national (but not local) party competition, and the extent of party contacting. As expected, the coefficient for national competition is negative—the smaller the gap in the perceived probability that the Liberals or the Conservatives would win, the more likely it is that someone would vote. As

TABLE 8.5 PREDICTORS OF VOTING TURNOUT AND ELECTION INTEREST,
2004 CANADIAN FEDERAL ELECTION

PREDICTOR VARIABLES	TURNOUT	ELECTION INTEREST
Influence-Discounted Benefits	.003*	.004***
Costs	-.27**	-.49***
Personal Benefits	-.09	.16*
Civic Duty	.33***	.58***
Election Interest	.62***	X
National Party Competition	-.01**	-.01*
Local Party Competition	.01	.00
Party Contact	.69**	.15
Strength of Party Identification	.30**	.26***
Social Trust	.15**	.07*
Party Evaluations:		
Governing	-.15	X
Representation	-.03	X
Democracy	.26**	X
Age Cohorts:		
Harper	-.51	-2.17***
Chrétien	.37	-1.26***
Mulroney	.07	-1.27***
Trudeau	.32	-1.11***
Diefenbaker-Pearson	.04	-.44
Education	-.19	.13
Gender	-.07	.52***
Income	.05	-.03
Region/Ethnicity:		
Atlantic	.12	-.31
Quebec French	.78**	-1.02***
Quebec Non-French	-.32	-.64
Prairies	-.18	-.03
British Columbia	-.32	.46*
Constant	-.55	
McFadden R^2 =	.25	.18
McKelvey R^2 =	.37	–
Per Cent Correctly Classified =	87.3	53.3
AIC =	649.65	1706.50

*** $p < .001$; ** $p < .01$; * $p < .05$; one-tailed test.
X—variable not included in model.
– not defined.
†—Akaike Information Criterion (AIC) —smaller values indicate better
model performance.

Note: Binomial logit analysis of turnout; ordered logit analysis of interest in 2004 federal election.

also expected, the coefficient for party contacting is positive, indicating that more contact promotes turnout.

Some of the predictor variables in the turnout model are noteworthy because they do *not* have significant effects. Education, a featured variable in the civic voluntarism and cognitive mobilization models, fails to make an appearance. Income and gender, two other variables frequently found in specifications of the civic voluntarism model, also do not achieve significance. However, perhaps most interesting is the absence of significant age-cohort effects. Although age and turnout rates are clearly correlated, the logit model shows no evidence of a *direct* effect once other factors are controlled. It is possible that the effect of age on turnout is *indirect*, operating through other variables. For example, we have already seen that there are age differences in feelings of civic duty. Table 8.5 shows that there are also age effects on levels of election interest; younger voters, i.e., those in the Harper, Chrétien, and Mulroney groups, were significantly less interested in the election than were older people.

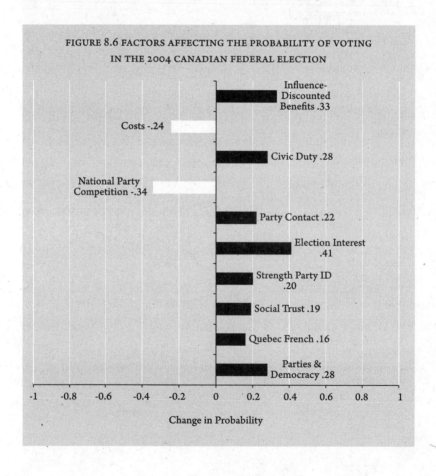

FIGURE 8.6 FACTORS AFFECTING THE PROBABILITY OF VOTING IN THE 2004 CANADIAN FEDERAL ELECTION

Several other variables also affect election interest in ways one would expect. Thus, civic duty, influence-discounted benefits, strength of party identification, and social trust all have positive effects on election interest, and costs have a negative effect. As for demographic characteristics, although education and income are not influential, there are gender and regional differences. Men were more interested in the election than women, Quebec francophones were less interested, and British Columbians were more interested than other Canadians.

Taken together, these findings indicate that several models can contribute to explaining voting turnout in Canadian elections. However, it is not clear which predictor variables are most important. Accordingly, we calculate changes in the probabilities of voting and being "very interested" in the 2004 election as each of the predictor variables is varied over its range while others are held at their mean values. The results, displayed in Figures 8.6 and 8.7, show that variables in the "soft"

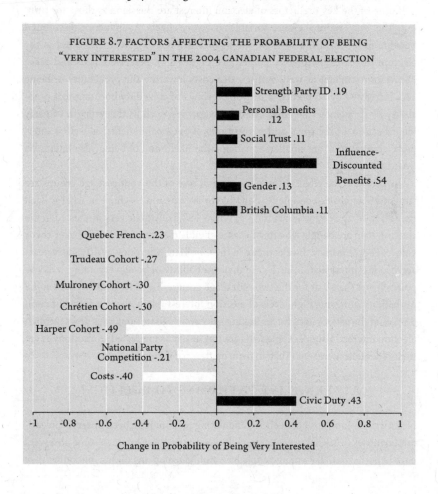

FIGURE 8.7 FACTORS AFFECTING THE PROBABILITY OF BEING "VERY INTERESTED" IN THE 2004 CANADIAN FEDERAL ELECTION

Strength Party ID .19
Personal Benefits .12
Social Trust .11
Influence-Discounted Benefits .54
Gender .13
British Columbia .11
Quebec French -.23
Trudeau Cohort -.27
Mulroney Cohort -.30
Chrétien Cohort -.30
Harper Cohort -.49
National Party Competition -.21
Costs -.40
Civic Duty .43

Change in Probability of Being Very Interested

rational choice model have sizable effects. As influence-discounted benefits and sense of civic duty increase from their lowest to their highest values, the probability of voting increases by 33 points and 28 points, respectively (see Figure 8.6). In addition, the probability of voting decreases by 24 points as perceived costs increase from their minimum to their maximum value. Several predictors from the civic voluntarism, cognitive mobilization, and social capital models also have sizable effects. For example, everything else being equal, heightened election interest can boost the probability of voting by fully 41 points, and being a strong party identifier does so by 20 points. Holding a very positive view of the contribution of parties to the functioning of democracy is influential, too, increasing the likelihood of going to the polls by 28 points. A strong sense of social trust does so by 19 points. Also, net of all these effects, perceptions of party competition and party contacting enhance the probability of voting by 34 and 22 points, respectively.[7]

Some of the key predictors of election interest are the same as those for turnout. The "soft" rational choice variables have big effects. As influence-discounted benefits move from low to high, the probability of being very interested in the election increases by fully 54 points (see Figure 8.7). Perceived costs and sense of civic duty matter as well, with greater costs lowering the probability of being very interested by 40 points, and strong feelings of civic duty boosting that probability by 43 points. The effects of other variables, such as the strength of party identification, social trust, and perceptions of personal benefits, as well as interparty competition, are smaller, enhancing the likelihood of being very interested by 11 to 21 points.

In contrast, the effects of membership in one of the youngest age groups are large. *Ceteris paribus*, people first eligible to vote in 2004—those in what we call the "Harper" age cohort—are fully 49 points less likely to be very interested in the election than are people who first became eligible to vote in the Diefenbaker era or before. People joining the electorate in the Chrétien, Mulroney, and Trudeau years are also less interested; in each case their probability of being very interested is 30 points lower than that for the two oldest age groups. These large differences in the probability of having high levels of election interest testify that a significant component of the set of causal forces linking age cohorts to turnout rates flows through election interest. Younger Canadians are not nearly as interested in elections as are their older fellow citizens. That, in turn, matters for voting turnout.

ALTERNATIVE PATHWAYS TO POLITICS?

Negative relationships between age and voting turnout have been observed in various countries (e.g., Clarke et al., 2004). Reflecting on these findings, some observers have hypothesized that young people have not "given up on politics," but rather they

TABLE 8.6 PARTICIPATION IN VARIOUS POLITICAL ACTIVITIES
BY AGE GROUPS, CANADA, 2004

Percentages Who Have Done Activity "Sometimes" or "Often"

Political Activities	Age Group 18-21	22-33	34-41	42-60	61-72	73+	Total	r†
Attend Political Meeting or Rally	2	7	12	22	26	36	18	.25
Work for Party or Candidate	2	4	8	15	21	26	12	.23
Donate Money to Party or Candidate	2	4	7	17	26	25	14	.27
Contact MP about Personal Problem	5	7	16	18	20	14	14	.16
Contact MP about Important Issue	9	15	16	19	27	28	19	.18
Sign Petition	52	60	60	65	73	61	63	.07
Join Boycott	16	35	43	45	47	30	40	.07
Participate Protest or Demonstration	5	14	17	18	11	12	15	-.04

†—correlation between extent of participation in various political activities and age in years.

Source: 2004 PSC post-election self-completion survey.

are embracing other types of political action (e.g., Thomassen, 2005). Although the hypothesis that young people are substituting other political activities for voting might be true in some countries, there is no evidence of it in Canada. Table 8.6 shows the percentages of people in various age groups who report participating in a variety of political activities including such things as attending rallies, working for parties, contacting MPs, signing petitions, joining boycotts, and engaging in protests and demonstrations. In every case but one, the correlation between age and participation in a particular type of activity is positive, thereby indicating that older people tend to participate more. In addition, the only negative correlation, that between age and protest is a miniscule -.04. There is, then, no indication that young Canadians have abandoned voting to become "specialists" in other forms of political participation.

Another way of looking for substitution effects is to examine the correlations between voting and other forms of political participation within different age groups. We do this analysis for two such groups, people in the "Harper" and "Chrétien" cohorts, i.e., those who first became eligible to vote in 1993, and all older people. If younger Canadians are engaging in substitution behavior, one would expect the correlations between voting and other types of political activity to be negative. However, all of the correlations (not shown in tabular form) for both age groups are weakly positive. Nonvoters, both young and old alike, tend not to be active in other ways. Thus far, young Canadians have not substituted boycotts for ballots.

VOTING TURNOUT IN THE UNITED STATES

For many years, political scientists believed that the United States had experienced a downward trend in voting turnout in national elections similar to that documented above for Canada.[8] However, McDonald and Popkin's (2001) recent recalculation of turnout rates suggests that this is not the case. The key idea underlying their calculations is the distinction between the voting age population and the voting eligible population. The latter figure is smaller than the former one and, for various reasons, the difference between them has tended to grow over time. McDonald and Popkin argue that if one uses the voting age figure rather than the voting eligible figure as the denominator in calculating turnout, the effect will be to induce an artifactual downward trend. Updated McDonald-Popkin turnout figures for presidential and mid-term congressional elections since 1948 and 1950, respectively, are displayed in Figure 8.8. As can be seen, the gap between turnout calculated using the "voting age" and "voting eligible" baselines has grown over time.

Although McDonald and Popkin deny the existence of a downward *trend* in turnout in American national elections, this does not mean that there has not been a decrease over time. In this regard, a number of analysts have conjectured that the mechanism for this downward movement was provided by the 26th Amendment to the Constitution passed in 1971 that enfranchised 18-year-olds. The hypothesis is that this produced a downward "step effect" in turnout. Here, we test this hypothesis, and the alternative of a long-term, but gradual, downward trend in voting rates in presidential and off-year congressional elections using the regression models shown in Table 8.7.

TABLE 8.7 MODELS OF VOTING TURNOUT AS A PERCENTAGE OF
THE ELIGIBLE POPULATION, AMERICAN NATIONAL ELECTIONS, 1945–2006

Predictor Variables	PRESIDENTIAL ELECTION YEARS		MID-TERM CONGRESSIONAL ELECTIONS	
	B	s.e.	B	s.e.
Constant	58.49***	1.83	45.07***	.99
Linear Trend	.57	.36	.26	.20
26th Amendment	-8.46**	3.21	-7.83***	1.74
Adjusted R^2 =	.32		.75	
Durbin-Watson d	2.20		1.57	

*** p < .001; ** p < .01; * p < .05; one-tailed test.

FIGURE 8.8 TURNOUT IN AMERICAN NATIONAL ELECTIONS, 1948–2006

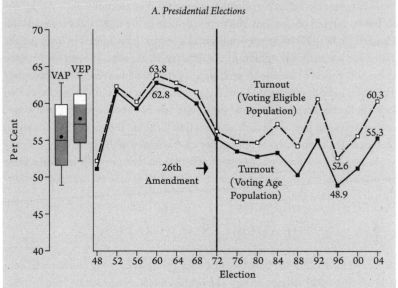

A. Presidential Elections

Note: VAP = turnout as percentage of voting age population.
VEP = turnout as percentage of voting eligible population.

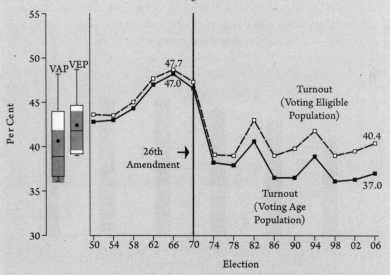

B. Mid-Term Congressional Elections

Note: VAP = turnout as percentage of voting age population.
VEP = turnout as percentage of voting eligible population.

Source: McDonald and Popkin (2001); http://www.electons.gmu.edu.

These analyses support the hypothesis that there has been no general downward trend in turnout in either presidential or congressional elections since World War II. For both types of elections, the trend coefficients are statistically insignificant. However, in both cases the step-shift variable indexing the impact of lowering the voting age is statistically significant. As anticipated, the effect is negative, with the enfranchisement of 18-year-olds producing a permanent decrease of approximately 8 per cent in both presidential and congressional elections. As the analyses also indicate, the impact of allowing 18-year-olds to vote has been considerably stronger on congressional than on presidential election turnout. The variance explained in turnout in the former case is fully 75 per cent, whereas in the latter one, it is only 32 per cent. These figures are consistent with the idea that, generally speaking, there are more transitory events and conditions driving turnout in presidential elections than in mid-term elections.

THE AMERICAN AGE GRADIENT

Similar to their Canadian counterparts, younger Americans are less likely to vote than are their older fellow citizens. The relationship between age and turnout displayed in Figure 8.9 shows that, in 2004, the percentage of ANES respondents who reported voting increased from 58 per cent among newly eligible voters (18–21 age

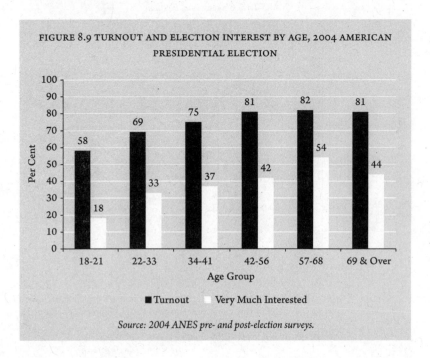

FIGURE 8.9 TURNOUT AND ELECTION INTEREST BY AGE, 2004 AMERICAN PRESIDENTIAL ELECTION

Source: 2004 ANES pre- and post-election surveys.

group) to 81 per cent among those 69 years and older. Also similar to Canada, the age gradient in election interest is steep, with the percentage stating that they were "very much interested" in the 2004 election increasing from 18 per cent among the youngest age group to 54 per cent among those in the 57–68 age group. It then declines to 44 per cent among the 69 and older age group.

As in the Canadian case, it is difficult to discern whether these relationships are products of life-cycle or generational processes, or some combination of the two. However, estimating models of voting turnout using age in years and age in years plus the five age-cohort dummy variables indicates that the latter do not add significantly to the variance explained in turnout over and above what age in years can do by itself (chi-square = 7.78, df = 5, p = .169). However, replicating this analysis with election interest as the dependent variable reveals that the age-cohort variables collectively produce a significant increment in variance explained (chi-square = 19.33, df = 5, p = .002). These results suggest that the relationship between age and voting turnout has an age-cohort component that works indirectly by affecting election interest which, as we now show, affects turnout.

TURNOUT MODELS

The 2004 ANES contains some, but not all, of the variables needed to replicate the Canadian turnout analyses. Noteworthy by their absence are measures of civic duty and the costs and personal benefits of participation. However, the variables needed to measure several other important concepts are present, and they allow us to perform an analysis of a composite US turnout model. The results, displayed in Table 8.8, indicate that election interest has a predictably large positive impact, with an increase in interest being able to bolster the probability of voting by 33 points.[9] Influence-discounted benefits, a key component in soft rational choice models of turnout also have large statistically significant effects. Variations in influence-discounted benefits can alter the probability of voting by 41 points. Education and income, predictor variables from the civic voluntarism model, make sizable contributions as well. Moving these two predictors from the minimum to maximum values increases the probability of voting by 35 and 31 points, respectively. Another variable in this model, strength of party identification, also has a moderate and predictably positive effect. Other things being equal, people with very strong partisan attachments are 17 points more likely to go to the polls than are those without a partisan tie.

Cognitive mobilization theory also finds support. In addition to the significant effects of election interest and level of formal education just mentioned, political knowledge has a positive impact. As the political knowledge index goes from its minimum to its maximum value, the probability of casting a ballot is enhanced by 17 points. To investigate how judgments about the workings of political institutions and

TABLE 8.8 PREDICTORS OF VOTING TURNOUT,
2004 US PRESIDENTIAL ELECTION

PREDICTOR VARIABLES		TURNOUT	CHANGE IN PROBABILITY OF VOTING
Influence-Discounted Benefits		.004***	.41
Election Interest		.70***	.33
National and State Party Competition		.31a	.07
Party Contact		.54***	.25
Political Knowledge		.12*	.17
Strength of Party Identification		.39***	.17
Social Trust, Civic Engagement		.25***	.38
Election Evaluations:	Representation	.17*	.18
	Fairness	-.04	X
Age Cohorts:	Bush II	-.08a	-.13
	Clinton	-.48a	-.11
	Reagan, Bush I	-.72*	-.16
	Carter-Nixon	-.37	X
	Kennedy-Johnson	-.25	X
Education		.26***	.35
Gender		-.17	X
Income		.06***	.31
Race/Ethnicity:	African American	.62**	.14
	Hispanic	.30	X
	Other	-.48a	-.10
Region:	South	-.50**	-.14
Constant		-2.56***	
McFadden R^2 =		.33	
McKelvey R^2 =		.54	
Per Cent Correctly Classified =		83.4	
AIC =		831.97	

*** p < .001; ** p < .01; * p < .05; a p < .10; one-tailed test.
X—not a statistically significant predictor of voting turnout.
†—Akaike Information Criterion (AIC)—smaller values indicate better model performance.

processes affect turnout, we employ measures of the perceived fairness of elections and the quality of representation they provide. The latter variable has a significant positive impact, such that people who believe elections are effective instruments for representing public opinion are 18 points more likely to vote than those who believe otherwise. Social capital, as indexed by a combination of social trust and civic engagement, is relevant, too, having the capacity to bolster the probability of voting by 38 points. In addition, although perceptions of electoral competition are not significant, party contact has the anticipated positive effect. Other things being equal, as the party contact variable increases across its range, the likelihood of casting a ballot goes up by 25 points.

Among the remaining predictors, as anticipated by the analyses described earlier, the age-cohort variables have only weak effects. The impact of race/ethnicity is also weak, with the analysis suggesting that, all other things being equal, African Americans were actually more likely to vote in 2004 than were whites or Hispanics. Asians and members of various "other" racial/ethnic groups were slightly less likely to do so. Finally, consonant with traditional patterns in American politics, residents of the South were somewhat less likely to vote than were people living in other regions. However, the effect was not especially large—again, all else being equal, the probability of voting in 2004 was 14 points lower if one lived in the South.

In sum, the analyses of turnout in American national elections produce results quite similar to those for Canadian federal elections. Key predictor variables from several competing models of electoral participation make sizable contributions to explaining who votes.

CONCLUSION: COUNTERVAILING FORCES

Political scientists and other observers often use turnout rates in national elections to gauge the health of democratic polities. This practice has long prompted worry among students of American voting behavior, because turnout rates in the United States have been well below those for most other mature democracies. Moreover, many believed that turnout was not only low but going lower. Historically, Canadians did not share these concerns; turnout rates in federal elections far surpassed those in the United States. However, as discussed in this chapter, this is no longer true. Over the past two decades, turnout in national elections in Canada has fallen sharply, such that rates of electoral participation in Canadian federal elections and American presidential elections are now similar.

In this chapter, we have explored the over-time dynamics of turnout in the two countries. Our analyses depict a Canadian pattern best characterized by a long-term decline, rather than an abrupt step downward concomitant with the advent of a new national party system in 1993. The US pattern is different; the lowering of the voting age to 18, not a significant factor in Canada, was accompanied by a thus-far permanent 8 per cent drop in turnout in both presidential and mid-term congressional elections. However, consonant with other recent research, our analyses contradict the old conventional wisdom of an ongoing decline in turnout in the United States. In the post-World War II period, at least, the American aggregate turnout story is one of trendless fluctuation around a downward step associated with enfranchising 18-year-olds. Turnout is down in both countries, but the patterns are different.

At the individual level, there are many similarities in the forces driving turnout in Canada and the United States. Key variables from a variety of different theories of electoral participation have significant effects. Some of these effects are very sizable.

Proponents of soft rational choice theory, civic voluntarism theory, cognitive engagement theory, and social capital theory all can claim that featured variables in their models influence turnout. Lurking behind some of these relationships, such as those involving election interest and civic duty, are interesting age differences. The pattern is uniformly one where factors prompting participation are attenuated among younger age groups. Moreover, there is evidence—not definitive but suggestive—that these age differences are at least partially generationally based. The implication is that Canadian turnout rates may not easily recover, and American ones may continue their mediocre course.

That is the bad news. The good news in the analysis is that many variables influence participation in particular elections. When voters perceive large differences in the benefits on offer by competing parties, when inter-party competition is close, when parties campaign vigorously, and when parties and elections are seen to perform the roles ascribed to them in democratic theory, interest in elections and turnout rates increase. In any particular election, these latter effects can work to offset longer term factors working to depress turnout.

There is more. The possibility that currently younger voters constitute a political generation that is less likely to vote than older generations is not written in stone. One of the major themes of this study is that voters can and do change. There is no reason that this cannot apply to voting turnout, as well as to party and candidate choice.

Notes

1   The Durbin-Watson statistic is a diagnostic test for first-order autocorrelation in the residuals. Values close to 2.0 indicate a lack of autocorrelation (see Hendry, 1995).

2   The χ^2 test places the null hypothesis of a lack of difference in fit between the two models against a rival hypothesis that the model with the age-cohort variables provides a superior fit. Since there are six age cohorts, there are five degrees of freedom for the test.

3   For estimates of the closeness of the national race used in the multivariate analyses, we generated a variable that was the natural logarithm of one plus the absolute value of the difference between the respondents' estimations of the Liberals and Conservatives winning the election. For the respondents' predictions of the closeness of the race in the ridings, we first determined the two parties that the respondent deemed to be the closest competitors. In Quebec there were four options because of the presence of the Bloc Québécois (BQ). Outside of Quebec, respondents were asked what they thought the chances were that the Liberals, Conservatives, and NDP would win in their riding. After ascertaining the two closest parties, we constructed a variable that was similar to the one created to measure the respondents' perceptions of the closeness of the national race.

4   A principal components analysis (PCA) yielded three factors. The eigenvalue for the first factor measuring attitudes about how well parties govern was 2.7; the eigenvalue for the second factor measuring
attitudes about the parties' ability to facilitate representation and participation was 1.2; and the eigenvalue on the third dimension that largely captured citizens beliefs about the parties' ability to facilitate
democracy was 1.0. The three factors explained 50 per cent of the variance for the 10 variables, and after
verimax rotation, all of the indicators had loadings of greater than 0.5 on their respective dimensions.

5   Respondents were given a score of one for each trusting answer, and a score of -1 for each distrusting
answer in response to the "people take advantage," "people try to be helpful," and "people can be
trusted" statements in Figure 8.5. Those stating that they were "not sure" or "did not know" how to
respond to a statement were scored zero on that statement.

6   In the logit and ordered logit analyses, gender is coded one if the respondent was a male. Income is
an eight-category variable that ranges from one through eight and is coded four if the respondent
refused to give their income. Education is coded one if the respondent had less than a high school
education or declined to state their education, two if the respondent completed high school, three
if the respondent had some post-secondary education, and four if the respondent had obtained at
least a university degree. The strength of party identification variable ranges from zero to four, with
nonidentifiers coded zero, not very strong identifiers coded one, fairly strong identifiers coded two,
and very strong identifiers coded three.

The party contact variable has a range of zero to four and each type of contact (mail, telephone, in
person, e-mail) increases a respondent's score by one. Election interest is a variable with a range of
zero to three, with respondents with a score of zero indicating on the pre-election study that they
were not at all interested in the election, while those with scores of three reporting that they were
very interested in the election.

The benefits, duty, and cost variables are factor scores obtained after a PCA of questions that asked
respondents whether: a) they would be seriously neglecting their civic duty if they did not vote; b)
being active in politics was a good way to get benefits for themselves and their families; c) being active
in politics takes too much time and effort; d) being active in politics is a good way for people to get
benefits for groups that they care about; e) most of the respondents' families and friends thought that
voting was a waste of time; f) the respondent would feel guilty if he/she did not vote in a general election; and g) these days many people were so busy that they did not have the time to vote. Questions
related to civic duty [i.e., questions a) and f)] loaded on the first factor that yielded an eigenvalue of 1.8,
and the factor scores obtained from the PCA comprised the civic duty variable in Table 8.5. Questions
b) and d) had high loadings on the second factor that yielded an eigenvalue of 1.3, and factor scores
from this second dimension comprise the personal benefits predictor variable in the multivariate
analysis. Questions g), e), and c) had loadings on the third dimension (with an eigenvalue equal to

1.1), and factor scores from that variable were used as measures of the respondents' perceived costs of voting in the analyses.

The influence-discounted benefits variable in the multivariate analysis was an interaction between an 11-point question ascertaining the respondents' perceptions of how much political influence they believed they had and the average absolute pairwise difference in feeling thermometer scores (on a scale of zero to 100) of the three (outside of Quebec) or four (inside of Quebec) competing political parties.

7   To generate predicted probabilities, we used the CLARIFY software package for STATA. To assess the impact of various predictor variables, we assumed that the combined values of other predictors yielded an expected probability of voting equal to the 2004 Canadian turnout rate, 60.5 per cent.

8   For a list of such studies, consult McDonald and Popkin (2001).

9   For estimating the impact of the predictors of American voter turnout, we followed the procedure described in endnote seven. The probability of voting for this analysis was set to the 2004 US turnout rate, 60.3 per cent. In the multivariate analyses, gender is coded one for men and zero for women. Income is a 23-point variable that summarizes household income (with a range of less than $2,999 coded 1, to having more than $120,000 coded 23; missing values were coded at 15). Education is a seven-point variable ranging from one (where the respondent has eight or fewer years of schooling), to seven (where the respondent holds an advanced degree). Respondents not answering the education question were coded one.

The election evaluation variables are the two factor-score variables generated from a principal components analysis of five variables: a) two separate five-point scales measuring how fair the respondents thought the 2000 and 2004 elections were, with higher scores indicating a greater belief that each election was fair; b) a dichotomous variable based on a question asking whether the respondent believed that there was a party that represented their views; c) a dichotomous variable based on a question asking whether elections make people pay attention; and d) a dichotomous variable based on a question asking whether elections ensure that people's views are represented. Variables b), c), and d) loaded on the first dimension, and the two variables concerning the fairness of the 2000 and 2004 presidential elections loading on a second factor. The two components explained 58 per cent of the variance in the five variables.

The social capital variable is an index created by summing two factor-score variables, one measuring social trust and one measuring extent of civic engagement. The strength of partisan identification variable ranges from zero to two in the American case, with nonidentifiers coded zero, weak identifiers coded one, and strong identifiers coded two.

The political knowledge variable ranges from zero to six, and the respondent receives one point for correctly identifying each of the following political actors and situations: the party with the most number of seats in the House of Representatives; the party with the most number of seats in the Senate; the speaker of the House of Representatives, the vice president, Tony Blair, the chief justice of the Supreme Court.

The party contact variable is an index ranging from zero to two, with respondents earning points if they were contacted by a party or a candidate during the campaign. The national and state party competition variable also ranges from zero to two, with the respondents receiving one point for stating that the presidential election would be close nationally and another point for stating that the presidential race would be close in their state. The election interest variable has a range of zero to two and taps interest the respondent had in the election as stated in the pre-election interview. The discounted benefits question is the interaction between a five-point scale measuring how strongly the respondent believed their vote made a difference and the absolute value of the difference in feeling thermometer scores for Bush and Kerry as measured in the post-election survey.

CHAPTER NINE

Political Choices Reconsidered

S tudies of voting behavior have a lengthy history. In the United States, the "Columbia" studies of the 1940 and 1948 American presidential elections by Bernard Berelson, Paul Lazarsfeld, and their associates employed what came to be called the sociological model to explain the choices voters make. The principal problem with the model was that most of the sociodemographic attributes of voters change little, if at all, in the interim between elections. However, candidate images and issue concerns do vary from election to election. Issues that have great salience in one election can rapidly recede from public view, and party leaders, previously focal points of media attention, can quickly exit the political stage. Most important, the way people vote and the outcomes of elections change over time. Fundamentally, the sociological model failed because it tried to use things that did not change to explain things that did. An outcome such as the victory by General Dwight Eisenhower, the candidate of the seemingly permanent minority Republican Party in the 1952 US presidential election, presented scholars using sociological models with a puzzle that was beyond their explanatory reach.

The social-psychological or "Michigan" model of voting appeared to solve "the puzzle of 1952" by addressing the problem that had stymied the Columbia school. The Michigan model had both static and dynamic properties. Introduced by Angus Campbell and his colleagues in their landmark studies, *The Voter Decides* (1954) and *The American Voter* (1960), the Michigan model attracted favorable international attention and popularized the idea that voters develop durable psychological identifications with political parties. Although Campbell and his colleagues never actually made the claim, many of the scholars who enthusiastically embraced the Michigan model thought of partisan identification as a great "unmoved mover." Candidates and issues came and went, but party identifications were widespread in the American electorate and directionally stable. Democrats remained Democrats, Republicans remained Republicans, and these partisan attachments shaped how voters saw the political world and how they behaved at the ballot box. Party identification was the principal long-term force on electoral choice.

Although the Michigan model continues to have many supporters, the privileged position assigned to party identification has prompted a variety of criticisms. In the United States, some analysts argued that beginning in the mid-1960s, a series of highly charged issues such as the Vietnam War and the civil rights movement sharply divided Americans and cut across party lines, weakening the intensity and incidence of identification and making issues a more prominent factor in voting decisions. Others argued that because of candidates' increased use of advertising and survey research specialists to market themselves to voters via the mass media, political campaigns had become increasingly candidate-centered. A principal consequence of these several changes was to increase the impact of candidate images and issue orientations on electoral choice, while decreasing the importance of party identification.

Students of congressional elections also argued that although candidate-centered campaigns weakened partisanship in the 1960s and 1970s, following the election of Ronald Reagan in 1980, the congressional parties became more cohesive and organized around a number of highly visible and deeply divisive domestic and foreign policy issues. In turn, core supporters of the two parties became more polarized around these issues. The Rochester or issue-proximity model appeared to provide an explanation of voting that was well-suited for this type of political environment— one where salient position issues held sway. The issue-proximity model had achieved its initial popularity because of Anthony Downs's (1957) landmark study in which he proposed that voters are rational actors who try to maximize their utilities by supporting parties that take positions in a one-dimensional or multidimensional policy space that are closest to voters' own positions in that space. In addition, since political parties are also rational actors whose raison d'être is to win elections, they try to position themselves in the same issue space so as to maximize public support. Voters' positions on the issues dictate where the parties go.

The Downsian spatial model quickly gained a large and devoted cadre of adherents who were attracted by its theoretical parsimony and promised predictive power. Over the years since it was first introduced, variations of the model have remained popular despite an early harsh critique offered by Donald Stokes. In what soon became a widely cited and highly influential article, Stokes (1963) did not dismiss the importance of issues, but rather contended that what he termed *valence issues* were typically key for understanding voting behavior and election outcomes. Valence issues, as we have observed in preceding chapters, are ones on which virtually everyone either agrees or disagrees.

Clarke et al. (1979, 1996) argued that Stokes's formulations could be combined with a long-standing theory of party behavior in Canadian federal elections, termed the "brokerage politics" theory, to provide a powerful theory of voting behavior. This is the valence politics model of electoral choice. The principal components of the model were valence issues, party leader images, and party identifications. An important point was that party identifications have dynamic properties.

Early Canadian criticisms of the Michigan model by Jenson (1976) and Clarke et al. (1979) had focused on attributes of party identification, such as intensity, directional stability, and consistency across levels of the federal system. A crucial part of their argument was that many Canadians lacked durable party identifications. Instead, partisanship in Canada was flexible—it could encompass identifications with different federal and provincial parties, and it could change in response to changing assessments of party and party leader performance on relatively routine policy issues. Partisan instability in federal and provincial politics was an ongoing phenomenon, not simply a product of infrequent cataclysmic events and conditions such as major wars or economic depressions.

In the introductory chapter of this book, we argued that the valence model of electoral politics provides the single best explanation of voting behavior in Canada and the United States. We noted that we had selected eight national elections—four in each country—to test our claim. The Canadian elections were the 1988, 1993, 2004, and 2006 federal elections. The American elections were the 1980, 2000, and 2004 presidential elections, and the 2006 congressional elections. In analyses of voting in each of these eight elections the explanatory power of the valence model would be tested against various rivals, including sociological and issue-proximity models. By analyzing the determinants of electoral choice in these eight elections, the generality of the valence politics model would be tested not only cross-nationally but over time and for different political offices. We also argued that although the inclusion of rival models in a "composite" model specification might augment the explanatory power of the valence model, the valence model would be almost as powerful as the more elaborate one. Explanatory gains provided by the composite model would be marginal.

We also wanted to address a second great question that has bedevilled and intrigued students of voting in Canada, the United States, and other democracies—why some people vote and others do not. For this purpose, we again studied the ability of several competing models to explain turnout in Canadian and American national elections. Survey data gathered in Canadian and US national election studies conducted in 2004 provided the empirical bases for investigating the factors affecting voter turnout.

We began our analyses in Chapter Two by studying voting in the 2006 Canadian federal election that brought the new Conservative Party of Canada (CPC) to power after 13 years of Liberal rule. The CPC, under the leadership of Stephen Harper, waged an almost perfect campaign. This, and a continuing scandal from which Liberal Party leader Paul Martin could not distance himself, enabled Harper and his CPC colleagues to drive the Liberals from office and form a minority government. In Chapter Three, the focus was on voting in the 2004 Canadian federal election, and why Harper and the CPC almost succeeded, but ultimately failed in their quest to prevent the Martin-led Liberals from returning to power after an exciting, closely fought campaign.

In Chapter Four we turned our attention to an American presidential election. In 2004 George W. Bush won re-election, overcoming several major obstacles facing him and his fellow Republicans. The most serious of these obstacles stemmed from Bush's decision in March 2003 to initiate a war with Iraq and his subsequent handling of what had become a bloody, protracted, and unresolved conflict. In the 2000 election, the subject of Chapter Five, Bush had become president by securing a razor-thin majority in the electoral college while receiving fewer popular votes than his chief rival, Democratic candidate Al Gore. In 2004, Bush secured majorities both at the ballot box and in the electoral college. Valence factors, especially Bush's positive image as a "strong leader," were critically important for both his initial victory and his re-election.

Valence factors were also important in the 2006 congressional election, the focus of Chapter Six. In this election, Bush's stewardship of the increasingly unpopular Iraq War and a series of scandals involving GOP congressmen and other prominent Republicans produced "a big blue wave" of public support for Democratic candidates across much of the country. The wave swept a large number of Republicans out of office, and the Democrats regained control of the House and the Senate, both of which they had lost 12 years earlier.

Analyses in Chapter Seven demonstrated that the valence model proved its mettle in three important earlier elections, the American presidential election of 1980, and the Canadian federal elections of 1988 and 1993. At first blush, it might appear that we had "stacked the deck" *against* the valence model by selecting these elections. The 1980 presidential election was one in which the Republican challenger, Ronald

Reagan, a self-described ideological conservative, ousted the incumbent Democrat, Jimmy Carter. This election campaign generated a firestorm of policy controversies and ideologically charged debates about the appropriate scope and power of the federal government.

Similarly, the 1988 Canadian federal election featured sharp inter-party controversy concerning a deeply divisive position issue, a free trade agreement with the United States. During a hotly contested election campaign, Liberal leader John Turner warned that if the agreement became law, there would be dire economic, political, and cultural consequences, and Canada would quickly become a lackey of its powerful southern neighbor. Although the free trade issue dominated the campaign, a plurality of voters refused to buy Turner's argument and Prime Minister Brian Mulroney and the Progressive Conservatives were returned to power with a comfortable parliamentary majority. However, this was the Conservatives' last hurrah. Only five years later, in the 1993 federal election, the party suffered a devastating defeat, losing all but two of its 151 seats in Parliament. The NDP also suffered serious losses, and two new ideologically based parties, Reform in the West and the Bloc Québécois in Quebec, emerged as serious players on the Canadian political stage. Analyses of voting in these two elections revealed that although positional issues had significant effects on voters' decisions, valence issues held their own as explanatory variables.

Chapter Eight considered why many Canadians and Americans fail to take advantage of their right to vote. Over the past two decades, the percentage of Canadians participating in successive federal elections has declined substantially. Similar downward trends in turnout also have occurred in several other mature democracies, but the United States is an exception. In the US, voter turnout has long been quite low in comparison to many other democracies including, until recently, Canada. Analyses clearly show that there are strong age-related differences in turnout, with younger people being much less likely to vote than are older people. Although it is difficult to disentangle life-cycle versus generational differences in these relationships, recent research suggests that there is a distinct generational component. The implication is that as they age, currently young people will not vote as frequently as their elders do. In addition, there is no evidence of "substitution effects," i.e., that young Canadians and Americans have abandoned the ballot box to participate in politics in other ways. In both countries, voting turnout tends to be positively, but weakly, correlated with other forms of political activity among both younger and older age groups.

Age differences are not the only story about electoral participation in the two countries. Testing rival models of turnout shows that several variables have significant effects. Expected benefits of having one party or candidate in power; perceived costs of voting; social capital (i.e., sense of social trust and membership in networks of civic engagement); expectations that an election will be a closely fought contest;

evaluations of the quality of representation provided by the electoral and party systems; local party campaign activities; and levels of political knowledge, education, and income all come into play. Controlling for these several factors, our Canadian analyses show that sense of civic duty makes a large difference. People with strong feelings of civic duty are much more likely to vote. Here, age differences are again apparent—reflecting their lower level of voting turnout, younger Canadians tend to have a much weaker sense of civic duty than do their older fellow citizens.

VALENCE POLITICS: SMART ENOUGH

In this book, the conjecture that valence models offer the single best explanation of the electoral choices people make has been strongly supported by analyses of voting behavior in several Canadian and American national elections. Why do valence factors have such strong explanatory power? We believe that the answer is that voters employ partisan identifications and images of leaders as heuristic devices—as shortcuts to make decisions about matters such as the relative importance of different election issues and the claims of competing parties and their leaders who say they can "do the job" and "deliver the goods." The importance of these heuristic devices stems from voters' inability to acquire and process the information needed to make fully informed and rational decisions about the consequences of electing one party or candidate rather than another. Unable to forecast the future, voters must make decisions in political environments of high stakes and substantial uncertainty. Leader images and flexible partisan attachments that encapsulate a storehouse of information about past party and party leader performance provide easily accessible cues that enable voters to make their decisions quickly and at relatively low cost. In a sense, voters are "smart enough" to know that they are "not smart enough." Recognizing their limitations, they react by making use of partisan and leader cues to select a "safe pair of hands" to steer the ship of state. The result is that valence factors regularly exert strong direct and indirect effects on electoral choice.

The functions that leader images perform for voters become especially important under a condition of actual or threatened crisis. In such an environment of heightened tensions, people's perceptions of who is the strongest and most competent leader become especially critical. This is because they want someone to lead them who can diminish their anxiety and make them feel physically, psychologically, and economically secure. What is intriguing are the different types of political leaders who, in such heightened electoral environments, have seemingly been viewed as "strong" and "competent" by voters.

Consider, for example, the longest period of economic crisis in the past century. The Great Depression began in October 1929 and continued relatively unabated until the beginning of World War II. In the United States, the handsome, distinguished, and patrician Franklin D. Roosevelt became president in 1932. At the very beginning of his presidency, Roosevelt, taking advantage of his public-speaking ability, employed the relatively new medium of radio to assure millions of Americans that "the only thing they had to fear was fear itself." Not hunger, which was felt by many, not joblessness, which was widespread, but fear. And millions of Americans, even many of those who had not voted for him in 1932, believed him enough so that four years later they gave him what then was the greatest election victory in American history. He was re-elected in 1940 and was able to rally a nation stunned by the surprise Japanese attack on the American Pacific Fleet in Pearl Harbor, Hawaii, on December 7, 1941. Despite that calamity and other lesser ones that followed, America and its allies were on the verge of victory when he was elected for an unprecedented fourth term in November 1944. Americans re-elected him although it was obvious from pictures that he was a very sick man who might never live to the end of his term.

In sharp contrast to Roosevelt was Canada's vanilla-plain, pear-shaped William Lyon McKenzie King, he of the wintry smile and the three strands of side-combed hair, whose most memorable public line may have been, "Conscription if necessary, but not necessarily conscription." After leading the governing Liberals in the 1920s, King became prime minister again after the 1935 election. The next four years were a period when Canada's economic woes generally were considered greater than those of its southern neighbor. King was re-elected in 1940 and led Canada through World War II. In contrast to the bold and innovative Roosevelt, King was regarded by his contemporaries as an archetypical conflict-avoider, conciliator, and deal-maker, and a highly skilled practitioner of the quintessentially Canadian art of brokerage politics. Despite his preference for the broker role, the foundations of Canada's welfare state, together with the economic policies that facilitated the country's post-war prosperity, were laid during his lengthy tenure as prime minister. Also important, he kept the country together in World War II when many Quebeckers voiced strenuous opposition to employing Canadian troops in combat roles overseas (Dawson, 1958).

Nor were Roosevelt and King the only leaders seen by voters to possess the qualities of strength and competence. Far from it. In Canada, there were the Conservatives Diefenbaker and Mulroney, and the Liberals Pearson, Trudeau, and Chrétien, and in the United States, the Republicans Eisenhower, Nixon, and Reagan, and the Democrats Truman, Johnson, and Clinton. Despite their many differences, what distinguished these leaders was that they were not "one and done." Rather, their electorates had sufficient confidence in their abilities that they chose them to lead more than once.[1]

The argument that valence issues differ from positional ones because the latter divide people whereas almost everyone is of the same mind about valence issues—they are either for them (e.g., economic prosperity, good health care) or against them (e.g., crime, terrorism)—has been reiterated throughout this book. Election outcomes can and do turn on the ability of contesting parties and their leaders to convince voters that they have "the right stuff" to deliver on a salient valence issue. However, it bears emphasis that valence issues are not written in stone. The near unanimity or opposition with which they are regarded can change over time. For example, the widespread belief in the benevolence of a market economy untrammelled by government regulation ended abruptly during the Great Depression. In turn, its successor, substantial government intervention guided by the theoretical precepts of Keynesian economics, received a severe jolt in the decade after the 1973 Arab-Israeli War. The enormous increases in energy costs helped generate a stagflated economy with simultaneously high unemployment and high inflation, a malady for which Keynesian prescriptions were seemingly of no avail. More recently, the war in Iraq, because of steadily increasing public opposition to it, has taken on the qualities of a valence issue, with large majorities of Americans voicing opposition to continued participation in the conflict, and large majorities of Canadians voicing opposition to getting involved.

Another example of the mutable character of valence issues is immigration. Canadians celebrate the contributions that immigrants and their descendents have made to the country's growth, economic prosperity, culture, and, when necessary, defense. In the United States, the Statue of Liberty, the first sight of America for millions of immigrants, and Ellis Island, through which they were processed in the nineteenth and early twentieth centuries, have become virtual shrines. However, immigration has now become an issue that sharply divides many Americans. As this is written, small armies of Democratic and Republican candidates for their respective parties' 2008 presidential nominations, although they disagree on many points, are unanimously agreed that America must "safeguard its borders," a code phrase for stemming the tide of illegal immigrants from Mexico. Although immigration is not yet the sharply divisive issue in Canada that it has become in the United States, it could well achieve that status if the trickle of illegal immigrants into the former becomes the raging flood that many Americans are convinced their country has experienced for more than a decade. In sum, what makes an issue a valence issue is a one-sided division of opinion, and opinion distributions can and do change.

In this book we have not only tried to explain for whom people will vote but also whether they will do so. Analyses show that people vote in part because of a sense of civic duty. It is simply the right thing to do. There are, of course, other reasons. People vote because parties encourage them to do so, and because of cost-benefit considerations. Although, objectively speaking, there is only a miniscule probability that someone could actually decide an election outcome with their single ballot, people believe they, and people like them, have political influence and that it is in their interests to cast a ballot. They also vote because of the intensity of their partisanship, their perceptions of the qualities of leaders and candidates, and their concerns about issues. Valence factors, in short, help explain the propensity to vote, as well as the direction of voting.

Regardless of why people turn out to vote, similar to many other countries, younger cohorts of Canadians and Americans consistently vote less frequently than do older people. Also, even though younger people vote less than older ones, millions in the latter group also do not avail themselves of the opportunity. In the recent Canadian federal and American presidential elections, only about three people in five bothered to cast a ballot. In American congressional elections only about two people in five bother to do so.

The question arises as to whether the good health of democracies could be facilitated if more of their citizens voted, even if they were compelled to vote. Compulsion, of course, immediately smacks of authoritarianism to many people and so, other than in a few instances, it has not been put into practice. A somewhat more benign suggestion is that since the political socialization processes in mature democracies are relatively haphazard, why not change that? Why not employ an instrument of the state, the educational system, to socialize successive generations of young people to vote, by inculcating a belief that participating in elections is a major responsibility of good citizenship. It is something you *must* do. The problem with using the educational system in this way is that, like compulsion, it would raise concerns in democracies such as Canada and the United States that their governments have embarked on a slippery slope that could lead to tyranny. Plus, it might not work. Successive generations of students have been exposed to the idea that voting is an aspect of good citizenship, and turnout has not increased.

Consequently, it seems likely that substantial numbers of citizens in the two countries, especially younger ones, will continue to be nonvoters. This is a matter of concern. Indeed, if the age-turnout relationship has a generational basis, the implication is that electoral participation will decline further in the future as younger generations with higher proportions of nonvoters become larger proportions of the Canadian and American electorates. Also, as observed above, there is currently no indication that large numbers of younger people are embracing alternative forms of political participation that would substitute for attempts to exercise influence via the ballot box. Encouraging citizens, young and old alike, to continue making political choices will challenge Canadian and American democracy in the twenty-first century.

ELECTIONS, DEMOCRACY, AND VALENCE POLITICS

Voting in national elections is one of the most important and by far the most frequent political act in which citizens in mature democracies such as Canada and the United States engage. Questions regarding the competence of ordinary people to perform this act knowledgeably and to be entrusted with the responsibility of deciding who will govern are long-standing. In Canada and the United States, reservations about the intellectual capacity of a mass electorate was a primary reason that a popularly elected House of Commons and House of Representatives shared the tasks of governing with appointed Senates. Skepticism about the competence of average citizens to exercise their vote intelligently and responsibly was also manifested repeatedly in the long process through which both countries moved from a limited electorate of white men of a certain age and economic status to their current electorates—one person, one vote for all citizens 18 years of age and older. Over the past half-century, worries about the quality of the choices voters make have been repeatedly spurred by findings from the now lengthy series of studies of voting behavior that began with the pioneering research by Paul Lazarsfeld and his colleagues at Columbia University in the 1940s (Lazarsfeld, Berelson, and Gaudet, 1948; Berelson, Lazarsfeld, and McPhee, 1954).

Lazarsfeld had emigrated to the United States from central Europe after the Nazis came to power in 1933. He was accustomed to ideologically based, multiparty political systems in which the contesting parties tried to sharply differentiate themselves from one another and in which inter-party conflicts were not restricted to verbal disputes. In the 1920s and early 1930s, both the Nazi and Communist parties had private armies that engaged in violent street clashes and regularly tried to break up each other's meetings and rallies. Given his background, Lazarsfeld was probably surprised and somewhat dismayed by his survey data indicating that most Americans lacked political awareness, interest, and especially information.

Data from the Michigan studies of Campbell et al. (1960) confirmed and reiterated these findings. Perhaps the best known work in this area was Philip Converse's essay "The Nature of Belief Systems in Mass Publics" (1964), in which he argued that political elites and ordinary citizens see the political world and think about politics and public affairs in very different ways. Converse drew a profile of the American public in the mid-1950s which indicated that only about 10 per cent of the public, whom he labelled "ideologues," could correctly use concepts such as "left/right" and "liberal/conservative" when discussing the political parties and their presidential candidates. This small group was able to think about issues in clusters that indicated that they knew "what goes with what." In Converse's language, their political thinking exhibited "constraint." Approximately the same proportion of voters, whom he labelled "near-ideologues," also used ideological terms, but used them in ways that revealed that they really did not know what they were taking about. The modal category (about 40 per cent) thought about parties and their leaders in very concrete group-interest terms (e.g., the Democrats are better for unions and Republicans for business). The rest of the electorate were what he called "nature of the times" or "no issue content" voters. The former tended to associate parties with major events and conditions such as "Democrats and wars" and "Republicans and economic recessions." Many of the no issue content people, who were approximately twice the number of ideologues, talked about parties and presidential candidates in ways that had nothing whatsoever to do with issues, e.g., Eisenhower is bald, Stevenson is divorced.

However, that was 50 years ago. Surely, things are different now with the massive technological and informational advances because of television, 24/7 cable news networks, computers, mobile phones, fax machines, and the Internet, all of which are utilized by populations which, on the whole, have considerably higher levels of formal education. Given the torrent of easily accessible information now available, surely voters must be much more knowledgeable about politics and public affairs.

Yet this does not seem to have happened. Over the years, survey after survey and poll after poll have indicated that large numbers of Americans and Canadians have very limited factual knowledge about politics. Many do not know the names of their Members of Congress and Parliament; cannot cite an issue in an election campaign or do not know what the issues they have just cited are about; give responses to policy questions that are contradictory; and take opposite positions on the same issue at different time periods, suggesting they may be doing nothing more than not wanting to appear ignorant when they answer public opinion surveys. Therefore, the question arises whether, from a democratic theory perspective, the idea that a representative democracy is composed of an involved informed electorate making rational decisions and selecting their leaders has any validity.

Scholars such as Samuel Popkin (1991, 2006) insist that the answer to that question is "yes." Even the Columbia studies noted that in each of the two elections they studied there was a minority of people who were well informed, aware of the issues, and interested in the outcome of the election. This group of "opinion leaders" provided cues and information to others to use in making a voting decision. More generally, it can be argued that everyone makes use of heuristics when making important decisions, political and otherwise (e.g., Lupia, 1994, 2006; Lupia and McCubbins, 1998). Indeed, even political elites use heuristics, since abstract concepts such as liberal/conservative are themselves information shortcuts (Menand, 2004). Even many political scientists in the two countries would be lost if party names such as NDP, Liberal, Conservative, BQ, Democrat, and Republican were not attached to candidate names on ballots.

Similarly, for millions of Americans and Canadians, leader images are cues that at times can speak volumes. A Canadian prime minister (Paul Martin) who was a very senior Quebec MP and had spent several years as minister of finance, who claims ignorance about a major scandal in his province, may be saying something to voters about his honesty. Another prime minister who dismissively tells Western farmers that he does not have to sell their wheat and, that if they want his attention, they should vote for his party, may be telling them something about his sensitivity to their needs. A Republican president's lack of familiarity with a food market scanner may be telling average Americans how out of touch he is with their lives, and a Democratic presidential candidate who will not defend himself against outrageous charges can make millions of voters nervous about his ability to lead the nation during a period of crisis.

Some four decades ago the late V.O. Key, Jr. (1966) famously argued that "voters are not fools." We agree. Voters use cues provided by party leader and candidate images, together with information stored in flexible partisan attachments and judgments about party performance on salient issues, to guide their electoral choices. As argued in this book, the issues of concern typically—not invariably—are valence issues dealing with the fundamentals of economic and physical security, broadly defined. Making political choices according to this valence politics model violates the canons of "full information rationality," but this is an impossibly high standard for political decision-making (Conlisk, 1996). Voters, with real concerns for the security and prosperity of themselves and those they care about, are "smart enough" to know this.

Note

1   Truman and Johnson were both elected once as president after being successful vice presidential candidates in a preceding election. In both cases, they initially became president when an incumbent president died in office.

REFERENCES

Achen, Christopher H. 1992. "Social Psychology, Demographic Variables, and Linear Regression: Breaking the Iron Triangle in Voting Research." *Political Behavior* 14: 195–211.

—. 2002. "Parental Socialization and Rational Party Identification." *Political Behavior* 24: 151–70.

Adams, James, Samuel Merrill, and Bernard Grofman. 2005. *A Unified Theory of Party Competition: A Cross-National Analysis Integrating Spatial and Behavioral Factors.* Cambridge: Cambridge U P.

Aldrich, John H. 1993. "Rational Choice and Turnout." *American Journal of Political Science* 37: 246–78.

Barber, James David. 1992. *The Presidential Character: Predicting Performance in the White House.* 4th ed. Englewood Cliffs, NJ: Prentice Hall.

Bartels, Larry M. 1996. "Partisanship and Voting Behavior, 1952–1996." *American Journal of Political Science* 44: 35–50.

Bartolini, Stefano, and Peter Mair. 1990. *Identity, Competition, and Electoral Availability: The Stabilisation of European Electorates 1885–1985.* Cambridge: Cambridge U P.

Bercuson, David Jay, J.L. Granatstein, and W.R. Young. 1986. *Sacred Trust? Brian Mulroney and the Conservative Party in Power.* Toronto: Doubleday Canada.

Berelson, Bernard, Paul F. Lazarsfeld, and William N. McPhee. 1954. *Voting: A Study of Opinion Formation in a Presidential Campaign.* Chicago: U of Chicago P.

Bishop, George F., Alfred J. Tuchfarber, Andrew E. Smith, Paul R. Abramson, and Charles W. Ostrom. 1994. "Question Form and Context Effects in the Measurement of Partisanship—Experimental Tests of the Artifact Hypothesis." *American Political Science Review* 88: 945–58.

Blais, André. 2000. *To Vote or Not to Vote? The Merits and Limits of Rational Choice Theory.* Pittsburgh: U of Pittsburgh P.

Blais, André, and Agnieszka Dobrzynska. 1998. "Turnout in Electoral Democracies." *European Journal of Political Research* 33: 239–61.

Blais, André, Elisabeth Gidengil, Richard Nadeau, and Neil Nevitte. 2001. "Measuring Party Identification: Britain, Canada, and the United States." *Political Behavior* 23: 5–22.

—. 2002. *Anatomy of a Liberal Victory: Making Sense of the Vote in the 2000 Canadian Election.* Peterborough: Broadview Press.

Bloom, Howard S., and H. Douglas Price. 1975. "Voter Response to Short-Run Economic Conditions: The Asymmetric Effect of Prosperity and Recession." *American Political Science Review* 69: 1240–54.

Bowler, Shaun, Todd Donovan, and Trudi Happ. 1992. "Ballot Propositions and Information Costs—Direct Democracy and the Fatigued Voter." *Western Political Quarterly* 45: 559–68.

Box-Steffensmeier, Janet M., David C. Kimball, Scott R. Meinke, and Katherine Tate. 2003. "The Effects of Political Representation on the Electoral Advantages of House Incumbents." *Political Research Quarterly* 56: 259–70.

Boyd, Richard W. 1989. "The Effects of Primaries and Statewide Races on Voter Turnout." *Journal of Politics* 51: 730–39.

Broder, David S. 1972. *The Party's Over: The Failure of Politics in America*. New York: Harper & Row.

Brooks, David. 2000. *Bobos in Paradise: The New Upper Class and How They Got There*. New York: Simon & Schuster.

Budge, Ian. 2001. *Mapping Policy Preferences: Estimates for Parties, Electors, and Governments, 1945–1998*. Oxford: Oxford U P.

Burden, Barry C., and David C. Kimball. 2002. *Why Americans Split Their Tickets: Campaigns, Competition, and Divided Government*. Ann Arbor: U of Michigan P.

Burnham, Kenneth P., and David R. Anderson. 2002. *Model Selection and Multimodel Inference: A Practical Information-Theoretic Approach*. 2nd ed. New York: Springer.

Butler, David, and Donald E. Stokes. 1969. *Political Change in Britain: Forces Shaping Electoral Choice*. New York: St. Martin's Press.

Campbell, Angus, Gerald Gurin, and Warren E. Miller. 1954. *The Voter Decides*. Evanston, IL: Row, Peterson, and Company.

Campbell, Angus, Philip E. Converse, Warren E. Miller, and Donald E. Stokes. 1960. *The American Voter*. New York: Wiley.

—. 1966. *Elections and the Political Order*. New York: Wiley.

Campbell, James E. 1997. *The Presidential Pulse of Congressional Elections*. 2nd ed. Lexington: U P of Kentucky.

Cannon, Lou. 2000. *President Reagan: The Role of a Lifetime*. New York: Public Affairs.

Caro, Robert A. 2002. *Master of the Senate, the Years of Lyndon Johnson*. New York: Knopf.

Carsey, Thomas M., and Geoffrey C. Layman. 2004. "Policy Balancing and Preferences for Party Control of Government." *Political Research Quarterly* 57: 541–50.

Carty, Roland Kenneth. 2002. "The Politics of Tecumseh Corners: Canadian Political Parties as Franchise Organizations." *Canadian Journal of Political Science* 35: 723–45.

Carty, Roland Kenneth, William Cross, and Lisa Young. 2000. *Rebuilding Canadian Party Politics*. Vancouver: UBC Press.

Charemza, Wojciech, and Derek Deadman. 1997. *New Directions in Econometric Practice: General to Specific Modelling, Cointegration, and Vector Autoregression*. Aldershot, UK: Edward Elgar.

Clarke, Harold D., and Allan Kornberg. 1996. "Partisan Dealignment, Electoral Choice and Party-System Change in Canada." *Party Politics* 2: 455–78.

—. Forthcoming. "The Valence Model of Electoral Choice and Canadian Election Studies." In *Four Decades of Canadian Election Studies: Learning from the Past and Planning for the Future*. Edited by Antoine Bilodeau, Mebs Kanji, and Thomas J. Scotto. Vancouver: UBC Press.

Clarke, Harold D., Allan Kornberg, John MacLeod, and Thomas Scotto. 2005. "Too Close to Call: Political Choice in Canada, 2004." *PS—Political Science & Politics* 38: 247–53.

Clarke, Harold D., Allan Kornberg, and Peter Wearing. 2000. *A Polity on the Edge: Canada and the Politics of Fragmentation.* Peterborough: Broadview Press.

Clarke, Harold D., Allan Kornberg, Thomas Scotto, and Joe Twyman. 2006. "Flawless Campaign, Fragile Victory: Voting in Canada's 2006 Federal Election." *PS—Political Science & Politics* 39: 815–19.

Clarke, Harold D., David Sanders, Marianne C. Stewart, and Paul Whiteley. 2004. *Political Choice in Britain.* Oxford: Oxford U P.

Clarke, Harold D., Jane Jenson, Lawrence LeDuc, and Jon Pammett. 1979. *Political Choice in Canada.* Toronto: McGraw-Hill Ryerson.

—. 1996. *Absent Mandate: Canadian Electoral Politics in an Era of Restructuring.* 3rd ed. Toronto: Gage Educational Publishing.

Clarke, Harold D., Jon Rapkin, and Marianne C. Stewart. 1994. "A President Out-of-Work—A Note on the Political-Economy of Presidential Approval in the Bush Years." *British Journal of Political Science* 24: 535–48.

Clarke, Harold D., and Motoshi Suzuki. 1994. "Partisan Dealignment and the Dynamics of Independence in the American Electorate, 1953–88." *British Journal of Political Science* 24: 57–77.

Conlisk, John. 1996. "Why Bounded Rationality?" *Journal of Economic Literature* 34: 669–700.

Converse, Philip E. 1964. "The Nature of Belief Systems in Mass Publics." In *Ideology and Discontent.* Edited by David E. Apter. London: Free Press of Glencoe.

—. 1966. "The Concept of a Normal Vote." In *Elections and the Political Order.* Edited by Angus Campbell, Philip E. Converse, Warren E. Miller, and Donald E. Stokes. New York: Wiley.

—. 1969. "Of Time and Partisan Stability." *Comparative Political Studies* 2: 139–71.

Converse, Philip E., and Gregory B. Markus. 1979. "Plus Ça Change ...: The New CPS Election Study Panel." *American Political Science Review* 73: 32–49.

Cover, Albert D. 1977. "One Good Term Deserves Another—Advantage of Incumbency in Congressional Elections." *American Journal of Political Science* 21: 523–41.

Curtice, John, and Michael Steed. 1982. "Electoral Choice and the Production of Government: the Changing Operation of the Electoral System in the United Kingdom since 1955." *British Journal of Political Science* 12: 249–98.

Dalton, Russell J. 2006. *Citizen Politics: Public Opinion and Political Parties in Advanced Industrial Democracies.* 4th ed. Washington, DC: CQ Press.

Dalton, Russell J., and Martin P. Wattenberg, (eds.). 2000. *Parties without Partisans: Political Change in Advanced Industrial Democracies (Comparative Politics).* Oxford: Oxford U P.

Dawson, Anne. 24 June 2004. "Party with Most Seats Governs: PM: Martin Backs Away from Talk of Ruling If Tories Win More Seats." *National Post,* p. A1.

Dawson, Robert MacGregor. 1958. *William Lyon Mackenzie King, a Political Biography.* Toronto: U of Toronto P.

Denver, David T., and Gordon Hands. 1997. *Modern Constituency Electioneering: Local Campaigning in the 1992 General Election.* London: Frank Cass.

Downs, Anthony. 1957. *An Economic Theory of Democracy.* New York: Harper.

Eichenberg, Richard C. 2005. "Victory Has Many Friends—US Public Opinion and the Use of Military Force, 1981–2005." *International Security* 30: 140–77.

Eichenberg, Richard C., Richard J. Stoll, and Matthew Lebo. 2006. "War President—the Approval Ratings of George W. Bush." *Journal of Conflict Resolution* 50: 783–808.

Elkins, David. 1978. "Party Identification: A Conceptual Analysis." *Canadian Journal of Political Science* 11: 419–35.

Engelmann, Frederick C., and Mildred A. Schwartz. 1967. *Political Parties and the Canadian Social Structure*. Scarborough: Prentice-Hall of Canada.

Epstein, Leon D. 1964. "A Comparative Study of Canadian Parties." *American Political Science Review* 58: 46–60.

Erikson, Robert S., Michael MacKuen, and James A. Stimson. 2002. *The Macro Polity*. New York: Cambridge U P.

Fallows, James. 1979. "The Passionless Presidency." *Atlantic Monthly* 243: 33–48.

Feaver, Peter, and Christopher Gelpi. 2004. *Choosing Your Battles: American Civil-Military Relations and the Use of Force*. Princeton: Princeton U P.

Fenno, Richard F. 1978. *Home Style: House Members in Their Districts*. New York: HarperCollins.

Filer, John E., Lawrence W. Kenny, and Rebecca B. Morton. 1991. "Voting Laws, Educational Policies, and Minority Turnout." *Journal of Law and Economics* 34: 371–93.

Fingerhut, Eric. 17 October 2002. "Evangelicals Rally in Support of Israel." *Washington Jewish Week*, p. 4.

Fiorina, Morris P. 1981. *Retrospective Voting in American National Elections*. New Haven: Yale U P.

—. 1981. "Some Problems in Studying the Effects of Resource-Allocation in Congressional Elections." *American Journal of Political Science* 25: 543–67.

—. 1992. *Divided Government*. New York: Maxwell Macmillan International.

Fiorina, Morris P., Samuel J. Abrams, and Jeremy Pope. 2005. *Culture War? The Myth of a Polarized America*. New York: Pearson Longman.

FitzGerald, Frances. 2000. *Way Out There in the Blue: Reagan, Star Wars, and the End of the Cold War*. New York: Simon & Schuster.

Frank, Thomas. 2004. *What's the Matter with Kansas? How Conservatives Won the Heart of America*. New York: Metropolitan Books.

Franklin, Charles H. 1992. "Measurement and the Dynamics of Party Identification." *Political Behavior* 14: 297–309.

Franklin, Charles H., and John E. Jackson. 1983. "The Dynamics of Party Identification." *American Political Science Review* 77: 957–73.

Franklin, Mark N. 2004. *Voter Turnout and the Dynamics of Electoral Competition in Established Democracies since 1945*. Cambridge: Cambridge U P.

Garand, James C., and Marci Glascock Lichtl. 2000. "Explaining Divided Government in the United States: Testing an Intentional Model of Split-Ticket Voting." *British Journal of Political Science* 30: 173–91.

Gartner, Scott S., and Gary M. Segura. 1998. "War, Casualties, and Public Opinion." *Journal of Conflict Resolution* 42: 278–300.

Gelman, Andrew, and Gary King. 1993. "Why Are American Presidential-Election Campaign Polls So Variable When Votes Are So Predictable?" *British Journal of Political Science* 23: 409–51.

Gelman, Andrew, Gary King, and W. John Boscardin. 1998. "Estimating the Probability of Events That Have Never Occurred: When Is Your Vote Decisive?" *Journal of the American Statistical Association* 93: 1–9.

Gelpi, Christopher, and Jason Reifler. 2006. "Casualties, Polls, and the Iraq War—Reply." *International Security* 31: 194–98.

Gelpi, Christopher, Peter D. Feaver, and Jason Reifler. 2005. "Success Matters—Casualty Sensitivity and the War in Iraq." *International Security* 30: 7–46.

Gidengil, Elisabeth, André Blais, Richard Nadeau, and Neil Nevitte. 1999. "Making Sense of Regional Voting in the 1997 Canadian Federal Election: Liberal and Reform Support Outside Quebec." *Canadian Journal of Political Science* 32: 247–72.

Green, Donald P., Bradley Palmquist, and Eric Schickler. 2002. *Partisan Hearts and Minds: Political Parties and the Social Identities of Voters.* New Haven: Yale U P.

Green, Donald P., and Jonathan S. Krasno. 1988. "Salvation for the Spendthrift Incumbent—Reestimating the Effects of Campaign Spending in House Elections." *American Journal of Political Science* 34: 884–907.

Greenstein, Fred I. 2000. *The Presidential Difference: Leadership Style from FDR to Clinton.* New York: Martin Kessler Books/Free Press.

Held, David. 1996. *Models of Democracy.* 2nd ed. Stanford: Stanford U P.

Hendry, David F. 1995. *Dynamic Econometrics: Advanced Texts in Econometrics.* Oxford: Oxford U P.

Hochschild, Jennifer L. 1981. *What's Fair? American Beliefs about Distributive Justice.* Cambridge: Harvard U P.

Holland, Keating. 21 October 2000. "CNN Poll: Bush Gains Solid Post-Debate Lead over Gore." Available from <http://edition.cnn.com/2000/ALLPOLITICS/stories/10/21/tracking.poll/index.html> (21 February 2007).

Howell, William G., and Jon C. Pevehouse. 2007. "When Congress Stops Wars." *Foreign Affairs* 83: 95–107.

Hunter, James Davison. 1991. *Culture Wars: The Struggle to Define America.* New York: Basic Books.

—. 1994. *Before the Shooting Begins: Searching for Democracy in America's Culture War.* New York: Free Press.

Inglehart, Ronald. 1971. "Changing Value Priorities and European Integration." *Journal of Common Market Studies* 10: 1–36.

Jackman, Robert W., and Ross A. Miller. 1998. "Social Capital and Politics." *Annual Review of Political Science* 1: 47–73.

Jackman, Simon. 2005. "Pooling the Polls over an Election Campaign." *Australian Journal of Political Science* 40: 499–517.

Jackson, Robert A. 1997. "The Mobilization of US State Electorates in the 1988 and 1990 Elections." *Journal of Politics* 59: 520–37.

Jacobson, Gary C. 2001. *The Politics of Congressional Elections.* 5th ed. New York: Longman.

Jelen, Ted G. 1997. "Culture Wars and the Party System: Religion and Realignment, 1972–1993." In *Cultural Wars in American Politics: Critical Reviews of a Popular Myth*. Edited by Rhys H. Williams. Edison, NJ: Transaction Publishers.

Jennings, M. Kent, and Richard G. Niemi. 1974. *The Political Character of Adolescence: The Influence of Families and Schools*. Princeton: Princeton U P.

Jenson, Jane. 1976. "Party Strategy and Party Identification: Some Patterns of Partisan Allegiance." *Canadian Journal of Political Science* 9: 27–48.

Johnston, Richard. 1992. "Party Identification Measures in the Anglo-American Democracies—A National Survey Experiment." *American Journal of Political Science* 36: 542–49.

Johnston, Richard, André Blais, Henry Brady, and Jean Crête. 1992. *Letting the People Decide: Dynamics of a Canadian Election*. Montreal: McGill-Queen's U P.

Johnston, Richard, Michael Gray Hagen, and Kathleen Hall Jamieson. 2004. *The 2000 Presidential Election and the Foundations of Party Politics*. Cambridge: Cambridge U P.

Jones, Charles O. 1998. *Passages to the Presidency: From Campaigning to Governing*. Washington, DC: Brookings Institution Press.

Kaufman, Burton Ira. 1993. *The Presidency of James Earl Carter, Jr.* Lawrence: U P of Kansas.

Kelley, Jr., Stanley, and Thad W. Mirer. 1974. "The Simple Act of Voting." *American Political Science Review* 68: 572–91.

Key, V.O. 1966. *The Responsible Electorate: Rationality in Presidential Voting, 1936–1960*. Cambridge: Belknap Press of Harvard U P.

Kiewe, Amos, and Davis W. Houck. 1991. *A Shining City on a Hill: Ronald Reagan's Economic Rhetoric, 1951–1989*. London: Praeger.

Klarevas, Louis J., Christopher Gelpi, and Jason Reifler. 2006. "Casualties, Polls, and the Iraq War." *International Security* 31: 186–94.

Klingemann, Hans-Dieter. 2006. *Mapping Policy Preferences II: Estimates for Parties, Electors, and Governments in Central and Eastern Europe, European Union and OECD 1990–2003*. Oxford: Oxford U P.

Kornberg, Allan, and Harold D. Clarke. 1988. "Canada's Tory Tide: Electoral Change and Partisan Instability in the 1980s." In *The Resurgence of Conservatism in Anglo-American Democracies*. Edited by Allan Kornberg, Barry Cooper, and William Mishler. Durham: Duke U P.

—. 1992. *Citizens and Community: Political Support in a Representative Democracy*. Cambridge: Cambridge U P.

Kornberg, Allan, Joel Smith, and Harold D. Clarke. 1979. *Citizen Politicians—Canada: Party Officials in a Democratic Society*. Durham: Carolina Academic Press.

Kornberg, Allan, and William Mishler. 1976. *Influence in Parliament, Canada*. Durham: Duke U P.

Krause, George A. 1997. "Voters, Information Heterogeneity, and the Dynamics of Aggregate Economic Expectations." *American Journal of Political Science* 41: 1170–200.

Krueger, James S., and Michael Lewis-Beck. 2007. "Goodness of Fit: R-Squared, SEE and 'Best Practice.'" *The Political Methodologist* 15: 2–4.

Lacy, Dean, and Quin Monson. 2002. "The Origins and Impact of Votes for Third-Party Candidates: A Case Study of the 1998 Minnesota Gubernatorial Election." *Political Research Quarterly* 55: 409–37.

Laxer, James, and Robert M. Laxer. 1977. *The Liberal Idea of Canada: Pierre Trudeau and the Question of Canada's Survival*. Toronto: James Lorimer.

Lazarsfeld, Paul Felix, Bernard Berelson, and Hazel Gaudet. 1948. *The People's Choice: How the Voter Makes up His Mind in a Presidential Campaign*. 2nd ed. New York: Columbia U P.

LeDuc, Lawrence. 2005. "The Federal Election in Canada, June 2004." *Electoral Studies* 24: 338–44.

Lewis-Beck, Michael S. 1988. *Economics and Elections: The Major Western Democracies*. Ann Arbor: U of Michigan P.

Lipset, Seymour Martin. 1990. *Continental Divide: The Values and Institutions of the United States and Canada*. New York: Routledge.

Long, J. Scott. 1997. *Regression Models for Categorical and Limited Dependent Variables*. Thousand Oaks, CA: Sage Publications.

Long, J. Scott, and Jeremy Freese. 2001. *Regression Models for Categorical Dependent Variables Using STATA*. College Station, TX: STATA Press.

Lumsden, Ian. 1970. *Close the 49th Parallel Etc. The Americanization of Canada*. Toronto: U of Toronto P.

Lupia, Arthur. 1994. "Shortcuts Versus Encyclopedias: Information and Voting Behavior in California Insurance Reform Elections." *American Political Science Review* 88: 63–76.

—. 2006. "How Elitism Undermines the Study of Voter Competence." *Critical Review* 18: 217–32.

Lupia, Arthur, and Mathew D. McCubbins. 1998. *The Democratic Dilemma: Can Citizens Learn What They Need to Know?* Cambridge: Cambridge U P.

Manchester, William. 1978. *American Caesar, Douglas MacArthur, 1880–1964*. Boston: Little, Brown.

Mayhew, David Raymond. 1974. *Congress: The Electoral Connection*. New Haven: Yale U P.

McDonald, Michael P., and Samuel L. Popkin. 2001. "The Myth of the Vanishing Voter." *American Political Science Review* 95: 963–74.

McFaetters, Ann. 12 September 2004. "No Way to Run a Campaign: Lack of Focus Threatens to Make Kerry a Loser." Available from <http://www.post-gazette.com/pg/04256/376928.stm> (7 January 2007).

McGinniss, Joe. 1969. *The Selling of the President, 1968*. New York: Trident Press.

Meisel, John. 1975. *Working Papers on Canadian Politics*. 2nd ed. Montreal: McGill-Queen's U P.

Menand, Louis. 30 August 2004. "The Unpolitical Animal: How Political Science Understands Voters." *The New Yorker*: 92–96.

Merrill, Samuel, and Bernard Grofman. 1999. *A Unified Theory of Voting: Directional and Proximity Spatial Models*. Cambridge: Cambridge U P.

Miller, Warren E. 1991. "Party Identification, Realignment, and Party Voting: Back to the Basics." *American Political Science Review* 85: 557–68.

Miller, Warren E., and J. Merrill Shanks. 1996. *The New American Voter*. Cambridge: Harvard U P.

Milstein, Jeffrey S. 1974. *Dynamics of the Vietnam War: A Quantitative Analysis and Predictive Computer Simulation*. Columbus: Ohio State U P.

Mitchell, Glenn E., and Christopher Wlezien. 1995. "The Impact of Legal Constraints on Voter Registration, Turnout, and the Composition of the American Electorate." *Political Behavior* 17: 179–202.

Monahan, Patrick. 1991. *Meech Lake: The Inside Story*. Toronto: U of Toronto P.

Morris, Edmund. 1999. *Dutch: A Memoir of Ronald Reagan*. 1st ed. New York: Random House.

Mueller, John E. 1971. "Trends in Popular Support for Wars in Korea and Vietnam." *American Political Science Review* 65: 358–75.

—. 1973. *War, Presidents and Public Opinion*. New York: Wiley.

Nadeau, Richard, and Michael S. Lewis-Beck. 2001. "National Economic Voting in US Presidential Elections." *Journal of Politics* 63: 159–81.

Nelson, Michael. 2005. "The Setting: George W. Bush, Majority President." In *The Elections of 2004*. Edited by Michael Nelson. Washington, DC: CQ Press.

Nevitte, Neil, André Blais, Elisabeth Gidengil, and Richard Nadeau. 2000. *Unsteady State: The 1997 Canadian Federal Election*. New York: Oxford U P.

Nie, Norman H., Jane Junn, and Kenneth Stehlik-Barry. 1996. *Education and Democratic Citizenship in America*. Chicago: U of Chicago P.

Nie, Norman H., Sidney Verba, and John R. Petrocik. 1976. *The Changing American Voter*. Cambridge: Harvard U P.

Nordlund, Willis J. 1998. *Silent Skies: The Air Traffic Controllers' Strike*. Westport, CT: Praeger.

Norpoth, Helmut, Michael S. Lewis-Beck, and Jean-Dominique Lafay. 1991. *Economics and Politics: The Calculus of Support*. Ann Arbor: U of Michigan P.

Pammett, Jon H., and Lawrence LeDuc. 2003. *Explaining the Turnout Decline in Canadian Federal Elections: A New Survey of Non-Voters*. Ottawa: Elections Canada.

Panagopoulos, Costas. 2006. "The Polls: Public Opinion and Secretary of Defense Donald Rumsfeld." *Presidential Studies Quarterly* 36: 117–26.

Patterson, James T. 2005. *Restless Giant: The United States from Watergate to Bush v. Gore: The Oxford History of the United States*. Oxford: Oxford U P.

Patterson, Thomas E. 1980. *The Mass Media Election: How Americans Choose Their President, American Political Parties and Elections*. New York: Praeger.

Petrocik, John R. 1974. "An Analysis of Intransitivities in the Index of Party Identification." *Political Methodology* 1: 31–47.

Pomper, Gerald M. 1977. "The Decline of Party in American Elections." *Political Science Quarterly* 92: 21–41.

Popkin, Samuel L. 1991. *The Reasoning Voter: Communication and Persuasion in Presidential Campaigns*. Chicago: U of Chicago P.

—. 2006. "The Factual Basis of 'Belief Systems': A Reassessment." *Critical Review* 18: 233–52.

Porter, John A. 1965. *The Vertical Mosaic: An Analysis of Social Class and Power in Canada*. Toronto: U of Toronto P.

Putnam, Robert D. 2000. *Bowling Alone: The Collapse and Revival of American Community*. New York: Simon & Schuster.

Putnam, Robert D., Robert Leonardi, and Raffaella Nanetti. 1993. *Making Democracy Work: Civic Traditions in Modern Italy*. Princeton: Princeton U P.

Rallings, Colin, Michael Thrasher, and Galina Borisyuk. 2003. "Seasonal Factors, Voter Fatigue and the Costs of Voting." *Electoral Studies* 22: 65–79.

Riker, William H., and Peter C. Ordeshook. 1968. "A Theory of the Calculus of Voting." *American Political Science Review* 62: 25–42.

—. 1973. *An Introduction to Positive Political Theory*. Englewood Cliffs, NJ: Prentice-Hall.

Riley, Russell L. 1995. "Party Government and the Contract with America." *PS—Political Science & Politics* 28: 703–07.

Romer, Daniel, Kate Kenski, Kenneth Winneg, Christopher Adasiewicz, and Kathleen Hall Jamieson. 2006. *Capturing Campaign Dynamics: The National Annenberg Election Survey, 2000 and 2004*. Philadelphia: U of Pennsylvania P.

Romero, David W. 2006. "What They Do Does Matter: Incumbent Resource Allocations and the Individual House Vote." *Political Behavior* 28: 241–58.

Rozell, Mark J. 21 September 2004. "Bush's Wild Card: The Religious Vote." Available from <http://www.usatoday.com/news/opinion/2004-09-21-bush-religiousvote_x.htm> (7 January 2007).

Russell, Peter H. 1992. *Constitutional Odyssey: Can Canadians Become a Sovereign People?* Toronto: U of Toronto P.

Schwartz, Mildred A. 1974. *Politics and Territory: The Sociology of Regional Persistence in Canada*. Montreal: McGill-Queen's U P.

Scotto, Thomas J., Laura B. Stephenson, and Allan Kornberg. 2004. "From a Two-Party-Plus to a One-Party-Plus? Ideology, Vote Choice, and Prospects for a Competitive Party System in Canada." *Electoral Studies* 23: 463–83.

Senate Historical Office. 2003. *Albert Arnold Gore, Jr.: 45th Vice President: 1993–2001*. Available from <http://www.senate.gov/artandhistory/history/common/generic/VP_Albert_Gore.htm> (9 March 2007).

Shales, Thomas. 4 November 2000. "Presidential Bash: Hands Down Winner." *The Washington Post*, p. 1.

Smith, Chris, and Ben Voth. 2002. "The Role of Humor in Political Argument: How 'Strategery' and 'Lockboxes' Changed a Political Campaign." *Argumentation and Advocacy* 39: 110–29.

Sniderman, Paul M., H.D. Forbes, and Ian Melzer. 1974. "Party Loyalty and Electoral Volatility: A Study of the Canadian Party System." *Canadian Journal of Political Science* 7: 268–88.

Sniderman, Paul M., Richard A. Brody, and Philip Tetlock. 1991. *Reasoning and Choice: Explorations in Political Psychology*. Cambridge: Cambridge U P.

Sonner, Molly W., and Clyde Wilcox. 1999. "Forgiving and Forgetting: Public Support for Bill Clinton During the Lewinsky Scandal." *PS—Political Science & Politics* 32: 554–57.

Stewart, Marianne C., and Harold D. Clarke. 1998. "The Dynamics of Party Identification in Federal Systems: The Canadian Case." *American Journal of Political Science* 42: 97–116.

Stokes, Donald E. 1963. "Spatial Models of Party Competition." *American Political Science Review* 57: 368–77.

—. 1992. "Valence Politics." In *Electoral Politics*. Edited by Dennis Kavanagh. Oxford: Clarendon Press.

Thomas, Evan. 15 November 2004. "Fits and Starts." *Newsweek*: 42–53.

Thomassen, Jacques J.A. 2005. *The European Voter: A Comparative Study of Modern Democracies*. Oxford: Oxford U P.

Tomz, Michael, Jason Wittenberg, and Gary King. 1999. "CLARIFY: Software for Interpreting and Presenting Statistical Results." Cambridge: Harvard U, Department of Government.

Troy, Gil. 2005. *Morning in America: How Ronald Reagan Invented the 1980s*. Princeton: Princeton U P.

Tufte, Edward R. 1975. "Determinants of Outcomes of Midterm Congressional Elections." *American Political Science Review* 69: 812–26.

Verba, Sidney, Kay Lehman Schlozman, and Henry E. Brady. 1995. *Voice and Equality: Civic Voluntarism in American Politics*. Cambridge: Harvard U P.

Verba, Sidney, and Norman H. Nie. 1972. *Participation in America: Political Democracy and Social Equality*. New York: Harper & Row.

Walker, Iain, and Heather J. Smith. 2002. "Fifty Years of Relative Deprivation Research." In *Relative Deprivation: Specification, Development, and Integration*. Edited by Iain Walker and Heather J. Smith. Cambridge: Cambridge U P.

Watkins, Mel. 1968. "Foreign-Ownership and the Structure of Canadian Industry." In *Report of the Task Force on the Structure of Canadian Industry*. Ottawa: Queen's Printer.

Weisberg, Herbert F. 1980. "A Multidimensional Conceptualization of Party Identification." *Political Behavior* 2: 33–60.

Weisman, Steve R. 10 October 1999. "'The Hollow Man.' Rev. of Dutch: A Memoir of Ronald Reagan, by Edmund Morris." *New York Times Book Review*: 7–8.

White, Theodore Harold. 1973. *The Making of the President, 1972*. 1st ed. New York: Atheneum Publishers.

Whiteley, Paul F., and Patrick Seyd. 1994. "Local Party Campaigning and Electoral Mobilization in Britain." *Journal of Politics* 56: 242–52.

—. 2002. *High-Intensity Participation: The Dynamics of Party Activism in Britain*. Ann Arbor: The U of Michigan P.

Wilson, Graham. 1994. "The Westminster Model in Comparative Perspective." In *Developing Democracy: Comparative Research in Honor of J.F.P. Blondel*. Edited by Ian Budge and David McKay. Thousand Oaks, CA: Sage Publications.

Wilson, John. 1968. "Politics and Social Class in Canada: The Case of Waterloo South." *Canadian Journal of Political Science* 1: 288–309.

Wirthlin, Richard, and Wynton C. Hall. 2004. *The Greatest Communicator: What Ronald Reagan Taught Me about Politics, Leadership, and Life*. Hoboken, NJ: John Wiley & Sons.

Wlezien, Christopher. 2001. "On Forecasting the Presidential Vote." PS—*Political Science & Politics* 34: 24–31.

Wolfinger, Raymond E., and Steven J. Rosenstone. 1980. *Who Votes?* New Haven: Yale U P.

Woodward, Bob. 2006. *State of Denial*. New York: Simon & Schuster.

Zaller, John. 1992. *The Nature and Origins of Mass Opinion*. Cambridge: Cambridge U P.

INDEX BY NAME

INDEX BY SUBJECT